Echoes of Humanity

Exploring Human Wonders Through the Pages of:

Lessons, Affliction, Triumph, Victory and Brilliance

Copyright © 2024 Markey Writing Academy ECHOES OF HUMANITY

First published by Markey Writing Academy 2024

Find us on Facebook @KellyMarkeyAuthor, Instagram @Author_Kelly_Markey and LinkedIn @kellymarkey

Paperback ISBN: 978-0-6451968-6-3

E-Book ISBN: 978-0-6451968-7-0

Markey Writing Academy and the authors mentioned in this book have asserted their rights under the Copyright, Designs and Patents Act 1988 to be identified as the author of this work. The information in this book is based on the author's experiences and opinions. The publisher specifically disclaims responsibility for any adverse consequences which may result from use of the information contained herein. Permission to use information has been sought by the author. Any breaches will be rectified in further editions of the book.

All rights reserved. No part of this publication may be reproduced, stored in or introduced into a retrieval system, or transmitted in any form, or by any means (electronic, mechanical, photocopying, recording or otherwise) without the prior written permission of the author. Any person who does any unauthorised act in relation to this publication may be liable to criminal prosecution and civil claims for damages. Enquiries should be made to the publisher.

Cover Design: Markey Writing Academy
Layout: Markey Writing Academy
Typesetting: Markey Writing Academy

Markey Writing Academy
Central Coast New South Wales, Australia 2250

www.kellymarkey.com

Table of Contents

Kudos for Echoes of Humanity 1

Foreword 4

Poem 5

Publishers Preface 6

Introduction 12

Rising Above Your Circumstance and Embrace your Ubuntu within 23

Empowered Within 31

Nothing is Impossible if You Have No Other Option 37

Sharing Humanity Through Storytelling 50

The Alchemy of Me 67

Being There Untold 79

Holding On To Let Go 90

The Mundane and Exhilarating Expedition of Life 98

A Lifetime of Resilience: Picking Up the Pieces 115

In His Hands 122

I am ENOUGH 131

I Met a Man 141

Faith in the Fire 153

You are the Key 162

Breaking Through Old Paradigms: Thriving Amid Chaos 173

Yesterday's Scars are Tomorrows Seeds 188

The Resetting of Humanity Towards Victory Through Proven Social Change Practices 202

Afterword 214

Acknowledgments 222

Kudos for Echoes of Humanity

This is a judicious and practical book that provides the guidance we all need to break free from the tyranny of perpetual vanity and reclaim joy on purpose. Highly recommended for those that want to live intentionally.

CBS News, USA.

Kelly is a master with words. Just by reading the captivating preface makes me want to *"dive in"* and learn to become an author. She has a creative knack for putting words together and to create such a diverse collaborative piece is sheer genius. This book is a treasure for readers of various genres. The topics are also practical and would be a great resource for students. This book will certainly inspire many and change lives.

Lyssa-Ann Clarke (MBA, B.Ed.) Educator, Author, The Purpose & Creative Biz Coach and Holistic Healing Ministries Jamaica Director.

"Echoes of Humanity" is an anthology that Kelly Markey, an author herself has compiled. With great insights into the human psyche combined with her lived experiences Markey is an exceptional storyteller and invited a select few authors to contribute to this magnificent book. **Amongst her many experiences good, bad and indifferent, she talks about all facets of life are filled with teachable moments such as her visit** to an old Abbey in Normandy, France, she reflects *"I stood looking up at the celestial-blue stained-glass windows of The Mont-Saint-Michel Abbey in Normandy, France, marvelling at the craftsmanship, expertise and devotion of people that have long-vanished. It was surreal to enjoy the beauty of their work and I smiled as we all have the same opportunity to impact humanity now and into the future. Wisdom is man's true strength; may this book help you cultivate yours. This book is a collaborative effort, acknowledge the contributions."*

Kelly Markey believes *"Echoes of Humanity"* is one where storytelling also contributes to a world where the multitude of voices harmonise to create a symphony of shared experiences and collective wisdom. Every chapter of her books is enthralling. I am sure you will not want to put this one down!

Kelly Markey must be commended for her other books including *"Don't Just Fly, Soar," "Making Sage Decisions"* and the narrative of *"The Life of Jayandra…Shining the Light on Suicide."* This book will compel you to break taboos and create a new narrative. Highly acclaimed Kelly Markey won "TOP

BOOK OF THE YEAR AWARD 2024" 🏅 Best Book for Suicide and Human Welfare Awareness.

No doubt that *"Echoes of Humanity"* is of the same impeccable quality, grab a copy and enthral yourself.

Helen Glen: Author, Life Coach and Speaker, Sydney, Australia.

When peering through the window of life, we often submerge ourselves into the assumption that we have been dealt the wrong hand. Challenges weigh us down and every step forward causes us to drag along our past experiences. Joy seems a distant memory and the hope for the future is seen as practically non-existent. We fool ourselves into believing that we are imperfect in a perfect world. Echoes of Humanity brings to light the fact that all of us are fighting our own demons. Kelly Markey through her seasoned encouragement has unmasked the issues of life that dims the light of a positive future. This read is not just a compilation of stories but nuggets of hope and promise. Echoes of Humanity reminds me to reflect on my past failures and challenges, conduct introspection to envision change and growth and apply principles shared to ensure progress. I know that I am created with purpose and living a defeated life is not a part of God's plan for me. I have challenged myself to use my life's experiences to cause me to become a catalyst for change. Thank you, Kelly Markey, for fulfilling your purpose. You are a phenomenal writer, a talented wizard of words and a truly remarkable human being. You are blessed to be a blessing.

Lynn Claudia Naidoo, Entrepreneur, Motivational Speaker, Drama Coach, Talent Scout. Mrs Role Model of the Zulu Kingdom 2023/24. Empress of KZN 2023/24. Richards Bay, KZN, South Africa.

Chapter: Breaking through old paradigms: Thriving Amid Chaos!

Dr. Fletcher-Lartey has written with such humility about some very relational issues that affect women globally. Her story mirrors the lives of many women who struggle with work life issues, including myself who had to choose between work and my personal life and health matters. Making the decision to walk away from what is consistent and stable to uncertainty shows that it is possible for us to push beyond the status quo and to sacrifice to build generational wealth and strive to become entrepreneurs instead of committing a life to intrapreneurship. Dr. Lartey's actions shows the impact of possibility thinking and that there is power in words and one's belief, that they are able "*to do all things possible through Christ.*" She leads by example and demonstrates to the reader that faith and courage are important factor in purpose achievement and in overcoming fear.

Her determination to achieve her goals and to prosper using the strength, talents and gifts embedded within to build wealth, is instrumental for success in the new stratosphere wherein she is destined to operate; one where the greatness within her will come forth with such boldness and exuberance that many will ask about her formula for success in shifting from old paradigms into the new - the reformed masterpiece that was hidden among the ashes of the past, people's opinions, expectations and a restrictive mindset. Look out world! Dr Fletcher-Larty is poised for greatness as she is clothed with new strength and resilience like never seen before.

A writer par excellence whose literary work will connect many readers globally. This article makes you think and reflect. It motivates, inspires, and is supported by the word of God. It will propel many to take risks, eliminate fear and raise their faith. Congratulations and thank you for writing this exceptional story which will capture the hearts of many readers and parents of children with special needs; people affected by issues of the soul and those who are not operating in purpose, especially those who are feeling trapped who need to take a leap of faith.

Lyssa-Ann Clarke (MBA, B.Ed.) Educator, Author, The Purpose & Creative Biz Coach and Holistic Healing Ministries Jamaica Director.

Foreword

In *"Echoes of Humanity,"* you will embark on a journey through the myriad hues of human experience. This collection of stories transcends mere narratives; it embodies the essence of our shared existence, echoing the triumphs, trials, and transformations that define us. Through the lens of lived experiences, these tales illuminate the resilience, compassion, and courage that bind us together as a global community.

In a world often besieged by division and discord, these stories serve as beacons of hope, reminding us of our capacity for empathy and understanding. Each narrative is a testament to the indomitable spirit of humanity, showcasing how ordinary individuals can overcome extraordinary challenges and inspire positive change.

As you immerse yourself in these pages, may you find solace, strength, and inspiration to navigate the complexities of life. May these echoes resonate within you, igniting a spark of compassion and empathy that reverberates far beyond the confines of these stories, shaping a world where kindness and understanding prevail. For in the end, it is the echoes of our humanity that define us, binding us together in a tapestry of shared experiences, aspirations and dreams.

Dr Christina Di Arcangelo, Author, *"Rescuing Mom"* **USA.**

Poem

Once caught in a cycle of desperation and desolation,
Until the reality of Your love Lord Jesus, became a priceless revelation.
No longer am I bound by the enemy's devastation,
You embraced me as Your beloved child, in Christ a new creation.
You opened wide the prison doors of the past to set me free,
Undefeated I live as an overcomer in Christ, not enslaved by captivity.
Now with Your goodness and grace my life has been marked.
You have been with me faithfully throughout this journey on which I have embarked.

Poem By Sonam Rifkin

Sonam Rifkin

Sonam's creative expression is reflected through avenues of both poetry and visual arts resulting primary from her lived experience of following Lord Jesus Christ. Her gift of writing as a poet captures the powerfully transformational love of Lord Jesus. Her poems are predominantly written in a testimonial or worship style from her perspective and she also writes prophetically under the inspiration of the Holy Spirit.

As an artist she functions in a similar manner, regarding meditating on the love of God and creating visually from this place of worship and adoration towards Him. There are also times she draws inspiration from the Holy Spirit and is led by Him as she crafts unique pieces. The mediums she usually utilises include oil pastels, acrylic and water colour paints. The use of colour and imagery is largely symbolic unless otherwise stated.

It is a privilege for Sonam to glorify and honour Lord Jesus through her creative pursuits by sharing her poems and artwork with others.

Publishers Preface

"The true path to completeness is made up of significant detours, mistaken choices and an acute sense to learn from these experiences."

Kelly Markey

I am Kelly Markey, the literary maestro behind numerous page turner books that have captured the hearts and minds of readers worldwide. With a unique ability to seamlessly blend vivid lived experience with profound insights, I have crafted compelling narratives that transcend genres, transporting readers to uncharted worlds and offering fresh perspectives on the familiar.

In each masterpiece, I have woven a tapestry of emotions, intrigue, and intellectual stimulation, leaving readers eagerly turning pages and craving more. With a distinctive voice that resonates across cultures, the author Kelly Markey has become a literary sensation, celebrated for the artistry in storytelling and the profound impact on regular and global narratives.

From gripping inspirational stories that keep you on the edge of your seat to thought-provoking explorations of the human condition, I have redefined the literary landscape. With an uncanny ability to connect with readers on a profound level, my books don't just entertain; they leave an indelible mark, sparking conversations and fostering a deep appreciation for the power of storytelling and the mandate to change.

Join the millions who have been captivated by Kelly Markey's literary prowess, as each book unfolds a new chapter in the legacy of a bestselling author whose words have the power to transport, transform, and transcend. I gave birth to my first book during the COVID-19 lockdown and since then I have been inundated with requests to write more books. This anthology was born due to many people from around the world reaching out to me for help to share their own story.

My motto is to empower voices by guiding others to find their narrative mastery. In the realm of storytelling and authorship, there exists a noble responsibility to not only cultivate our own voices but also to empower others in discovering and expressing theirs. The journey of helping fellow storytellers find their voice is a rewarding endeavour that contributes to the richness and diversity of the literary landscape. This book is a product of the art of mentorship, encouragement and guidance in nurturing budding storytellers.

The mentor's role is to nurture seeds of potential. Becoming a mentor in the world of storytelling involves more than just sharing techniques and strategies. It is about instilling confidence, sparking creativity and providing a supportive environment for growth. A mentor serves as a guiding force, helping aspiring authors navigate the labyrinth of self-discovery and artistic expression.

Amidst the rolling war drums a few enthusiasts searched for fragments of hope to live a relentlessly redefined life. They grasped the opportunity to become great literary agents to foster hope and change. Unearthing such a motivated cohort at the helm is great for humanity, these enlightened thinkers share their lived experiences with the vision of preening society. Let's GO world changers! We do not have all the answers, but we have our experiences to help others. To manage aberrant behaviours where chaos ensues is a calling only few can bridge a gap to. I have listened to the plea of humanity for a better world and the desire for creators to have a platform to make a difference by sharing their lived experiences. I have heeded and learned and now put into action:

Active Listening and Understanding

To help others find their voice it is crucial to be an attentive listener. Understanding their unique experiences, passions and perspectives allows you to tailor your guidance to their specific needs. By acknowledging their individuality, you pave the way for the emergence of a distinct and authentic voice.

Unleashing Creativity through Exercises

Engage aspiring storytellers in creative exercises designed to unlock their imagination. These exercises could range from prompts that encourage reflection on personal experiences to collaborative storytelling sessions that promote spontaneity and innovation. Creating a safe space for experimentation fosters a sense of exploration and self-discovery.

Encouragement: The Fuel for Artistic Expression

In the challenging world of storytelling where self-doubt can be a formidable adversary, encouragement becomes a powerful tool. Positive reinforcement, constructive feedback and celebrating small victories are essential components of nurturing a fledgling author's confidence.

Recognizing Unique Strengths

Every storyteller possesses distinctive strengths, whether it be a knack for dialogue, a gift for world-building, or an ability to convey emotions vividly. A mentor's role is to identify and celebrate these unique strengths helping authors recognize the value they bring to their narratives.

Constructive Critique: Balancing Feedback

While encouragement is vital, so is constructive critique. Provide feedback that highlights areas for improvement without discouraging creativity. A delicate balance between positive reinforcement and constructive criticism encourages growth without stifling the individuality of the storyteller.

Guiding the Narrative Journey: Techniques and Strategies

Helping others find their voice involves sharing practical tools and strategies to refine their craft. From mastering the art of character development to creating evocative settings, offering guidance on the technical aspects of storytelling empowers authors to shape their narratives effectively.

Story Structure and Pacing

Introduce aspiring authors to the fundamentals of story structure and pacing. Understanding the nuances of plot development and maintaining a rhythmic narrative flow equips them with the tools to captivate readers from start to finish.

Characterization and Authenticity

Encourage the exploration of diverse characters and perspectives. Emphasize the importance of authenticity in character development, fostering relatable and compelling personas that resonate with readers on a deeper level.

Cultivating Resilience: Navigating Challenges

The path to finding one's voice is not without obstacles. As a mentor, prepare storytellers for the inevitable challenges they may face – whether it be writer's block, rejection or self-doubt. Teach resilience as a key attribute, emphasizing the importance of perseverance in the face of setbacks.

Embracing Failure as a Steppingstone

Failure is an inherent part of the creative process. Help authors view setbacks not as roadblocks but as opportunities to learn and grow. Sharing personal experiences of overcoming obstacles can inspire resilience and instil a sense of determination.

Building a Community of Voices

The journey of helping others find their voice extends beyond individual mentorship. Encourage the formation of communities where storytellers can support and inspire each other. Whether through writing groups, workshops or online forums, these spaces foster collaboration and provide a collective platform for diverse voices to thrive.

The act of helping others find their voice as storytellers or authors is a noble undertaking that contributes to the richness and diversity of the literary world. As mentors, advocates and fellow travellers on this creative journey, we have the power to inspire, encourage, and guide budding storytellers toward the realization of their unique narrative potential. By doing so, we not only enrich the landscape of storytelling but also contribute to a world where the multitude of voices harmonize to create a symphony of shared experiences and collective wisdom.

Even though talent maybe evenly distributed opportunities are not, and acknowledgement is rare. Opportunities do not always come knocking, some had to build their own doors. Some have no means to build their own doors, so I stepped up to help create new authors and facilitate publishing a world class product for those that are willing to change the world with me. Light a star that will keep burning long after you depart. Thus, this anthology was born.

Stories have been the heartbeat of humanity since our earliest days, weaving together the threads of our collective experience. Through tales spun by firelight or inked on parchment, we transcend the boundaries of time and place, sharing dreams, fears, and triumphs. In the dance of words and imagination, storytelling breathes life into history, kindles empathy, and ignites the sparks of understanding. It binds us in a tapestry of diverse voices, offering solace, inspiration, and the promise of endless possibilities. Embrace the power of storytelling - for within every narrative lies the potential to inspire, unite, and illuminate the path forward for generations to come.

LIFE EVENTS   STORYTELLING

Illustration to use your life experiences for greater good.

Embrace the stories. Grasp the inspiration and start a new narrative in your own story. The goal of Markey Writing Academy is to publish books that inspire, encourage, motivate, and fortify both the creators and readers. It is not about mass publication it is about living this vision to enable and equip society. Insofar as we know, when one person makes a considerable difference to their awareness it creates a significant ripple effect throughout the ecosystem and donates to the mass remedial of human consciousness. When you work in concert, either as a reader or creator you are assisting in achieving a profound vision.

I stood looking up at the celestial-blue stained-glass windows of The Mont-Saint-Michel Abbey, in Normandy, France marvelling at the craftmanship, expertise and devotion of people that have long-vanished. It was surreal to enjoy the beauty of their work and I smiled as we all have the same opportunity to impact humanity now and in the future. Wisdom is man's true strength; may this book help you cultivate yours. This book is a collaborative effort, acknowledge the contributions of others. During my visit to Mount St. Michael in France, nestled majestically atop its rocky island, I found myself profoundly moved by the echoes of history and humanity that resonated through its ancient walls. The abbey's rich tapestry of architectural splendour, steeped in centuries of religious significance and cultural heritage, sparked a creative awakening within me that eventually led to the inception of my book, "Echoes of Humanity."

As I wandered through the abbey's corridors, climbed its winding staircases, and gazed out across the sweeping vistas of the Normandy coast, I felt a deep connection to the countless generations of individuals who had sought solace and enlightenment within these very walls. Each stone seemed to whisper stories of triumph and tribulation, of faith and fortitude, weaving a narrative tapestry that transcended time itself. Captivated by this palpable sense of history and inspired by the enduring resilience of the human spirit, I embarked on a journey of introspection and creativity. "Echoes of Humanity" became not just a collection of stories, but a testament to the universal themes of love, loss, hope, and redemption that bind us all together as a global community. Each chapter became a homage to the echoes of humanity that reverberate through our shared experiences, reminding us of our interconnectedness in an ever-changing world.

As I reflect on my visit to Mount St. Michael and the profound impact it had on my creative journey, I am reminded of the power of travel to ignite our imaginations and awaken our souls. May "Echoes of Humanity" serve as a testament to the transformative power of inspiration and the enduring legacy of places like Mount St. Michael that continue to inspire generations of storytellers and dreamers alike. This anthology is possible by the collaborative efforts of all authors, whose expertise, experience and dedication have enriched every chapter - THANK YOU!

Kelly Markey
Publisher / CEO / Founder
Markey Writing Academy

Introduction

"My voracious readers: Life is not what happens to you but what you hold inside in the absence of an empathetic witness or having a noteworthy vista to observe and grow from. Look for pages of experience everywhere and every day and from everyone!"

Kelly Markey

In the tapestry of human existence, the threads of our individual lives are woven into the fabric of society creating a complex and ever-evolving narrative. *"Echoes of Humanity"* is an expedition of social change carved by lived experience that seeks to explore the profound impact of personal stories on the broader canvas of societal transformation. As we navigate the currents of change, this book endeavours to unravel the intricate connections between the intimate and the collective, demonstrating how individual narratives shape the course of history.

The impetus for this exploration arises from the recognition that societal shifts are not merely abstract concepts or statistical trends but are, at their core, reflections of the myriad lived experiences that comprise our shared reality. Through the lens of personal narratives, we embark on a journey to unveil the untold stories that have moulded cultures, ignited revolutions and propelled humanity forward.

The pages that follow are a testament to the belief that understanding the lived experiences of individuals is integral to comprehending the dynamics of social change. By delving into the intricacies of personal stories, we gain insight into the motivations, struggles and triumphs that propel individuals to become catalysts for transformation. Whether it be the quiet courage of everyday heroes, or the resilience born from adversity, these narratives illuminate the human spirit's capacity to shape the world.

This anthology brings together a diverse tapestry of voices, each contributing a unique hue to the portrait of social change. From the grassroots movements that reverberate through communities to the transformative power of individual choices, the narratives within these pages serve as both a mirror reflecting our shared history and a compass guiding us towards a more equitable and compassionate future.

As we embark on this exploration, let us embrace the richness of lived experiences and recognize the potential for profound social change inherent in every individual story. Through the collective understanding of our shared humanity, we may find inspiration, empathy and a collective call to action that transcends the boundaries of time and culture. *"Echoes of Humanity"* invites readers to engage with the stories that have etched their mark on the ever-evolving tapestry of our world.

In a world that often seems divided by boundaries, cultures and languages, there exists a unifying force that transcends these apparent barriers - the power of human inspiration. This anthology draws inspiration from around the world: the rare gems that sparkle vividly, is a testament to the remarkable capacity of individuals to ignite flames of hope, courage and determination that traverse every corner of our planet. Within these pages, you will embark on a journey that spans continents and embraces the rich texture of human experience. We have gathered the voices of extraordinary individuals, each an author and a storyteller, who have ventured beyond the ordinary, overcoming challenges and embracing their dreams with unwavering fervour.

From the bustling streets of the United Kingdom to the serene landscapes of the African savannah and the humming skyscrapers of America to the tranquil village called Tugela, this anthology brings you stories that resonate across borders, cultures and generations. These tales of triumph and perseverance remind us that the human spirit is a force of boundless potential, capable of surmounting even the most formidable obstacles. As you immerse yourself in the narratives penned by these authors, you will discover the strength of character that emerges from adversity, the profound wisdom that arises from introspection and the unbreakable threads of connection that link us all. Their words will touch your heart, provoke your thoughts and inspire you to rekindle the flames of your own dreams.

"Echoes of Humanity" is not just a collection of stories; it is a celebration of the universal human capacity to rise above limitations, to create beauty from chaos and to craft a life that echoes with purpose. These authors invite you to share in their journeys, to learn from their experiences and to embrace the infinite possibilities that lie within your grasp. May these stories remind you that no matter where you come from or where you are headed, the power to inspire and be inspired resides within us all. So, let the pages of this anthology be a reminder that even amidst the diversity of our world, the sparks of inspiration know no bounds.

During my expedition to England, I was fascinated by an abundance of vast history. My jaw dropped in awe and remained dropped so long that a flock of birds could have flown in, to roost. One of the captivations: Stonehenge is a prehistoric monument located in Wiltshire, England and it is one of the most famous and mysterious archaeological sites in the world. Although the exact purpose and significance of Stonehenge remain a subject of debate among scholars, there are several historical aspects and potential lessons that can be gleaned from its study.

Construction and Engineering Skills

Stonehenge is believed to have been constructed in several phases over a span of at least 1,500 years, with the earliest phase dating back to around 3100 BCE. The monument consists of large standing stones, known as sarsens, arranged in a circular pattern, with smaller stones, or bluestones, set within. The engineering and construction skills required to transport and erect these massive stones are a testament to the capabilities of ancient societies.

Astronomical Alignment

Stonehenge exhibits a remarkable alignment with celestial phenomena, such as the summer and winter solstices. The layout of the stones suggests an intentional alignment with the movements of the sun, moon and stars. This has led many to believe that Stonehenge may have had an astronomical or calendrical function, serving as an ancient observatory or a ceremonial site tied to celestial events.

Cultural and Religious Significance

Stonehenge is thought to have had religious or ceremonial importance for the ancient people who built and used it. The significance of the monument in the religious or spiritual practices of its builders is not understood, but it likely played a central role in their cultural beliefs. The lessons here involve the exploration of ancient belief systems and the role of monumental architecture in expressing and reinforcing cultural identity.

Community Collaboration

The construction of Stonehenge would have required a significant amount of labour and collaboration among the community members. The ability to organize and mobilize a workforce for such a monumental undertaking suggests a level of social organization and cooperation. The lessons here include the importance of community collaboration in achieving ambitious goals and the potential role of collective effort in societal development.

Adaptation and Evolution

Stonehenge underwent various modifications over centuries, indicating a continual process of adaptation and evolution. The builders responded to changing needs, preferences, or perhaps external pressures. This adaptability is a lesson in the dynamic nature of societies and their ability to evolve over time.

Cultural Preservation

Stonehenge has been a protected archaeological site for many years and its preservation is a lesson in the importance of safeguarding cultural heritage. The ongoing efforts to study, conserve and interpret Stonehenge contribute to our understanding of the past and its relevance to contemporary society.

While Stonehenge continues to be a source of fascination and mystery, ongoing research and archaeological investigations contribute to our understanding of ancient cultures and their achievements. The lessons from Stonehenge extend beyond its physical structure, providing insights into the social, cultural, and technological aspects of prehistoric societies. You also have the potential to create a legacy and rich history that will push more than just daisies after you have gone, just like Stonehenge. Are you going to take that leap? You are not here to match mediocre energy you are here to enhance the atmosphere and create a sustain change of the narrative.

Knowledge is only a speculation until it manifests in your lifestyle. Never bask in glories for the day while you have no vision of the droughts in the future. Don't adapt to the energy in the room, influence the energy in profound and subtle ways. You will breathe country and eat nation, change your words and change the narrative. Either on prayer or a whim grace and experience will take you places that hustling cannot. There is no restoration where there is no reflection. Stop, ponder and look at what life is teaching you from your own journey and other paths as well. Stop playing gymnastics with complacency, most people don't want to make decisions, but they want choices. Remember that we climb mountains not for the world to see us but to see the world. Elenore Roosevelt said, *"the future belongs to those who have the capacity to dream."*

Readers have overwhelmingly shared how my books have impacted their lives, leaving an indelible mark on their hearts and minds. Many express a deep sense of inspiration, describing my work as a transformative journey that stirred their emotions and ignited a newfound perspective on life. The eloquence of my words, coupled with the richness of my personal experience has carved the narrative that has resonated with readers on a profound level, prompting them to reflect on their own experiences and beliefs and lives.

Numerous reviews highlighted the way my books have acted as a guiding light during challenging times, offering solace and encouragement. Readers speak of my experience and themes lingering in their thoughts long after they have turned the last page, illustrating the lasting impression my storytelling has made. Some share personal anecdotes of implementing the lessons learned from my books into their daily lives, attesting to its practical wisdom and applicability.

In essence, the consensus among readers is that my books transcend the boundaries of non-fiction, evolving into a source of empowerment, wisdom and emotional resonance. It's evident that my work has become more than just a story; it has become a catalyst for personal growth and introspection, fostering a sense of connection and understanding among its diverse audience.

"There is no greater agony than bearing an untold story inside you." - Maya Angelou. In 2022 during my book tour to South Africa, August is Women's month - I donated my books to an organization to help women. The receiving organization farmed out my books to women that they deemed needed to read something inspirational.

Months later it was 3.00am in Australia and a reader that was gifted one of my books was gripped, she found me online from South Africa and instant messaged me via messenger. She began to narrate how my book was impacting her. She then asked if she could call me as she just wanted to hear my voice, talk to me and confirm if I was real. I confirmed yes sure, I am available for you to call me. She was in tears when she first began to talk to me. *"For the first time in months I feel like I have hope. Your story gives me HOPE. I have not had a proper meal or sleep in the last 6 months. My husband killed himself on my birthday! I am still numb from the pain (she cried bitterly. He was a son of pastors and a drug addict, so they did not want us to talk about the daily dramas of our lives. Even now after his death I feel like I am suffocating as I have no real support and no one understands my grief as they are unaware of my journey. Thank you for sharing your life with me in your book, it gives me courage to live for tomorrow. Today was the first day I tried to eat something substantial and sleep for a while. Your experience, endurance and comeback instilled courage in me."*

This is just one example where my books have impacted readers around the world. People place limits on themselves and manifest a restricted destiny based on their current circumstances. Our traumas are real and for eons we have played prolonged victims on the stage of life. By sharing my story, it helped so many people in other countries realign their lives. Our past can be washed by the river of shared stories that gushes forth new light and propels us forward. When society experiences tragedies the emotional roller-coaster that is unexpressed and expressed diverge from the inner turmoil. So much is hidden and the unfortunate person must trudge through life trying to find solutions to a bleak situation. We tend to create a mental trapeze act - dangling in between past and present then creating delusions between reality and illusions.

When we are riddled by grief and trauma it is too hard to see the silver lining and grasp a sensible future however some of us have the knack to grasp from the lived experiences of others. It gives them a thread of hope, it reassures them that there is light at the end of the tunnel. I have taken the liberty to create this book so readers can identify, acknowledge and remedy their suboptimal choices and learn from them. Always remember that God will be your balm to all the things you have not advertised. He will heal the places where you were assassinated even when no one models rationale to you.

I had a radio interview with a renowned Australian radio host. Prior to the interview he obtained a copy of my book *"Don't Just Fly, Soar."* While we were live on air, he confessed to me and his listeners:

"I normally do not read non-fictional books. I gravitate to fictional books to help me escape from the reality of my life. I am reading the latest Star Wars book and I had to put it down several times to pick up your book, "Don't Just Fly, SOAR" had me hooked. Your life experience had me engrossed and in awe!"

As the radio host delved into the pages of my non-fiction book, a profound sense of emotion swept over him. The carefully crafted words painted vivid pictures and unravelled powerful narratives that resonated on a personal level. The host found himself moved by the authenticity and raw honesty that permeated every chapter, creating an intimate connection with the material. In the quiet moments between sentences, the host couldn't help but reflect on the profound impact my words had on him, expressing genuine admiration for the courage and vulnerability revealed within the pages. It was a reading experience that transcended the airwaves, leaving the radio host touched by the transformative journey my non-fiction book invited him to embark upon - I was certain that he was now converted to the brighter side of dabbling with other genres.

The same is applicable in life, you do not have to always do the same old thing. Try something new, you may learn something new, or expand your horizon to other possibilities. Connections exists to make us conscious rather than boxed in. Influences are established when we share our stories, pain and joy. Serendipity is reaped in a profound fashion. As an author, professional, publisher and explorer I can witness to an archetypal resolution that presents when we share our life journey with others. It utilizes case vignettes to illustrate various principles, values, lessons and serves up hope in bucket loads.

People are tormented by hungry ghosts of trauma and the plight of life, sharing our stories are essential on life's savannah's. It creates the vast chasm between enthusiasm and despair - the dance of life. It cements the reality and everyone is doing the same dance of life with good and bad circumstances just with different intensity. My voracious readers: Life is not what happens to you, but what you hold inside in the absence of an empathetic witness or having no noteworthy vista to observe and grow from. Look for pages of experience everywhere and every day and from everyone!

I still pinch myself when I receive reviews and feedback of how my written work has touched lives in a profound way. My lived experience has created a trajectory that is leaving a profound echo on humanity.

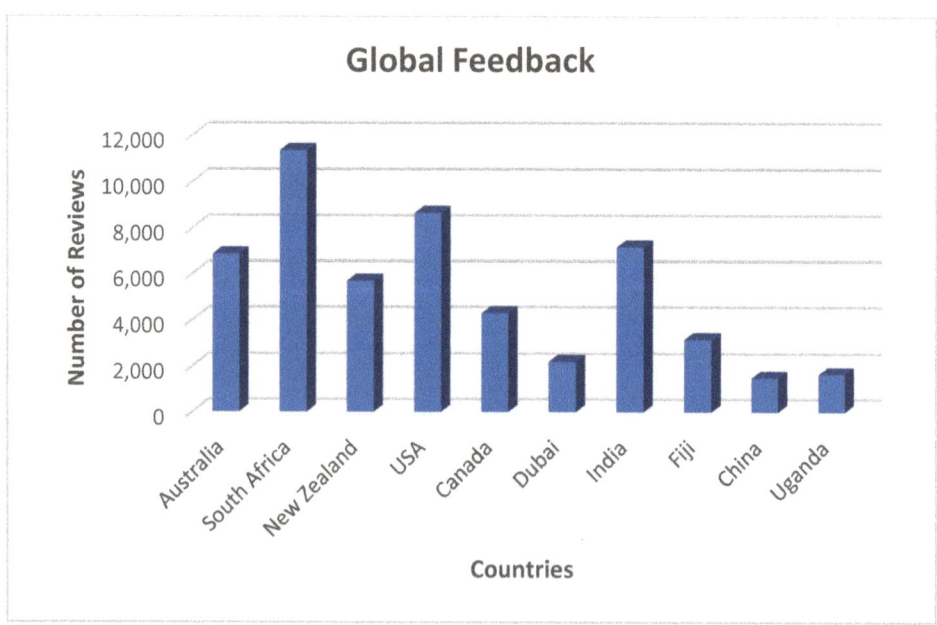

Graph of my reader reviews from top ten countries.

In the vast complexity of human existence, woven with threads of triumph and tribulation, lessons learned in moments of affliction echo through the corridors of time. Each page of our collective stories is imprinted with the indelible marks of distress, the resonance of victory and the dazzling brilliance that emerges from the crucible of experience. *"Echoes of Humanity"* embarks on a profound exploration of these intricate facets, inviting readers to traverse the diverse landscapes of our shared journey.

This literary odyssey unfolds as a mosaic of narratives, revealing the profound lessons imbibed during times of adversity, the enduring human spirit that rises in the face of distress and the symphony of triumph that accompanies the pursuit of victory. Through the lens of our collective experiences, this book aims to illuminate the intricate dance between challenges and growth, sorrow and joy, defeat and triumph.

As we navigate the pages of *"Echoes of Humanity,"* we encounter stories that transcend borders and cultures, threading a universal narrative that binds us all. From the depths of affliction, characters emerge as resilient protagonists, their tales etched with the wisdom gained from life's trials. In the ordeal of hardship, we find the raw material for triumph and within the folds of victory, we uncover the brilliance that defines the human spirit.

This exploration seeks to celebrate the diversity of our shared experiences, acknowledging that each lesson, each trial and each triumph contributes to the grand mosaic of our existence. Join us on this literary journey, where the pages of *"Echoes of Humanity"* resonate with the timeless cadence of our collective wonders, unveiling the profound beauty woven into the fabric of our lives.

The perks and pitfalls of reminiscing offers us a visual testament and oh so many opportunities to realign life. Presenting you the opportunity to use your human cogs to transform into an intrepid connoisseur rather than a victim of life. Every obstacle has a solution, discover your sacred compass to nurturing on purpose. Don't just whistle pass the graveyard and ignore what the setback it is teaching you. Find your radius of respect and change with discipline. Wherever your travels may take you let it also take you within for introspection. Life is not about the perception of Pinterest perfections. It is about learning to navigate your flaws and I hope this book will shed some light to you in achieving just that.

This is a book that invests talents, time, energy and resources in telling stories from lived experience, creating moral vistas, painting pictures of models, navigating ethical judgments, discerning integrity, negotiating social dilemmas, establishing blue prints, wiping tears, ignoring the pain you dispense, mastering the art of self-awareness, becoming perceptive about the hurt you prescribe, stopping to smell the roses even when thorns are around and finding your mojo in church, temple or where ever. The target is to glean from others and grow to be uninhibited from the cosmic dread. When people see themselves in your story, they relate and feel less alone. All facets of life are filled with teachable moments. These are docile gems that are not only to be gleaned but mandatory to pass on to future generations. Just as Stonehenge stands the test of time due to safeguarding, we need to establish a culture that values the lessons of stories shared. The mantle is now passed onto you! Now is the best time to start becoming the person you want to be.

"Character cannot be developed in ease and quiet. Only through experiences and suffering can the soul be strengthened, vision cleared, ambition inspired and success achieved." - Helen Keller.

Echoes of Humanity

Kelly Markey

An evergreen blacklist multiple award-winning and bestselling author - Kelly Markey. Both Kelly and her books are referenced as inspiration and motivation on international platforms. Her books have saved lives, revolutionised mindsets, featured on Times Square billboard in New York City and galvanised organisations. Markey's work has achieved immortality.

Kelly Markey is cut from a different cloth and that cloth is rarely produced now! Kelly's passion is to nourish humanities leap to their apex of possibilities. Kelly's craft ignites the prowess in every reader. Your mental library expands as you read and implement Markey's books. These are resources associated with gallantry and invincibility. An authentic walking inspiration banner.

A literary virtuoso and an unparalleled polyglot whose mastery of languages is as enchanting as her storytelling. With a linguistic repertoire that spans across continents, Markey seamlessly weaves motivation in a multitude of tongues, creating a rich tapestry of narratives that transcends cultural boundaries.

Her ability to fluently speak and write in languages as diverse as Afrikaans, Zulu, Hindi, Tamil and now learning German, allows Markey to delve into the nuances of different cultures, bringing authenticity and depth to her stories and settings. Each book that she pens becomes a linguistic journey, inviting readers to explore the beauty and complexity of language through the lens of her compelling narratives.

Kelly's linguistic prowess not only sets her apart in the literary world but also serves as an inspiration for aspiring writers and language enthusiasts. Her work embodies the belief that language is not just a means of communication, but a powerful tool that can unlock new worlds and perspectives.

As a talented polyglot, Kelly Markey continues to captivate readers with her ability to transcend linguistic barriers, creating a literary legacy that celebrates the universal thrill of words. Kelly is a talented book illustrator and brilliant poet.

Her corporate vocation in Health Information Technology has offered her the opportunity to design and implement numerous strategic systems around the world. Kelly has significantly enhanced healthcare for both patients and clinical software users around the globe.

Other Books by Kelly Markey

- Don't Just Fly, SOAR
- Glean, Grow and Glow
- Making Sage Decisions
- Legacy Playbook
- The Life of Jayandra…Transcending Beyond the Shadows of Suicide.
- Lady Diversity Power - Co-author
- Heart Warrior - Co-author

Future Book Releases by Kelly Markey

- Contentment Unravelled
- The Enchanted Language Garden (A multi linguistic kid's book)
- Beacon of Hope, Anthology – intaking author submissions now.

Contact kelly@kellymarkey.com for current/future publishing enquiries.

Kelly Markey Business Card

1

Rising Above Your Circumstance and Embrace your Ubuntu within

"YOU are not your CIRCUMSTANCES."
Loschinee Reddy

October 1976 - As the blinding sun cast its golden hues across the breathtaking South African landscape, my mother lay 6 months pregnant. As she watched the sky became a canvas of vibrant oranges, purples and pinks, melding seamlessly with the nearby rolling hills a gentle breeze was blowing carrying the scents of the earth and whispers of stories untold.

In this moment where the day bid farewell and twilight embraced our rural, small home on the north coast of Durban, Mandini, my mum found herself feeling grateful. She reflected on her journey up until this point in her life as she was only three months away of giving birth to her baby girl, a moment she had always dreamt of.

It is within the embrace of the captivating South African sunset that my story takes shape - a story of perseverance, love and the unyielding spirit of Ubuntu - an African philosophy emphasising interconnectedness, compassion and community. Through my personal narrative I encourage you to explore the transformative power of rising above circumstances, choosing one's attitude and redefining self-identity. My hope is that my story not only serves as a testament to the indomitable human spirit but also offers practical insights into how we can all embrace Ubuntu within ourselves, regardless of our circumstance.

My mother stared blankly as she found herself within the sterile confines of the ice-cold hospital theatre room in Stanger, South Africa. It was in this space that my mum describes a time in her life where time seemed to stand still and the air being heavy with anticipation. The clinical ambiance, devoid of warmth and familiarity, created an eerie backdrop for the extraordinary events that were about to unfold.

Sure, our bodies have limits, but at the end of the day your only limit is you and your mind. You can either hang out on the side lines and watch life pass you by or you can dive in, push yourself and prove to yourself and the world how limitless you are. Do you make the **choice** to live without limits and rise above your circumstances in life?

It was in this unforgiving environment that the pronouncement of my departure from the world echoed through the room, sending shockwaves of despair and heartache. My mum screams and cries out loudly: *"What do you mean my baby did not make it? Please I am begging you to do something. Do something to save my baby please. I beg you, doctor, anyone, save my child."*

The flickering fluorescent lights cast a cold, unwavering glow, intensifying the gravity of the confusion and panic felt by all in the room. Yet, in this stark setting, something miraculous occurred - perhaps even a divine intervention that defied all medical or human logic.

The doctor's faces etched with a mixture of disbelief and resignation, who just proclaimed my life as extinguished, now showed a faint flicker of hope. It was as if the icy grip of the room was momentarily thawed by an otherworldly presence, breathing life into me - a being who was only moments before deemed lifeless.

In that pivotal moment when all seemed lost, the room transformed into a sanctuary of fascination and wonder. Through the unwavering belief of my precious mother and the miraculous intervention of an old doctor, my faint heartbeat was heard by the 11th doctor who came to examine my mum, defying all odds and as if through some divine presence, their combined forces brought me into the world.

My mother recalls that 10 doctors who preceded him declared me dead and they were amid a procedure to remove the foetus but almost out of nowhere came this grey-haired doctor whose almost angelic presence challenged the certainties of science. The disbelief transformed into awe as the realisation dawned that a higher power had certainly different plans for me - plans that would shape my purpose in life and the lives of those I would touch as I navigated through my journey.

This profound experience reinforced the power of faith deep within and serves as a testament to the ability that I can rise above my circumstances. From that pivotal juncture, my path became intertwined with an inner need to serve almost as an *"Earth Angel"* - an embodiment of love, kindness and compassion. Just as the hospital theatre room was once a place of uncertainty and then became a symbol of transformation, so too is my personal testament to the resilience of the human spirit irrespective of temporary circumstances.

Whilst life and death danced a delicate tango, a divine intervention shifted the course of my existence. It birthed a purpose that would radiate warmth, compassion and strength - a person who tries to live her life, lighting the way for others so that they too can transcend their own circumstances and discover the limitless possibilities that reside deep within their own souls.

Through the subsequent chapters of my life I found myself rising above my own circumstances, defying limitations and embracing the profound responsibility to uplift others. Almost like an angel walking among others, sometimes even without realising it, I found that my purpose would unfold. I would be the one guiding those in despair to find hope, empowering them to rise above their challenges and reclaim their own will to keep going on. My story of resilience, triumph and overcoming must be rooted within my DNA because those that walked before me almost planted those integral seeds into the core of my mother's womb.

From the struggles faced by my ancestors to my own personal journey of triumph and resilience, I can bear witness and testimony to the indomitable spirit that has guided me through adversity. Anchored in love and kindness, my parents embodied the Ubuntu philosophy, transcending circumstances and inspiring others to rise above their own challenges.

My grandfather who was born in Kanchipuram, India joined the first indentured labourers that were transported across the seas from India to South Africa. Despite the tragic loss of his parents at a tender age of 6 years he persevered and created a self-sustaining life in South Africa. He together with my precious grandmother (Aya) cultivated their own food and tended to cattle to put food on the table for their thirteen children.

Chellan (Thatha) as he was affectionately known explored the enduring legacy of resilience and self-reliance that shaped my family's journey, providing a foundation for overcoming the adversities faced by subsequent generations. The core legacy that my grandfather left for us is that he introduced his children and then us his grandchildren to the fundamental concept of personal agency-the ability to make conscious choices irrespective of our circumstances. Through Thatha, we learnt of the distinction between being a victim and an active participant in life. He demonstrated through his life that our circumstances do not define us. Each one of us have the power to reconstruct our own perspective, choose to be in the present moment and take ownership of our own narrative.

In May 2023 amidst the vibrant tapestry of India, a land steeped in rich history and cultural heritage, my family embarked on a journey of discovery from the UK to India - a journey that held deep significance and profound symbolism for us as a family. It was not just a holiday but rather a voyage that transcended borders, spanning generations and carried with it the echoes of resilience that flows through our bloodline.

As we set foot on the soil that birthed my family's legacy, the air became infused with a palpable sense of connection - a tangible thread that wove together the stories of our ancestors with our present reality. In the bustling streets of India, amidst the kaleidoscope of colours and sounds, I felt the pulse of my heritage resonating within me. For my parents this journey to India was a stark reminder of the unwavering determination that courses through our family's history. It served as a testament to the sacrifices made by my grandfather, who defied the odds and travelled vast distances from India to South Africa in search of a better life for his own family. His remarkable courageous journey became the cornerstone upon which my family's story, my story was built. An enduring testament to the unyielding spirit that refuses to be defined by circumstances.

Just as my grandfather's voyage symbolised a pursuit of a brighter future, my own journey from South Africa to the United Kingdom echoed the same resolute spirit. By stepping beyond the boundaries of my familiar homeland, I embraced the call of my own purpose, refusing to let my circumstances dictate the trajectory of my life. My life's journey has encompassed love and heartache, understanding that once your purpose has been fulfilled in a person's life, they will disappear from your life, often in a way that you cannot understand or fathom but must trust as part of your continuing purpose.

In 2011 I suffered one of the worse levels of pain when I lost my baby girl at the exact same stage that I was brought into this world, having my mother in the hospital room with me to relive this nightmare that she lived when I was declared dead at birth.

In 2017 despite having been told by medical experts that it will be impossible to bear children, I gave birth to a bouncing bundle of joy, my beautiful daughter, Arabella (her name is of Latin origin meaning yielding to prayer), exactly a year after God decided that I was to become a mother to another daughter, Sraddha. From having no children, I became a mother to two beautiful girls in one year. In that bold leap of faith, I reaffirmed the legacy of resilience and unwavering determination that has now been passed down through the generations.

2 Corinthians 4:17: *"For our light and momentary troubles are achieving for us an eternal glory that far outweighs them all"*. This verse reminds me that the challenges we face in life are temporary and transient. They serve a purpose in shaping us, but they do not define us. Our true essence and potential lie in the eternal glory that surpasses any earthly circumstance.

For my father, being the youngest of thirteen children and now not having a single member of his own family here on earth, this journey to India, held deep personal significance for him. It carried within it the seeds of resilience and the transformative power of embracing the belief that you are not your circumstance. As my father ventured into the land that bore witness to his family's beginnings, India, he stood at a unique crossroad in his own life. He found himself at a stage where the ties to his birth family had been severed, leaving him with a profound sense of solitude. Yet, it was within this moment of introspection and soul-searching that he discovered the extraordinary strength that resides within him.

The notion that you are not your circumstance took root within him as he witnessed the resilience and tenacity of the people he encountered on his journey. Their ability to rise above poverty and adversity, to find joy and purpose amidst challenging circumstances, served as a profound reminder that one's inner strength and mindset are the true determinants of a fulfilling life. In embracing this empowering belief, my father has transcended the limitations imposed by external circumstances and has chosen to live his best life. Through resilience, determination and an unwavering spirit, he has forged his own path, shaping a future that defies the constraints of his past.

As we visited the ancient temples and bustling cities in India, we were reminded that the power to shape your destiny resides within you. The journey became an affirmation that the path I have chosen is not defined by the circumstances that surround me, but rather by the unwavering belief in my own potential and the unyielding drive to fulfil my own purpose. In the heart of India, where the past and present co-exist I discovered a profound truth - that my family's story is an embodiment of the human spirit's capacity to rise above adversity, to transcend borders and to create a legacy that defies the limitations of time and place. It served as a reminder that you are the author of your own narrative, etching my own indelible mark upon the world, just as my ancestors did before me.

As we ventured back from India to the United Kingdom, we carried with us the memories and the lessons imprinted upon our hearts, our family's journey became more than just a physical journey or holiday. It was a testament of resilience and the unbreakable bond that connects us to our roots and a testament to the extraordinary power that lies within us to shape your own destiny, no matter the distance or the odds.

My life which encompasses both triumphs and tribulations is one that extends far beyond the borders of my birthplace and the confines of any circumstance. As a daughter out of Africa I am determined to lay a strong foundation for my daughters instilling within them the unshakable belief that they are not their circumstance. Through my own journey of resilience, I have witnessed the power of rising above adversity and of defying the limitations imposed by outside or external forces. It is this invaluable wisdom that I seek to impart to my daughters - to plant within their own hearts a deep-seated understanding that their circumstance no matter how daunting it may seem, does not define who they are, at their core.

I long for my daughters to embrace the truth that God's plan and purpose for their lives is far superior to the limitations of the present moment. It is in aligning themselves with this divine guidance that they will discover their inherent strength, their unwavering resilience and their limitless potential. I yearn to nurture within them a profound sense of self-worth, reminding them that they are beautifully crafted by a loving Creator, bestowed with unique talents and abilities that surpass any temporary, external situation or circumstances. I want them to understand that the challenges they encounter along their journey are opportunities for growth and that within the depths of their souls lies an unquenchable flame, ready to ignite their spirits and move them forward, to the next chapter of their life.

By sharing the stories of my family's legacy, from my grandfather's courageous life from India to South Africa, to my own journey from South Africa to the United Kingdom, I hope to infuse hearts with a resolute belief - that you too can rise above any circumstance and fulfil your purpose in this world. I encourage you to walk through life with your head held high, anchored in the knowledge that your worth is not measured by the external markers of success or the challenges you may momentarily face. Instead, remember that your worth lies in your ability to tap into your inner strength, to trust in God's plan and to rise above any circumstance with grace, determination and unwavering faith.

May you carry this profound truth within your hearts as a guiding light, illuminating your path through life's challenges and triumphs. May you be empowered to create your own narratives to live authentically and to fulfil the divine purpose that has been woven into the very fabric of your core being. I stand steadfast in my commitment to cultivate this strong foundation within my daughters, the unshakeable belief that they are not their circumstance. I entrust them to the embrace of the divine, knowing that their journey will be marked by courage, resilience and an unwavering faith that they are destined for greatness.

Just as diamonds undergo a transformative process to unleash their inherent brilliance, I too have embarked on a daily journey of self-discovery, continuous learning and growth. Through my life's trials and triumphs, I have been refined, re-defined, shaped, moulded and polished by the hands of experience and the lives I have touched along the way.

As a daughter born in Africa, I proudly embrace the symbolism of a diamond - a precious gem that emerges from the depths, uncut and raw, waiting to be polished and transformed into radiant brilliance. Like a diamond, I recognise the unique rarity within me and I am humbled and grateful for the honour bestowed upon me to share my love and kindness with the world.

Loschinee Reddy

Loschinee, from the United Kingdom, a daughter of the Highest, an accomplished Legal Eagle, a Jay Shetty certified Holistic Life and Success Coach, a loving wife and devoted mother to two adorable girls, shares a powerful, empowering and insightful story in this book. She shares a compelling narrative of triumph over adversity, how she conquered tough roadmaps born from a personal journey of facing overwhelming challenges, to inspire others. From navigating through seemingly insurmountable obstacles to overcoming setbacks, Loschinee candidly narrates her experiences, through the lens of her family's legacy and offers invaluable lessons on harnessing inner strength to transcend limitations. Through personal experiences and practical advice, Loschinee illuminates the transformative power of resilience, courage and perseverance and offers a roadmap for anyone facing difficulties, revealing how resilience and determination can lead to a fulfilling life. *"Rise Above Your Circumstance"* isn't just a story, it's a guide to unlocking inner strength and embracing a brighter and more empowered future.

2

Empowered Within

"I am Empowered to Inspire."
Dr Adama Kalokoh

"I am Empowered to Inspire" is my favorite tagline which I developed as my personal statement during my college years. This was my daily reminder that I was created with greatness to do amazing things in the world. Never did I know this inspirational affirmation would lead me into becoming a Global woman leader and humanitarian.

Let's ponder a question: Do you ever feel that there is a constant battle between the inner voices in your head? From the voice of doubt telling, you that you're not good enough to the voice of power telling you, *"I Can Do This."* Many may think that the voices of others dictate your actions, but I've come to realize over the years, it's what we speak to ourselves daily that really matters. Afterall, we are what we think we are! As I embraced my phrase *"Empowered to Inspire,"* I really created my own victory story to overcome life's challenges and inspire the world. This voice of empowerment has motivated me to keep going despite difficulties on my journey and to turn my burdens into my brilliance. I did not discover my true strength until I began opening my mouth and using my voice to be a motivation and inspiration on various platforms. I am honored to share my journey of empowerment which led to my purpose, my growth, my victory and a lifetime of humanitarian service.

One thing I believe is you must be inspired to do something great in the world, big or small. Inspiration comes from within, a deep place in your heart that is fuelled into a positive action. Inspiration is influenced by people we know personally or those who we know from afar. Growing up, I was always inspired by men and women who did acts of service such as feeding people, providing clothes and putting smiles on the faces of those in dire situations. As a woman of faith, I grew up seeing my parents serve in church and in their community. I loved the good feeling of service even at a young age. I grew up with a natural passion to serve others and it always brought me complete joy to see others smile from my giving. I was inspired by a combination of factors. To begin with my parents, James I. Conteh and Harriet M. Sesay who migrated to the US from Sierra Leone for a better life, birthing 5 children. They always instilled in us a deep sense of pride and appreciation for their Sierra

Leonean heritage. My parents were my early mentors and greatly influenced my love for humanity as well as our home country of Sierra Leone. My parents always inspired my siblings and I to not only work hard, but to make sure we help others along the way. They also encouraged us to love our African roots and embrace all aspects of our culture.

My parents instilled in me a deep sense of pride and appreciation for our Sierra Leonean heritage. My parents imbued in me the importance of being a proud African child that must never lose sight of my heritage. My mother never allowed me to be defined by the whims of others and to always remember that *"greatness lies within me;"* which is the driving force of my inspiration. My parents both migrated here in the late 70's looking to better themselves and achieve the *"American dream"*. Like many of their fellow Sierra Leonean counterparts, they sought to make a name for themselves within the African community. As I look back, I got my first taste of humanitarian service from my parents as a little girl.

Empowered to Speak

The most powerful tool we have in life is our voice and I am a strong believer in the notion that our words matter. Our words can open and close doors of opportunity. When we don't speak up we miss opportunities. Most of my life growing up was spent as a shy young woman filled with insecurities over her looks.

I marvelled at seeing powerful people speak on stage, especially women. My insecurities kept me in a box for many years and can still creep up in my adult life. I never thought my voice mattered and concluded being in the background would suffice for my life. Little did I know that my destiny and purpose was too great for me to remain in the background. You may wonder, how did you get to a point from being shy and quiet into a woman who now loves public speaking and using her voice. By building confidence in myself, surrounding myself with great mentors, I realized my capacity to impact others and that my desire to help humanity cannot be done in silence. We all have a calling on our lives, to do something greater than our imagination. To fulfill our calling we must come out our shells and use our voice in a mighty way. Within each of us are treasures, gifts and talents that can help us achieve the impossible and lead us to our greatest destiny! Once you realize your gift and believe me it may take time, you must nurture and grow in your gift. Never let your circumstances cripple you from using your gift. With determination, will power and quality networking, you will overcome hurdles and reach your success.

Reflect with me for a moment- how has your voice propelled you to your destiny, your potential and your purpose. Life is too short to waste our gifts and talents. Start with the belief that you are enough and with hard work, your light will shine bright and make a difference in the world. Just take a trip to the cemetery and see all the people buried with their dreams. They are under the earth and can no longer be bold and achieve. If you have breath, you have hope. I always remember my brothers Saidu and Musa who both died too young, using my voice and platform to honour them. Anyone who has a voice to speak and does not speak always reminds me of caterpillars trapped in jars. These trapped caterpillars cannot grow, be nurtured and reach their fullest potential. They will not get their wings and become the butterfly to soar high above. Our voices will catapult us into soaring experiences and when I realized this, my attitude about myself changed. I then looked at myself as a beautiful black butterfly.

Empowered to Serve

My career path began in the military (US Air Force) where I was honoured to serve military personnel at various leadership levels, guiding them on maintaining great nutrition. My thirst for public health and wellness was born during my military service and has been a major part of my leadership journey. The military brought out skills in me I never knew existed. The military taught me keen leadership and organizational skills that would later be a great benefit to my future career. I developed a huge passion for Public Health and wellness not to mention great customer service skills during my time of service. After graduating from college with honours, I performed two years of service as an AmeriCorps Fellow under the Corporation for National and Community Service. My seed of service began in the military, continued in college and led me to a lifetime of serving others.

I learned so many valuable leadership tools while in this role and started to see a glimpse of where I would thrive most in the world...serving as a Non-profit leader. These latest accomplishments all had a common theme and that was community service. I found that many doors of opportunities opened once I embraced serving. It wouldn't be long that my service in the United States would then transform into a love for serving Africa. My seed of service began in the military, continued in college and led me to a lifetime of serving others. After graduating with Honors with a bachelor's degree in public health, my next chapter propelled me into my greatest destiny.

Empowered to Lead

I am a proven example that when you connect your roots, your culture and your passion, your true purpose is born. I had to remember who I was to dive into what was inside of me, therefore becoming the true woman leader I was destined to become. Although my love for Sierra Leone was not as strong in my early years, it was the death of my father in 1997 which triggered in me a strong love and desire to do great things for Sierra Leone. I felt a strong sense of duty to honour his memory by impacting and making a difference. In 2003, I travelled to Sierra Leone as a descendent, discovering my roots. Little did I know I would discover my passion, my purpose and my destiny.

My status as a first generation born West-African positioned me with having unique skills to be a leader in international development. I could serve as a bridge between the US and Africa and be a powerful force! After my first visit to Sierra Leone, I began volunteering with local organizations connected to Sierra Leone but soon realized I had to strike out with my own organization to reach my greatest potential as a leader. After many years of wondering what my purpose was, it was crystal clear that I needed to use my skills and strengths to empower, uplift, inspire and transform the minds of those in extreme poverty with focus on Sierra Leone and within the United States. In 2019, after letting go of my fear of failure and learning so much about the Nonprofit sector, I launched 'Impact Sierra Leone' so I could better serve communities at greater capacities. I hope that my efforts will inspire other descendants of Africa to embrace their culture and impact their home country. As founder of this organization, I've been able to work with great people and providing services to orphans, farmers, students, women and young girls.

Through my organization I have been able to provide communities in Sierra Leone with hope and inspiration by giving them a voice, meeting them where they are and working with them to improve their lives and outlook on life. Through our anchor initiative called the Seeds of Life, we are revamping the community school, starting a literacy program that will benefit the students and women of the community. We will also be launching a skills training program for young women and girls soon. None of these projects would be possible if it were not for the support from other women on my team who see the value in making sure that women have a voice and a seat at the table when decisions are made on the local, national and international levels.

My efforts have garnered me numerous awards and accolades over the years including an Honorary doctorate for my Missionary work in 2020 for which I am proud of. As a devoted mother of two children I hope people will not just see me as an individual but a valuable stakeholder and change agent that is making a difference for future generations to come. I have no regrets in my life of service for serving in any capacity allows you to be a beacon of light the world so needs. For those interested in connecting with my cause, please go to our website at www.impactsierraleone.org or contact me at; adama_kalokoh@yahoo.com

To every person reading this chapter, I encourage you to never stop dreaming or pursuing your goals. I leave you with some best practices that have guided my leadership journey: inspire and motivate others with your platform; pursue personal development; do everything with compassion and humanity; create a legacy that will have impact; live life to the full. You are empowered for greatness!

Dr Adama Kalokoh

Dr Adama Kalokoh is a global humanitarian, Global Goodwill Ambassadors Foundation (GGAF), Chairperson; Sustainable Development Goals (SDG) Advocate; Motivational Speaker; Author, Women Empowerment Leader and Founder of Impact Sierra Leone. Dr. Kalokoh, a proud descendant of Sierra Leone, has always had a passion for helping others and international development. As a former active-duty member of the U.S Air Force who honorably served for 4 years, Dr. Kalokoh is a strong advocate for women and girls in Sierra Leone as well as sustainable development. She received an honorary Doctor of Philosophy degree from Oved Dei Seminary Institute in 2020 for her global missionary work. She hopes that her mission will inspire other descendants of Africa to embrace their culture and positively impact their home country.

3

Nothing is Impossible if You Have No Other Option

"The bar is always so low. People with disabilities are treated as if they are invisible, a burden or with disdain. Humanity created this world and we can also change it."
Nompilo Maphumulo

Growing up under unfortunate circumstance I believe it made who I am today, I can't say I was poor because I had a warm meal every night and warm clothes even though it was not best of the best, I had my basic needs met. It was still the apartheid era in South Africa, but we survived. Given an opportunity to look back to my childhood journey which had a fair share of challenges. The long kilometres we travelled to school through the summer heat, icy winters and heavy rains crossing the rough rivers. It was also our childhood routine to fetch water from those rivers unsupervised by adults, in and those cold dark morning during the winter. It was horrid but giving up then was never an option which built up the resilient muscle that I never knew I had util life threw curve balls at me. This was the most important muscle that I needed for survival, for then and for my future.

I grew up in deep rural village. I had my big dreams just like many children those dreams were great, now that I think about it: they were perfect in my world without any challenges at that time even though I knew that one would need to work hard for them, but those dreams were amazing full of happiness and everything I needed. There was no trace of struggle, pain and sorrow it was just pure happiness for a successful life. That was young naïve me, I didn't know what life had in store for me. I was raised by a strong independent woman who had a stronger belief in God.

In my village especial in rural areas women are raised to get married, if you had child out of wedlock is taken as a taboo then you can settle for any old man who will marry you. However my mother chose me and my twin brother, she went to the nearest town and found a job as a domestic worker and raised us as a single parent against all odds she was alone as *"she broke all the rules."* And created a new rule book. Due to this I grew up and had labels with specific names attached to me. Obvious this was not the greatest start to life. I was judged for deeds that did not belong to me, discrimination soaked by bones, I was tagged a mistake and my birth was ridiculed. The cards of life gave me little hope, but I marched on, each day with pain however my resilient muscle grew bigger and even stronger.

My mother taught us that we were a blessing despite the way we were born and that we are created in the image of God and that's how my faith in Christ was born. When the community and family could not see my value, I was reassured by the Creator Himself. God knew the plan and the need to create me according to his image. This is pure love, right? However, the damage was done because of that situation I had already decided that my very own child would not go through the same trauma that I went through and the decision was made based on that experience that should I have children they must be in marriage. The decision that was supported by the Christianity path that I have chosen where I felt sense of belonging.

Despite all the experience I have had, the big dreams were still there while as growing up. I finished my high school and was ready to conquer the world not knowing that when my journey of the reality will start. Being raised in a disadvantages family and community obviously there was no funds for higher education. That when I had to face reality and study short courses and volunteered at few nonprofit organisations and started odd jobs at the supermarkets.

I began to think that dreams do not come true. Dreams are just that dreams of a fantasy world. Not knowing that the sun was about to shine bright and Gods mercy was upon me I got married to an amazing partner and I was the happiest women on earth, studied towards achieving my awesome social workers degree and blessed with wonderful children who also become my world, everything was perfect living my best life unaware what was to happen.

Had three beautiful children who were special to me not knowing that indeed two of them are special kids. The eldest is 14 years, second is 12 years old and last born 10 years as we speak today, they are my everything. My children are 2 years apart from each other. Even though I almost lost the last one I was told that he was not worth saving because of his condition at the age of 6 months. I had to find my resilience button rather than reacting.

When my eldest child turned 4 years we had a diagnosis of Autism, my whole world shattered as this was the new monster that entered our home and we knew nothing about it and all we heard was that there was no cure. We had to learned that autism is a neurological and development disorder that affects how people communicate, learn and behave. No parent wants to hear that about their child, their first born, their son. Parents supposed to make their children better yet I'm sitting with something that I cannot do anything with it as a mother I felt helpless, useless and less of the mother, a failure. The journey with him was arduous, feeling like uphill, as we knew that there was no cure. The dark abyss that trapped both my family and me. I had to dig deep the find that resilient button and pushing it with tears.

Before I could make a sense of what this autism was the younger one at the age of 6 months was rushed to the hospital diagnosed with hydrocephalus and he was in bad shape as his head as overgrowing and his body could not carry it anymore, he could not sit anymore. He was taken for shunt insertion surgery which was already bad as his aneurysm has busted already and after the surgery he was taken straight to Intensive Unit Care and continued with numerous surgeries. My entire life turned upside down, nothing make sense in my life anymore. I was sitting with a child with autism and a baby with hydrocephalus.

I asked myself how I got here, what have I done wrong, why me and what sins have I committed to be punished like this. The list of questions bombarded me and I struggled to find that resilience button amidst tears. It surfaced but the current of an unfair life kept swirling me in more turbulence. Where I come from, I was taught to believe that disabled, deformed, special needs kids were the curse and here I am having two. I dreamt to be this powerful woman who can change society and change this history coming from humble beginning and be successful, I wanted to show young girls from my own village it can be done. That girl who once had those amazing dreams of conquering the world died inside me in 2014, with not a chance of revival or resuscitation. My dreams and hope vanished with no assurance to return.

I cried a river then had to dry my own tears to fend for my children. A new mother, not just any typical mother but a mother with a shield, armour and a spear, was born that very same day because I was a MOTHER to two special needs boys. We had a challenge but together with my husband we were going to stand up and fight for our children. We did not buy into any beliefs of cursers, to us they were our blessings from God. We did not know even where to start but we decided that we will never give up on our children.

Even though I thought I was ready to fight and defend for my children, I soon realised that the world is full of stigma, discrimination and cruelty against people living with disabilities. It was a battle uphill all the way. Our developing country offers almost no support or extended services for the disabled or their family. I got home after sitting in hospital for the period of three months watching my son fighting for his life going through numerous surgeries to try and relieve the pressure of excessive fluid in his brain, I had my fair share of emotional torture and rollercoaster topped up with suffering from the post-traumatic stress disorder. The resilience button was almost invisible, but I still did not give up.

I started my own research being in denial and believing that I can find the cure for my children but at the end I had to accept the reality and start assisting my children with therapy for them to reach their full potential. Nonetheless, I had educated myself on the matter in the pursuit of a cure. The time and effort were not wasted. It helped us along the way. We noticed that nobody takes time to sit you down to help you understand what is going on with either of the kids. Our journey of two having two different types of disabilities was a new experience for the family. We had choices: sink, swim or carve out more resilience.

Through all this experience my faith towards God for some reason grew even more strong due to loneliness, confusion and tiredness of listening to people's insult, opinion about my kids even though they don't even have a clue what I go through each day raising them. It was not a walk in the park, but society was so eager to judge yet stumbled to help. These moral choices create echoes in our lives and some continue to haunt me. I am writing about my lived experience so that others in my shoe do not have to endure the same pain, in addition to give the community new options to focus on. Lend a helping hand rather than judging.

I have learned to be strong every day because I don't know who I will meet and what that person's opinion will be about my kids. Sometimes I will go for days without sleeping when they're sick, struggling with new routine and on top of all that I still have a daughter that needs her mother by her side as well even though she might be a normal child, she has her own needs. I have learned to not care much about myself and dedicate my entire self in trying to ensure that they are all well taken care off. It is a hard road and it gets tougher when people that don't know me throw stones at me. No human can always have their resilience button on. Stop and ponder how you treat people, think about the scars and echoes you create by cruel behaviour.

Believing that God has trusted me with them and no one else but me and my husband gives us some relief - we must have the skills for the job. The confidence was not by default, we stumbled before we found our feet. We have now flexed the resilient muscle and when I look back, I wonder how we made it. There were days when we saw no light at the end of the tunnel, but we kept pushing. I have learned not to complain or blame anything on my children. If one is in hospital due to limited resources in the area that we are in, the hospital that can attend to them is 171 km away from work. I will drive

344km to and from work without being late neither leaving early nor asking for annual leave since God trusted me with them and provided me with strength to handle every situation that him my way. My resilience, fortitude and ethics was carved in adversity and for this I thank God. He made me a better person. The character that I did dream of. Ah dreams do come true. It just did not happen the way I expected. Frankly I prefer learning from the school of hard knocks. It aligns me to what is wholesome. No, I would not bater my deal with anyone, I have accepted it and I am thriving despite the circumstances. Resilience on steroids.

Sometimes people wonder why I act like a super woman and do not request any help. Why do I go to such an extent? To me it simple my children are not a burden, so I am not going to blame everything on them. I would rather sit with a smile on my face and get my work done. Taking care of the one child while making sure my daughter doesn't feel excluded while the other one is on the operating table in hospital, without telling anyone the anxiety, fear and worry that I am going through at that time not because I am a super woman but because my children cannot become an inconvenience and or burden to anyone but me. If society wants to help, then they will find a way to care and make a material difference.

Even though I have tried my best to ensure that my children do not become inconvenience to the world out there however the stigma and discrimination do not go away. It suffocates us daily; I pray for a world that is fair. Perhaps it is another dream but if we all work for positive sustained change, we can introduce policy and legislation or better behaviour that will change the landscape. I must fight for my children and other children so I can leave better echoes for the future of humanity.

I have been told that my kids are a burden to me, they are holding me back, the financial constraints I go through because of them, hospital bills, therapy, special schools' fees, emotional stress etc, is not by choice but unconditional commitment. People have suggested that I should place my autistic child in a home for adoption and went to the extent to conduct special prayers for my hydrocephalus child to rest in peace because of his needs being demanding and requiring special, there is no resilience button to endure stupidity! I have been in and out of hospital numerous times. But what puzzles me the most is that they haven't lift a finger to help but their comments hurt like a ton of bricks, like the spear that have stabbed right through my heart. How do I summon resilience here?

But maybe they are correct. It just the denial in me? However I am a mother that gave birth to these children after carrying them for 9 months, I have special bond with them and I have chosen to not abandon them. If they are a burden well, they are my burden to carry hence why I don't trouble anyone by asking for help. I understand yes, they are not going to become what society believe that a child should grow up and become a lawyer, nurse, judge, pilot etc, but for me they are my God Blessed children. My love is unconditional regardless of their condition.

The world might view them as the disabled and useless or a burden maybe it because they haven't seen them through my eyes. When my first boy was diagnosed by a professional, I tried to find him a special school but had to go through psychologist that yet still today I am angry at because he wrote off my son completely. He indicated that I must keep him at home, love him because he will never become anything. The best is he must be kept busy by trying to fetch the red ball in the that I will tire on the tree for him. This is the future a skilled professional had for my child. I often ask myself then why I expect more from society. The bar is always so low. People with disabilities are treated as if they are invisible, a burden or with disdain. Humanity created this world and we can also change it. The narrative is in your hands period. This inhumane response was an insult to my son, I believed that he was capable of more than that. As the saying goes raising a child with disability does not come with a manual but with a parent who never gives up.

My child could speak or socialise even with his own siblings. Loving touches and embraces was not always possible. My heart ached for him. Those early years he could not even speak or even communicate well. He would make a loud noise and flap his hands walk up and down the whole day. That report from the psychologist fuelled me up, it enraged me, it angered me like nothing I ever felt before. Mercy did not come out, but I must show mercy to society that is mean to me and my family.

I researched special needs schools like my entire life depended on it, tried numerous schools that insisted on putting him on medication that made my son a different creature that I didn't recognise. In addition, we also realised that special needs children were not well catered for in this area and if they are available, they are not as easily accessible like normal schools, let alone the exorbitant fees. We never stopped until I found the private school that catered to his special needs. The school is 131KM away from home which meant my little angel will need to board at the school. I was so anxious and worried as to how this little person is going to survive without his mother. I was wondering how I am going to feel without him, he is my heartbeat. How will I protect him, who will love him like I do, how will he survive without his familiar home. A few years later my son started talking, little socialisation began, he started making eye contact when speaking.

As parents we don't celebrate birthdays, orators win, karate achievements or soccer tournaments, for us the milestones with special needs children are different yet rewarding just the same. By his hard work and our support, he later started school, he is in grade 4 at the age of 14. To a mother that was told to orphan the child or keep him busy with a red ball - they didn't know my tenacity, courage and resilience. To me as a mother it is amazing to see his achievements whether he makes it in life or not that is in God's hands but I am a proud mother that against all odds I have made it this far and it was never any easy journey and I am not counting my chickens yet because I know the journey may become even more difficult. However, every little achievement deserves a celebration. In my eyes they are not burdens but soldiers fighting everyday for their place in the society. They are the hope and light to many other parents that have doubts about their children with special needs, they are the ones that will help society remould and rethink their position when it comes to disabled children and adults. We are fighting this fight, much bigger than just my two special needs children. We are creating a path that will change the trajectory.

My younger boy with hydrocephalus is my hero and I thank God for giving me the opportunity to raise my very own hero. I feel so privileged to raise him. When he was only six months, he had a shunt inserted to drain the water from his brain as he was diagnosed with dandy walker hydrocephalus, but the pressure was so intense that he had an aneurysm bust which spilled the blood in his entire brain which was already floating on water. The doctors worked around the clock to try and save him but he was critical surgery after surgery, the doctor were ready to give up on him and said that this child have suffered enough and maybe it time to let him go because he is not going to make it and they had to perform last surgery that may take his life because he was still young therefore his nerves may not have developed enough for them to be able to conduct aneurysm coiling. Once again, I had to hunt for that resilience button!

Through my tears I watched him ventilated, with all the wires on top of him, surrounded by the machines before we could respond we saw the blood quickly filling up the bag so quickly through the pipe that was draining the blood from his head, we were chased out from his room and waited for what seemed like years. After 6 hours the doctors stabilised him and we were called back in. He laid there so peaceful, but the doctors were still worried. The next morning I reached out my hand to hold his and pray but something strange happened he held my hand so tight like he was confirming to me that he was still here and will make it through this surgery. We signed the papers like it was the end for him and us, but he made it through that surgery and fought through thick and thin to survive. The title of my chapter took a significant meaning in our lives so often, nothing is impossible when we have no option. No options yet society makes the choice to kick us when we are low. I often ponder who is really disabled when *"normal"* people have no concept how to treat another human especially when they are grappling with so much.

My hero made it, his ability to fight everyday make me the happiest person on earth. Yes 10 years later he is still not talking like normal kids or walking or running around like normal kids. He communicates with ums, singing and a few gestures of which we have come to understand now. He requires special care everyday but that is not a burden to me. He is my champion who has fought everyday to survive who refused to give up even though everyone was ready to give up on him. He still struggles with seizures, shunt irritation, blockages and often have numerous surgeries but always pulls through. His will to survive and keep me grounded is unmatched to none. It's like I need him more than he needs me.

He is the apple of our eyes; his smiles give us reason to wake up everyday and be ready to face each and everyday without any fear because if he can do it why can't we? Though I wake up everyday ready to fight for them, without any hesitation because if I don't, I would not only be failing them but God who trusted me with them. My children also give me strength to continue living every day. If my son can wake up every day take a handful of his tablets and medicine without cringing and still smile and sing, how am I to complain. His presence has humbled me.

The experience with my children has taught me to be modest and appreciate life in so many ways. I had big dreams of being powerful and successful, but I have grown to learn through my experience that life is more that important and precious how would we become who we are without life. I have learned to appreciate life so much to the fact that when my son is sick, home or hospital, I will not sleep safeguarding his soul not to leave his body as crazy as it might sound but because life is precious and once it is lost it is gone and can never be replaced. I have resolved not to have regrets. I am leaving the best legacy I can.

I appreciate the fact that I woke up and made someone smile because life is hard for everyone but again, we are here despite what we are going through, but we still given opportunity to live but we take it for granted everyday not understanding how fortunate we are. We often learn lessons the hard way, when we lose our loved one because we were too busy complaining chasing our dreams that we forgot to sit and appreciate life. Don't get me wrong people must dream and work hard to reach their dreams but not forget to sit back and appreciate that they woke up and they are ok. Simple pleasures of life are dreams coming true for me.

My focus has changed and my children have shaped my life and made me see life differently, as difficult as my life is, because if you have to walk a mile in my shoes, I believe you would return them before you even finish 10 steps of the mile, as I was saying as difficult as my life seems I can't complain because my mind is working. I have someone who can't use his or her mind because they are autistic, or their brain is damaged by water which is diagnosed as hydrocephalus. Really what should I complain about, if I can walk, talk and see where other people cannot. I am blessed.

Before we complain, have we thought about people who have legs but cannot walk, eyes that cannot see and mouth but cannot talk. There are masses that are unable to feed themselves, change their clothing or bath themselves, perhaps think how they may feel. Have we ever imagined what would it be like if we was in their situation yet we complain everyday and not appreciate the fact that we can do all those basic things.

I often hear others say that I am one of the strongest, resilient women that they have seen crossing their path. I appreciate the kind words however don't like them so much because to me they mean that I am going through stuff that was not supposed to go through, I am carrying the load that is too heavy for me, but I keep going. I would hate to think like that about my children. My job is to be a mother and that is what I am doing. To be the best mum because my children only have one mother and I cannot let them down. My different unique special children that I was blessed with and there is nothing that needs recognition there, I believe that every mother could have done the same by being there for her children. That's the real echoes we leave for humanity, how we trudge along when the chips are down.

Sometimes I even doubt myself. Wondering if I am I doing what needs to be done for my children but I have learned to trust in God and depend up His words and that sees me through every day, so I am not strong but I am the woman who is carried by God through each and everyday to try and do right by her kids under all the circumstances and challenges.

Juggling work, being a wife, being a mother to special kids and to my daughter and work has it fair challenges, sometimes I feel sorry for my daughter being raised in between this traumatic experience, but she enjoys being a big sister to both her elder brother and young one. The fear is that am I raising her to fit in what society feels is right or am I raising her to accept everyone or be compassionate towards others or not.

These experiences have shaped how I view life and gave me different perspective to life. My dreams have also changed, where dreams were be successful woman and influence others where I come from to become independent and change their story that has changed too. I'm content not being that person because that person was buried longtime ago. Now I prefer to be behind the scenes because everything that is celebrated in this world is not what I'm looking for. Nobody celebrate the achievements of the people living with disability and special needs or the challenges of the parents raising these children, even if they do some celebration, it for praising the parents, making them feel special but not recognising the actual people that live with disability because up until this day they are not fully accepted by society and nobody believes that they can contribute in making positive changes in the society.

My dream is to be that voice for the voiceless, eyes of those that can't see, hands that can make a different in their lives and be the feet that can walk mile for them. I strongly believe that God would not create a human being for the sake of creating them or make someone be in pain or experience humiliation everyday because of the way they look. God did not bless me with them for the sake of giving me children, but He had a purpose, I may not understand it yet, but I must fulfil it if I haven't yet. I have broken grounds in not hiding my children, not feeling embarrassed that are my children are not what the society define as normal. I had many people reaching out trying to understand why I am so brave to tell the world and putting my children out there and teaching my daughter to speak so proudly about them like nothing is wrong. Nothing is wrong, it's just their uniqueness. Why does society struggle to accept it? It's your ignorance not mine, what I am aware of these are my heroes who brought life to me each day, after all who hides their heroes. I am not ashamed of my loved ones.

People often ask how did I accept the fact that I have special needs children, my answer is always this question who told you that I have accepted, how can a parent accept that their children have a diagnosis that has no cure to it? How can I accept that one day my child could die, do you know even how it feels knowing that one day you may wake up and one of your children could have had seizures in his sleep and died. This requires more than just resilience!

None could ever accept that and why I spare no amount of money to leave no stone unturned. I would rather go barefoot to ensure that they get therapy and treatment that can help them to reach their full potential. If I could accept disability that means I would not be failing as a parent but would also be failing my children who fight to break barriers that were put in front of them as obstacles. I have learned to package work pass the trauma, stress and sadness that comes with the experience, I chose to look things that are positive in this journey because that gives life to me every day. Yes, I could have not gotten this far without God by side, my husband a man that have also broke boundaries on gender roles and inequality. People would be shocked that he can sleep with his child at hospital, bath, change him and even knows his medication. I remember when he was asking for leave at work they were under pressure and his employer hesitated to give him leave and asked him where your wife is, isn't she the one who supposed to stay with child in hospital. His response was he is my child too and I need to be beside him and my wife. These are the echoes of life that changes the trajectory for greater good.

He has been an amazing husband and father, together we have carried each other till this far, this experience has changed the narrative of this situation putting a strain on the marriage and often divorce, in hospitals and in schools are often surprised that we are still married but it can be only God's grace and support of our families and some friendships turned into families.

Truth be told it is a journey that filled with lot of emotions, sadness, happiness, loneliness and self-doubt, love and craziness because sometimes we laugh at things people called taboo such as my son coming back and mimicking the new school child disability. Often sad and lonely because your child has to go through all these sickness and therapy in between even if you try to explain how you are feeling, nobody real understands you and they try to encourage you to stay strong while all you need is to vent and they even make it worse by saying things like your children are a blessing, if mine is a blessing from God then is yours not? Some would say God would not give you a burden that you could not carry. I dislike the word burden with a passion because it labelled my kids bad while they did not choose the disability. It has tagged them unfairly and made them a target of disdain.

It is true if I had a choice to choose knowing what disability they would have, I would have never chosen, as would any other parent. However, Gods plan was one day I would be the champion for them and they needed me as much as I need them. My two special needs babies plus my daughter -my kids I'm glad that I did not have a choice because all three of them with their uniqueness are my world with their uniqueness, I would not trade them for anything in this world not even for billions because they have taught me that money is not everything in this world. Paying medical bills for them with no cure. If money failed to give me what I wanted most which is cure for my children, it cannot hold a higher valuable position in my life.

They have taught me to be there for others going through difficult times without being judgemental because I know what it feels like to be misunderstood and how lonely you become if you are going through hardship or difficult times. My brothers would fight with me a lot because sometimes I give so selfless and effortless but when it is my turn for the favour would not be returned. This did not bother me as it was my very own therapy. I know what it like to be in a lonely dark place. I might miss out on your success and celebration but will always shows up in difficult times because I am familiar with this place. I know about it too well. I will not treat others the way I was treated.

It is true what they say that through suffering, trial and tribulations that you may receive strengthening through all hardships; after enduring and persevering I guess one could emerge as a strong person that can withstand any challenge that may come my way. I guess one would have said I have emerged strong, they might even look up to me but one thing they must remember I was given a no choice, but I decided to not fall apart because to me failing apart and entertaining the nervous breakdown that I am entitled to was going to mean failing my children and that was definitely not an option.

I have shared a lot of tears throughout my journey and I am well aware that I will share a few in future but I am grateful everyday and if you ever thought that you can't cope with your special children well it not easy but learn not to accept what professionals have told you, they might be an expert in reading and have a higher qualification on the field but the best specialist for your child is you as a parent because you didn't read it from the book and practice through dolls, you have an experience of the real human being that you gave birth too and always remember that they have no one to fight for them for except you. Don't let anyone rush you in to making decisions about your child. Allow yourself to work through your emotions and take much time as you need and make an informed decision about your child.

Remember when it comes to your child the only expectation is that YOU are the parent, nobody else but you. What helped me was to take one step at a time which is one step each day and sometimes no step at all nothing changes overnight but trying is all that matters. You are the best for not giving up on your child nothing in this entire world that can be beyond that. If I can push through every day, I believe you can also it is no magic or proven scientific procedure. It is living in all its glory and it is called not giving up!

Nompilo Maphumulo

My name is Nompilo Maphumulo residing in a small town in South Africa KwaZullu Natal in a place called Gingindlovu. I am a wonderful wife, daughter, sister and a mother. I am a qualified social worker that started at LifeLine Zululand as a social auxiliary worker that have worked hard and many hours. I am now sitting as an operations manager even though for me it just a title, but the real satisfaction is to get the job done and work on the ground serving people in need, but my CEO tends to believe otherwise and possible see leadership skills that I have not seen myself.

I believe that circumstances may change your dreams, but never throw it away. My dream now is to one day see the centre that caters for special needs people only, others may say that will be discrimination but a person who has stand in the long que in hospital that is full of autistic children would understand what I mean. I am the person who stayed with my hydrocephalus child and I could not even move an inch to enable me to change my child's nappy, I am a mother driven by lived experience. My passion for change is palpable. I champion local and international Autism reforms. I am a victor for Hydrocephalus in my own right. I also support others on a similar journey via a What's App support group.

I envision a world for those with special needs that has no trace of discrimination. A person that can afford a car buys it and travels well. However, a person who cannot afford a car travel via public transport. Globally we have catered for public transport and this is not frowned on as catering so a specific sector. Similarly catering for their special needs would be not a discrimination but rather catering for unique basic needs. This is my story, we are not well to do nor are we high up on the corporate ladder, I work for an NGO, we are ordinary parents with ordinary jobs and making it day by day. If my story inspires one person to do better and create change for a better future my mission is accomplished.

4

Sharing Humanity Through Storytelling

This is a collaboration chapter between Julienne B. Ryan and Jerome Deroy.

"You are standing at the right spot in your life. You have learned new ideas and tools that you use to keep "bettering your best" efforts."

Julienne B. Ryan and Jerome Deroy

Overview

Jerome and I were taught to never show up anywhere empty handed to any life event, so we're bringing our back stories, lessons learned and some helpful listening and story sharing tips that you can apply to any part of your life.

"What Are We Bringing?"

When we have a story to tell, we like to create a map of where we are going so that our listeners can trust that they are in good hands.

Below is the map of this chapter, so you know where you'll be going and why.

1. Introduction: How'd you get here?
2. Our Why
    - Jerome's Why?
    - Julienne's Why?
3. A Deeper Dive - *"Context Matters"*
    - Jerome - The Box
    - Julienne - The School Yard
4. Narativ® Listening & Storytelling Basics
5. LEADERSHIP STORYTALKS, a podcast produced by Narativ®
6. Thank you. Goodbye for Now.
7. Biographies
8. Contacts

Introduction

Julienne - *"How'd You Get Here?"* was a frequently asked question in Queens, New York, where I grew up. The borough was a confusing place for visitors and locals alike to navigate. Road's stop, reappear and repeat without any visible logic. As a result, we were always looking for easier ways to travel from one point to another.

"How'd You Get Here?" was also the question I wanted answered when I checked out countless biographies from the many Queens Public Libraries that I frequented as a child. Reading artists, adventurers, historical and entertainer's back stories taught me lessons about how they overcame obstacles and found ways to utilize their talents and realize their dreams. Those stories were my best teachers because they showed me not only what was possible, but what existed outside my neighbourhood.

Then, through life's many twists and turns, the act of telling and sharing stories became an important tool in my work later in my adult life. Using personal stories enabled me to connect with others in performances, talks, workshops and coaching.

Over the years, I met many kindred spirits who recognized that the art of story-sharing allows people to heal and develop as individuals. One of those kindred spirits is Jerome Deroy, the CEO of Narativ®. When we met, we realized that while our paths had been very different, we shared the same story-sharing mission. We believe showing clients how to appreciate and share stories about the simple moments that shaped their life allows them to become more self-aware and develop the ability to connect with others on a deeper level.

We'd like to use our chapter to share the moments that led us to use storytelling in our work, share a few of our backstories and provide helpful story-sharing tips in the process so that you can listen for clues and shape your life in new and fulfilling ways.

Jerome - Our intention when sharing our stories is to model a specific methodology, which was developed by Narativ®'s founders during the HIV/AIDS global crisis of the mid-1990s. When people were dying, telling their story became a way to be remembered and to advocate for themselves and those who were suffering from the same type of stigma and discrimination. Storytelling offered an opportunity to express who people were and what mattered to them so that others would relate and want to take action to protect, defend, or make change.

The methodology that was developed then is the one we use today with people from all walks of life and all over the world. In fact, the Narativ® method has been used in more than 20 countries, in 10 different languages, by the likes of executives in Fortune 100 corporations and volunteers of grassroots non-profit organizations, over the last 25+ years.

The stories below follow a simple premise that we invite you to reflect on: Every story is the answer to the question *"What Happened?"* This means that we will rarely tell you about what we were thinking, feeling or what our opinions were about what happened to us. Rather, we will stick to the facts of our lived experiences so that you, our listener, can be free to have your own interpretations, feelings and even judgments about our stories. The job of the storyteller is to say what happened and trust that the audience will follow. Here are the stories of what brought us to do this work and why we've kept at it for the last two decades.

Our Why

We believe that everyone has an origin story. There's always a moment that when we look back, we can point to it and say, *"That's really where it all started."*

There can be many origin stories and indeed, you could argue that the stories we share in this chapter fit that description. These stories express our *"why"* and we hope these will inspire you to think of your own *"why,"* so that you can come up with a powerful origin story, using the Listening and Storytelling Basics we share further in this chapter.

Jerome - My Why

When I graduated from business school in France, I took an internship in a major global bank. At the end of the internship I was offered a position in Asia. In December of 1999 I walked onto the 15th floor of a glass building overlooking the streets and harbor of Hong Kong. I arrived wearing my new suit and tie and rang the bell. I was sent to meet with the director of personnel and was greeted with the words, *"Welcome, we're glad to have you. Before you meet anyone on the team, I need you to go through a few things."* She took me to a small windowless room and we sat down in front of a television and she popped a cassette tape into a VCR. It was a training tape that took me through compliance and what it was like to work at BNP Paribas. It looked like it dated from the 1980s and had lines that went down the screen and distorted the image. She then handed me two huge binders and said, *"I'd love for you to go through these in the next 48 hours,"* then promptly closed the door and walked out.

After a week, I had only met a handful of people on my team. After a month, I still didn't know what this company stood for or what purpose we were all fulfilling for the company. I wasn't completely clear on what my role was other than my job description. It was only when I shadowed the person I was meant to replace, that I really started to get what my role was about and why it was important to the company. But I couldn't tell you what the values of the company were and why what we did mattered in a bigger way.

I ended up staying in the company for another 4 years, but along the way I noticed that every 3 months, people would walk into my boss' office and come out a few minutes later with brilliant smiles on their faces. They then declared *"I quit!"* and they'd leave. Moments later, my boss inevitably came to my desk, put his hand on my shoulder and said *"Man, all these people are leaving...Other banks pay a lot more, you know. That's why they're all leaving."*

Finally, it was my turn to walk into his office in 2003. I said *"Lawrence, I quit."*

He said *"Well, what will you do?"*

I said, *"I'm not sure, but it's going to be creative and engaging!"*

I left and went to New York, where I met Murray Nossel, the founder of Narativ®, the company that I now run. When Murray Nossel told me about Narativ® and the power of storytelling to change mindsets and move people into action, the word that came up for me was *"engagement."*

When I was working in the corporate world, the disengagement I experienced was high and I wasn't alone. No one really knew what the values of the company were, or how they were lived in the world. What difference or impact were we making? I told Murray *"I think we can use this method of storytelling in businesses to help engage people. We can do this by connecting what they do with who they are and ignite a higher sense of purpose. Stories connect us with our shared humanity and make us feel like we belong."* We set out to create programs that tackled the disengagement problem and I suddenly felt like I was adding value and making an impact. That was in 2005. Now, 19 years later, I'm on the same mission to engage people at work and I get to share that vision with Julienne. Here's her own answer to the question *"Why?"*

Julienne - My Why

I am standing in a crowded conference room in Baruch College[1] Library. The Executives on Campus Mentorship Program (EOC) has organized a speed networking event for the students. The room is crowded and buzzing, with students moving from mentor to mentor as they give their mini *"elevator pitch"*[2] and receive feedback. The process has a beautiful dance-like flow as the students shake hands, speak and shake hands again before they move on to their next mentor partner. I had been meeting one student after another in rapid succession. I listened to their aspirations, made suggestions about their job search process and enjoyed their energetic, *"can do"* candour.

Suddenly, a student breaks through the crowd and strides towards me. He shakes my hand briskly and says, *"I don't think I will ever get a job. I don't have a good story to tell."* I ask him to tell me more. *"I don't look or sound like the other candidates I see when interviewing on Wall Street. I don't have time for clubs, sports, or anything I hear them talking about. What you must understand is that I am new to this country. I am the first in my family to go to college. All I have time to do is go to work and school, care for my family and sleep. That's it. That's why I am not going to get hired."*

I listen and then ask him if I can provide feedback. *"Listen, I have been hiring people and overseeing professional development for years. You are exactly the candidate I look for when recruiting for a position. You are a hard worker; you're motivated and disciplined. Your migrating to this country shows me you are a risk-taker. You have everything you need to be a great employee and successful. You must keep telling your story until the right person hears you. When this happens, you are going to do very well."*

The student begins to stand a little straighter as I speak and his shoulders relax slightly. I even see the hint of a smile emerge. Then suddenly, he looks at his watch and announces he must go to class. He shakes my hand and, turning away, disappears into the crowd. His words, *"I don't have a good story to tell,"* lingered...

---

[1] Baruch College is a part of the City University of New York (CUNY) Baruch College is a respected throughout the U.S. for making rigorous academic programs affordable for students who have been historically under-served by higher education. Combining excellence and access, Baruch is a recognized leader in advancing student, social, and economic mobility

[2] Elevator Pitch is a brief (think 30 seconds!) way of introducing yourself, getting across a key point or two, and making a connection with someone. It's called an elevator pitch because it takes roughly the amount of time you'd spend riding an elevator with someone.

He is the last student I speak to at this event. I leave the hall, head out to Lexington Avenue and hail a cab to take me to my office. As the cab weaves through traffic, I listen to the cab's TV playing. But I hear *"I don't have a good story to tell"* instead of tourist site promotions.

My heart felt heavy as I thought about how this student perceived himself and wondered, *"How many other students feel this way? Someone has made them feel less worthy and capable and they don't appreciate their backstory?"*

Then my *"Inner Queens Girl"* voice spoke up in a tone that always cuts directly to the heart of a matter. *"What about you, Sista? (Sister) Do you own your story and everything that made you?"* The answer was *"No."*

Weeks pass and the student's words, *"I don't have a good story to tell."* still surface at different times of my day. I am now in the middle of a work transition and am reflecting on my work in Human Resources. While I like interfacing with the employees and parts of my role, I feel something is missing. Of late, I have been spending a lot of time terminating employees because of conflict or mismanaged work expectations or communication challenges and mishaps.

So, I have started to do what any self-respecting HR professional does when they want to collect information. I have begun to *"survey"* my staff, peers and management, asking, *"Where do I bring value to my work?"*

Oddly enough, no one is getting very excited about my HR reports or successful hires, even when they are one of them! Nor are they waxing poetically about the numerous policies, procedures and employment laws they learned because of me. None of these matters.

But what surprises me is that one person after another keeps saying the same thing: *"You show up. You tell stories. You make us laugh. But while we're laughing, we're learning and, on some days, this makes all the difference."*

These are game-changing words. Every time I hear them, I feel myself filling up with positive energy like a character in a Marvel Comic Strip who starts to their superhero costume when the right elements occur. At the same time, I am aware that I am letting something go. I am releasing the belief that when *"I finally grow up and become less touchy-feely, I will evolve into a true corporate professional who communicates in perfect PowerPoint Slides and data dialects and only makes pithy comments. I will refrain from using colourful metaphors and stories. I will learn how to speak without smiling."*

Now, I am discovering that the employees value the real, true me. My stories and humour matter and I have been making a difference.

My conversation with the Baruch student and the employees changed my perspective and my path. I study narrative storytelling and use it in my talks, workshops and coaching. I use characters from my Queens upbringing and adult life in my writing and presentations. I even perform humorous stories in public venues. I am using all of me.

You may be wondering, *"Whatever happened to that young man? Did you ever hear from him?"* Oddly enough, even though I am connected to many former Baruch students, I have never heard from this young man. But that's ok. He's always with me when I step up to a podium and say, *"We all have a story to tell."*

A deeper dive - *"context matters"*

Below are stories that reveal our deeper connection with storytelling. They offer further context for the work we've done in the world as well as what you can learn from this chapter.

Jerome - The Box

I was a production manager for Oscar®-nominated filmmaker, Murray Nossel, PhD. One day, he said he had an idea to run by me. I went to his place on the upper West Side. When I got to the studio on the 21st floor on the corner of Riverside Drive and 103rd St., I took in the view of the Hudson River. We sat at a table that had nothing on it except for a shoe box. Murray told me that he'd founded a company called Narativ®, which mostly worked with non-profit organizations to teach people how to tell stories that could affect change. And then he said, *"I know you've got this background in business and finance and I wonder if you wouldn't mind taking a look at what we've created and whether we could do this in for profit businesses."* Then he slid the shoe box to me and said, *"It's all there."*

That night I took the shoe box back to my sublet in the East Village and I opened it. There were lots of papers in no order. I told my girlfriend: *"Boy, this is a mess. I'm not sure what I got myself into and whether this will lead to anything. Maybe I should just go back to finance."* I had just left a 3-bedroom apartment in the Hong Kong hills and a highly profitable position in a bank to pursue my dream of working in a creative field. After a year of being an intern and then a production manager for low budget movies, my savings were dwindling. She then said *"Don't give up now. Just look at what's in the box!"*

So, I made stacks out of what was in the shoe box and I wrote things like *"sales", "team building", "leadership development", "business development", "Employee engagement"* on post-it notes that I placed on each of the towers of paper. I then took my laptop out and opened PowerPoint and wrote *"Business Plan for Narativ®"* on the title slide.

A week later, sitting at the same table, I told Murray and his co-founder Paul Browde, MD: *"You've got something really special here, a way to engage people with personal stories that are relevant to what they do and will leave a lasting impression on their audience."* The mystery of the shoe box I opened revealed a company and for me, a sense of possibility. What unopened boxes are in your mind? What will they reveal when you remove the lid? If you've been hesitant to answer recurring questions you have about your life, career, etc. perhaps the unknown that comes with every mystery is too overwhelming. But if you start with exploring your own stories of vulnerability, strength and resilience, you'll build up the confidence to open the box and discover new opportunities that were just hiding in plain sight.

"The mystery box opens. What's inside? I don't know. I want to know, but at the same time, I don't want to know. The mystery is what fascinates me." **JJ Abrams, acclaimed filmmaker**

Julienne - A School Yard

Years ago, I started to use the *"Inner Queens Girl"* device in my talks, writing and workshops. I use it not because my life in Queens was perfect. It was quite the opposite, but my upbringing taught me many lessons. The studious, shy, smiling girl others saw in school, dance and music classes masked what I felt inside. I had a challenging upbringing with two parents who struggled with the effects of their extensive childhood traumas. They did their best under the circumstances, provided for me and ensured I obtained a college education. However, our home life was always challenging.

To complicate matters, I endured years of intense and horrible physical and mental bullying from 5th to 7th grade at the Catholic grammar school I attended. The incidents were never *"seen"* or addressed. This led me to feel like the *"other,"* and I was wary when I approached groups of people for years.

These experiences made me sceptical of the institution that was supposed to nurture and protect me. Through time and the gift of support, I now recognize that those children and adults were carrying their unfortunate, broken stories forward when they impacted my life.

However, all those biographies I read while I held a flashlight under my bed covers at night must have helped fortify me. Together with the actions of a few key people, I was able to begin to make important changes.

One of the first things I did was learn how to communicate. I willed myself to approach individuals and small groups of people. I challenged my shy, nervous, mumbling self to interact with peers and adults.

I had started teaching myself how to ask other people questions in a positive manner so I could listen and not have to speak. My listening skills-built trust and helped increase my confidence. Under the right conditions, I would even reveal my talent for making witty observations about everyday life. Without realizing it, I had begun to develop the skills that would serve me well later in life.

One of my best decisions was to attend a large private, co-ed Catholic High School that attracted students from all over Queens and Brooklyn. It was forward-thinking for its time and had a diverse student population. I began to find *"tribes"* of students I could relate to, students whose parents had also immigrated and/or had not attended college. These students were working hard to make their way forward.

I am sharing this back story at this point in my adult life not to bemoan my history but to own it. It's just *"what happened"* and the good and the painful bits that helped shape who I am today.

Today, instead of disavowing my past, I look for the gift of lessons learned. I am figuring out ways to repurpose them and find opportunities to play these lessons forward so that others can summon up the courage to view their stories with a fresh eye and make a change for the better.

The Queens experiences I tried to dismiss or forget have evolved into my *"Inner Queens Girl"* character. She *"appeared"* when I finally began appreciating my stories and giving myself the gift of being seen and heard. The *"Inner Queens Girl"* now serves as my witty, no-nonsense sidekick, my humourist's voice and plays an important part in my work.

The art of storytelling opened up and changed my life. Now, when I am given the privilege of listening to someone else's story, I know I am helping them create a path to do the same.

So, as I always say, *"The best stories are already in the room. It's up to us to listen and give them some space so they can emerge."*

NARATIV® STORYTELLING AND LISTENING BASICS

Below is a framework to support you in creating your own compelling narrative. We invite you to try this out!

Connection Matters - We have a word that represents the essence of what we're about: Connection. We are here to connect people through listening and telling business-relevant personal stories. We call our methodology the listening and storytelling method because listening is just as important, if not more important than storytelling.

Listening - is the *central focus* of our work and it cannot be stressed enough. Underpinning our storytelling methodology is the simple premise that there is a reciprocal relationship between listening and telling.

We support our listeners in being MORE than witnesses. They are shaping the story through their listening. Their listening is constitutive in as much as it both shapes and energizes the storytelling.

Let's turn to you. If listening influences the story so much, then you must *pay attention to the obstacles* that can get in the way of y*our ability to listen and be present.*

Listening Obstacles - We invite you to reflect on your own obstacles to listening.

- What routinely keeps you from listening?
- What practices or strategies could you use to set those obstacles aside?
- What do you think would become available if you did so?

Pay attention to how you listen, go deeper and see what happens when you give the gift of non-judgmental and open listening to someone else. Change starts with you. Don't wait for somebody to listen. Be the kind of listener you want to see in the world and change will follow.

That's what Julienne and I have experienced time and time again throughout our collaboration. We can't get to the kind of personal, vulnerable storytelling we've heard without first examining how we listen to others and to ourselves.

Why Story? Why Now?

The first question you need to answer before you even think about which story you will tell, is *"Why?"*

Why do you need a story? What matters to you so much that you need to communicate about it in a more effective way?

Why do you need a story NOW? Answering this question will create a sense of urgency for both you and your listener.

You may realize that you DON'T need a story and that's fine. Don't assume that storytelling is always the best way to communicate your point.

What's critical is to ask yourself these questions so that you can confidently move forward, with intention.

Tell what happened - When you can tell a story and you're not sure how to tell it, remember this: Every story is the answer to a simple question.

That question is: *"What happened?"*

This is the fundamental question in our storytelling methodology. The question invites us to deliver only empirical facts, i.e. anything which we can take in through our five senses: sight, sound, taste, smell and touch. When you enhance your facts with detailed descriptions, you will be able to convey the depth of your inner experience.

To tell a personal story well, you must be willing to let go of the tendency to coerce the listener into understanding your experience and worldview. Instead, look to the external world - use your senses - to craftily persuade the listener into seeing the world through your eyes.

You see, if you describe a situation to someone, the listener is free to come up with his own meanings and interpretations, which are not only different from yours, but may also be undesirable to you.

The *"what happened"* question imposes a limit on you, the storyteller and is a way of looking at your own life fairly and squarely, stripped of meanings and the judgments that you put onto your own story.

Telling *"what happened"* to the listener engages them and draws them in and stimulates his/ her own interpretations, feelings, meanings etc. in the process.

Know Your Ending - Have you ever had the experience of listening to a story that started with a bang, but then at some point, you felt like the storyteller didn't know where they were going, so you stopped listening?

There's a simple solution: *"Know your ending."*

Always think of your ending first. Next, craft your last sentence. Think of where you want to leave your audience - *"What do you want them to feel, think about or do?"* when you've finished your story.

Your last sentence will act as your anchor AND serve as your North Star so you can reach your desired ending. Stick to that last line and you will reach your story destination.

Podcast

In June 2019, Jerome and Julienne decided to collaborate and tackle the *"disengagement at work"* challenge we had experienced in our prior leadership roles in Finance and Human Resources and were noting in our coaching sessions.

When the COVID19 lockdown began, we had many, many conversations about what our clients and we were going through. We decided to open and expand our circle by starting a podcast called LEADERSHIP STORY TALKS.

We've had the privilege of speaking with thought leaders from all over the world whose backgrounds include Finance, Talent Management and Development, Education, Technology, Medicine, Global Health, Sustainability, Mental Health, Social Advocacy, Entertainment and more.

The podcast illuminates the methods, lessons and stories to help leaders and their teams be better at engaging their employees, clients, stakeholders and themselves! In the process of speaking to our various guests, we've built a community of peers that we'd love you to join.

Here's how to tune in:
- Podcast page: https://narativ.com/podcast/
- YouTube page: https://www.youtube.com/playlist?list=PLaWxpJS-bkdgmq1SAeEK3oJBFjwtohrcd

Thank you and goodbye for now.

Jerome and I were also taught to send our guests home with a little something to remember the event - maybe some food to enjoy the next day or in my case in Queens, it was food and *directions* so that our visitors could reach their homes the same day that they left. In this case we are going to share a parting thought.

"You are standing at the right spot in your life. You have learned new ideas and tools that you use to keep "bettering your best" efforts. You have our contact information. All you need to do now is "try." **Jerome & Julienne**

Jerome Deroy
CEO and Lead Trainer, Narativ®, Inc.

Jerome Deroy joined Narativ® in 2007. Jerome had recently left a position at BNP Paribas, Hong Kong and come to New York to pursue a career in film. When he discovered the transformative power of storytelling to engage leadership, employees and customers alike — he worked on adapting Narativ®'s listening and storytelling methodology to business messaging challenges.

Narativ®'s training programs include one-on-one coaching for senior leaders and executives and team engagement sessions to improve sales, employee engagement and collaboration.

Narativ® has also created an onboarding system where new hires learn from stories of their peers, helping to engage employees from Day 1 and throughout their career cycle.

As a lead trainer and certified professional coach, Jerome has worked closely with clients as diverse as Capital One, Meta, CIGNA, Prudential and Warby Parker.

He has guest lectured on the art of storytelling at Parsons the New School of Design in New York, Haas School of Business at UC Berkley and Cornell's Graduate School of Management.

Contact Jerome Deroy

Email: jerome@narativ.com
Website: http://www.narativ.com
Linkedin: https://www.linkedin.com/in/jeromederoy/
Youtube: https://www.youtube.com/@narativinc4338
Book: Powered by Storytelling (McGraw Hill Education, 2018) - https://narativ.com/resources/book/

Julienne B. Ryan

Julienne B. Ryan is a Communication Catalyst - She is a storytelling keynote speaker, humourist, facilitator, author and coach. She shows her clients how to listen better, by showing them how to use their voices, without raising their voices one authentic and informed conversation and story at a time.

Ryan accomplishes this by working with her clients in creative ways using improv, humour, storytelling and neuroscience in her coaching sessions, team building and communications workshops and keynotes!

Julienne works with businesses, organizations, educational institutions and non-profit agencies. Julienne brings to her work, her experience as a talent management professional, educator and performer. She has consulted with non-profits, academic institutions and multinational corporations. She holds a master's degree in organizational psychology and leadership from Teachers College, Colombia University and a dual B.A. in Psychology/Urban Studies from Manhattan College. Ryan is a certified Collective Brains Mentor , a AccuMatch Behaviour Intelligence Coach as well as Narativ® Storytelling Methodology Coach.

Julienne is the author of humorous *"The Learned-it-in-Queens Communications Playbook – Winning Against Digital Distraction"* and co-hosts THE LEADERSHIP STORYTALKS Podcast by Narativ® Inc with Jerome Deroy, the CEO of Narativ® Inc.

Julienne is a native New Yorker and is a married to her college sweetheart, a Dublin, Irishman who never met a sentence he could not make longer.

Julienne B. Ryan

Communication Catalyst
Keynote Speaker | Humourist | Storyteller | Coach | Facilitator
[AccuMatch BI Certified Coach](#) | [Podcast Co-Host](#)

LinkedIn| Narativ | Facebook | Instagram | YouTube
Website: https://jryanpartners.com
Email: Julienne Ryan <jryan@jryanpartners.com>
Phone: +1 914-310-1638

Transform your communication with my book:

The Learned-It-In Queens Communication Playbook - Winning Against Digital Distraction now available on Barnes & Noble and Amazon and other global bookselling platforms. Visit jryanpartners.com to stay tuned for upcoming events and podcasts.

5

The Alchemy of Me

"Go where your tribe is, those who will catch you if you fall, or even if you slipped a little. Life is full of positives and negatives, but one thing is for sure, life is meant to be lived, even if you trip over your own feet from time to time enjoy all the phenomenal things about this journey and about you!"

Mandy Douglas

Reflecting on times when uncertainty was divine. Innocence's glowed, and you were nothing but bold. Life with all its bitter sweetness will surely etch you into the person you need to be, eventually. All the anguish and turmoil, we took to be despondencies, will eventually reveal to be your fortitude.

Growing up in a home where I was always taught to be respectful, kind, loving, giving and accept what adults told us to be or do has honorable. Little did I know that these would lead to me being taken for granted, mistreated, abused if you will. I don't claim to be a victim, and I don't ever want to have a victim mentality. On the contrary, I am a woman learning to be her true authentic self from the lesson's life has provided. Growing up I always thought of my mom as a woman possessing an excessive wealth of knowledge. It perpetually seemed like she had inconceivable life experiences or had been exposed to the same undertakings I, myself had gone through. Later in my adult life I would learn that this was in fact the case, on so many levels.

Growing up with an extended family always present was a beautiful encompassment in our support system. This was our dual income, typical south African home. My granny used to take care of us while my parents were away. This day, at the age of 2 years old my mom said, she came home from work to find me lethargic, my mouth and lips swollen and bluish. My breathing was compromised. My gran said "she ate the leaf of this plant "while handing the half-eaten leaf to my mom. My granny was not educated and had not experience seeing this in any of her children or grandchildren, so she did not know what exactly she needed to do. She did what she thought would help by cooling my head and trying to keep my temperature down and trying to position me in a way that I was able to breathe a little better. At this point my mom could have yelled or cursed or spoken out of character to my granny, but she didn't, and her substance never allowed her to ever speak with disrespect to her in laws. My parents did not own a vehicle, so my mom turned to our neighbors for help. Thankfully the neighbor was able to drive my mom and I to the doctor's office. On arrival at the doctor's office, we found him locking up his "surgery" as it was called in those days. This will be my first encounter with death and my first torment. The doctor took one look at me and opened his office. He grabbed me and placed me on the examination table, started an intravenous line and gave me the medication he deemed I needed. We stayed at his office for almost 6 hours or more, before my breathing returned to somewhat normal. It was very late in the night. My mom had not eaten all day nor did she get a chance to change clothes or take a bath. I was her priority. The doctor told my mom there was nothing more he could do. He told my mom to take me home and see what happens. On arriving home my mom placed me on the bed and started anointing me with olive oil and started to pray earnestly. All night long with no sleep, nothing to eat, not even leaving my side to take a bath, she continuously prayed and kept encouraging me to drink fluids. My mom stated years later to me that she thought that night, she was going to lose her only daughter, but alas this is not what happened. This was the strength of a mother's prayers. Later I would mirror these same practices, whenever my own kids would be sick or in distress from injuries or childhood mishaps. From hearing how my mom handled this, I too sort God and prayer for the enigmas of life. I deal with me in laws in the same way too, with love and kindness and inclusion. I have learnt that misunderstandings are part of life, and the way people perceive you has more to do with them than it does with you. I have established over the years; my mom has more self-restraint than I do. This is an area of my persona I truly need to work on. Reflection is key to becoming a better version of yourself. Your own experiences or reflecting through experiences of others is awe-inspiring. We don't always have to go through something to understand it, that's the beauty of written and shared writings.

These circumstances we find ourselves in are not the situations we put ourselves in rather they are situations that come to ambush our innocence. At the age of ten, my family took a family trip with a few other extended family members. We drove from Durban to Cape Town in a minivan. After a long day of driving all day and all night, we stopped at this rest stop to freshen up. The sun with its glorious rays shone brightly in the east. We all had turns to freshen up as the bathrooms were smaller than we needed. The male and female bathroom were side by side. You had to pass by the male bathroom to get to the female bathroom. I was one of the last to go to the bathroom, but as I approached the female bathroom someone tried to grab my hand and pull me into the male bathroom I fought and managed to get away and I yelled and ran back to my family. The men in our group tried to look in the male bathroom for the culprit but they were nowhere to be found. We continued our trip like normal. Everyone shook it off, except me, because "nothing happened". This incident remained on my mind, especially after something similar happened again when I was twelve! This time I was in my own home, a man I grew up with thinking of as a brethren, would befoul my beliefs in humanity. This time too, I fought and ran to escape the depravity of my innocence's. I was home alone as I was twelve now and could take care of myself and my brother. I told my parents. My parents confronted this human, but he of course gave other rationalizations for what I apparently misperceived. My parents still asked him never to come near me again. This was not really reassuring because I was always alone, it was the necessity of the times, in a dual income family. Again because "nothing happened" No one really reassured or thought to ask how I was doing! The fear I felt the first time came crushing into my heart and mind. In adulthood I would finally understand this phase of my life. There are many women, who keep quiet about the trauma they've experienced in childhoods due to social norms. This changes, however, when we start discussing these and our communality is sculpted. The strength of a woman is all the encounters she lives through. Supporting each other becomes innate. I would say the next time you think you are the only one who has experienced something traumatic, try to talk it out with a friend, a sister or even a woman who seems approachable. You might be surprised at the support and care that can come from hearts that share the same experiences and traumas.

Travelling to a state where I was seen as rare. Apartheid was abolished yet the environment was still alienated and strained. Traits of my personality scrutinized, for being different in a world where the culture you came from was not understood by the conqueror of the times of this state. Something as simple as pulling your nose when it feels runny, was seen as you are being uncivilised. For me, who grew up in a small rural town with minimal affluence from the outside world, it was foreign to think that something so insignificant was causing that much annoyance to some people. I tried not judge, I did not even try to correct them, I tried not to do any of the "annoying stuff" in front of them.

Little beknown to me, this is more of what was shaping the way I handled dilemmas in life. I would shy away, suppressing who I had been, I saw their deficiencies, but still accepted them as they were but they could not do the same for me. Did it frustrate me at times, of course, I am but a mere mortal! I would later also realize that my flaws were not flaws with the right people around. My "flaws" were my strengths in and around the right tribe. "My Flaws" set me apart from the rest, it gave me the strength to achieve the impossible or difficult to reach aspects in my life. It also taught me that no matter how many mistakes you make along the way, your people will still appreciate you and see the good in you and ignore the bad, if there is actually bad.

Most people are not bad, they have habits that are not liked by some people. Making mistakes is the best teacher. Once I realized this, I stopped being so critical about the mistakes I made and started concentrating on how they can be prevented and how they reshaped our personality. I used to think making mistakes made you less than you were, until this point. Most of the time, people who are so judgmental have a low tolerance and a high worth of self. They stir turmoil and are satisfied speaking the insults even if it brought pain to the targeted individual. It was something I used to watch for, I would see people smirk as they said or did something to hurt me or anyone else. I could not bear this type of behavior. I would later realize there is a name for this, and for so many other behaviors that people with a limited consciousness of compassion. For me, helping and caring comes naturally but even that can be an annoyance to some. This reality astonished me. Growing up in a warm loving home. My parents were always genuinely kind people. I thought that being caring and kind was how we should be, and this is how I lived. I realized later that some people do actually see kind and caring people as weaker.

Life would show me I needed to set boundaries of what I would allow and what I would tolerate. The saddest truth was it took me so long to realize this basic life lesson. Realizing how different cultures perceive differences was a game changer, especially already being in a different country. In one culture taking care of and loving are good traits to have while in another they are seen as obstructive, intrusive, detrimental and prevent self-growth. Life is full of these variants. Raising kids with a person who has different upbring on these makes for an interesting yet terribly complicated variable. It's difficult to even know when to do what at times. You could be doing it right and, in someone else's eyes, it is perceived wrong. We can only do our best and pray it is the right thing at that moment. As a mom, our jobs in this life are extremely ridiculed. We know our kids. We communicate more than anyone else with our kids. We know not only what the world sees, but what our kids don't show the world and show to us. This relation itself is so important yet it also stems from the relationship you have with your own parents.

I see it often, how kids react to their parents and how parents react to their kids. A kid who was loved and supported and made to feel special will grow up to be an adult who raises their kids to feel this same way. A parent who was always criticized and made to feel they were insignificant or even not valued, will show up for their kids in this same way. Parenting is hard, just dealing with the personalities of your kids as they grow, learn and change, but doing it from a well of surplus negatives is a recipe for tragedy. Tragedy for the child and for the parent. Healing from these childhood traumas is so important. But how many of us truly do? Most don't even want to do the work.

They are happy to see themselves like they have been seen and never fix themselves. They don't believe anything is wrong.

They will constantly think that it's the other person who is the problem and never seek the help they need. This mentality bleeds on everything they touch. They hurt the ones they love because they never prioritize anyone but themselves. They are ok for short exposures of time but cannot handle people around them for long periods. Their need for seclusion is stronger. Children don't understand these types of behaviors, and then think they are rejected. As adults our thoughts always seem to be to do it the way we want and to hell with anyone else. Discrepancies are part of life, and some would say, do it your way and those who care will adapt and those that don't, do they even matter? This philosophy is why we have influenced this next generation without knowing that we needed to heal first ourselves. I understand the mentality of "If you are not hurting anyone, do what you want in life" but we do affect the people around us and we don't even realize this. We stress ourselves to the point where we live with anxiety, depression and self-loathing. And this spills over to the point where we can't recognize our true selves. We are so scared to be ourselves because of the experiences we had, that shaped us into being this way. We try to redirect ourselves and then something tragic happens and it sets us back down a different path. Healing is a non-stop process with setbacks and positive vibes all flowing together on this roller coaster of life. Heal anyway.

I then had the opportunity to go abroad. This was the most exciting and scariest part of my journey. I knew no one here and I did not speak the language of the land. People were already annoyed about my presence. I had landed here but a few days and I was called into a so called "conference". I was given the ground rules of the land by females who were intrigued and envious, but also had a malicious spiteful yearning to have me know, I was an outsider to the compound. I did not understand at the time. I stayed in my apartment. I would read and stay away from socializing, out of fear. Then a wise woman enlightened me about what was transpiring, she told me that these women were in fact not virtuous. That their intent was to patronize and keep me away from experiences that I would truly enjoy. She took me under her wings, we explored and had fun doing things that were permitted in this land for foreign travelers. This gave me exposure to people from a wealth of cultures and diversity of beliefs.

I would come to understand what this meant for them. There were but a few things that foreigners could do, and my presences set off an imbalance. I was young and naïve, innocent if you will. I had no want of the things they so wanted, the human lust for that of the flesh. I was happy dancing and spreading my wings to try new things. Rock-climbing, deep-sea diving, sand dune buggy driving and all these things to explore. The last thing on my mine was the opposite sex. They did not know my reasons for going there in the first place so intimidated were they, when in fact they need not have been. Once I set my sights to have fun and explore, I did not pay attention to the noise. I spoke with my dad and mom every day and their guidance helped to keep me on the right part. I knew why I went, and I focused on getting done with my task at hand.

Even these things I went through so unnecessarily, and it did tarnish a part of me. I was more subdued and only wanted to be around people who accepted me. I became more aware of how people assumed without knowing facts. Then again who truly knows a person, expect for themselves. What people perceive you to be is their issue, you keep staying true to who you really are. Living my life, true to myself became my fortitude. Experience brings about change. Change enhances our personalities in different ways. For me at this point in my life, I continued to be positive full of love, joy, happiness, sass, and whimsical. I was spreading my wings, and our vast world was open to all my naïve silliness. Life was for living and creating new adventures and boy did I create those adventures. I didn't let anyone subdue my spirit and emotionally I was well adjusted. Life is easy, it's the critics who hinder its ease.

Later, I would become more closed off and subdued, learning more about oneself from the opinions of others, especially negative ones, makes one a lot less confident. If anyone had told me at this point in my life, I would not have confidence in myself, I would have laughed at them. I was loved so dearly by my parents and those around me. Fueled with love and understanding from my parents and those around me, I would have never believed anything could break my spirit or crush me mentally, physically and emotionally. My career was taking off. I was living my dream of travelling and exploring this beautiful world of ours. I knew only of the love and care I felt. I would come to need this a lot more in my life. It's funny how we take for granted genuine love and care.

As youngsters we think we have all the time in the world for the people who are in our lives. Little do we know life changes so drastically in the blink of an eye. Mine did the day I lost my first love, my hero, my cheerleader, my everything, my Dad. This was the most unexpected thing to ever happen to me. I was overseas, far away from him. I was not doing well financially at that time. I had just had my second child and my dad had spent 4 months with me and my family here in the USA. We always got on so well, like two peas in a pod. We loved each other's company. My dad was a very hands-on type of dad, and he would help with the care of the kids, even bathing them. He was a remarkable man of God. He was loved by everyone who knew him. His death crushed my soul.

I couldn't breathe, I could not do anything. I had to go home but how would I do this. My pregnancy was very complicated and after delivering my son, my body was broken. My son and I had almost lost our lives multiple times due to complications during my pregnancy and at birth. I can truly say because of the prayers of my parents, the rest of our family, friends and my dad's congregation, we survived. I had been on bedrest for seven months of this pregnancy which meant income for seven months too. Post delivery I did not work either, which further inflicted challenges. We were barely surviving financially. God in his mercy always created a way for us through this trying time. I was at a loss, on what to do to make the trip to South Africa for my dad's funeral. Living abroad can be extremely beautiful but when you need to get back home for emergencies it can prove to be stressful and challenging. Distance is not your friend when you must return home to be with your family.

True to our Lords' teachings, he always coming through for us at the right time. He sent a living angel who without hesitation blessed us to go to South Africa. We made sure to return this blessing not only to her, but multiple times to multiple others. Throughout life we have angels that come into our lives daily. Some of them we brush off due to misunderstanding and others we embrace. These angel human beings are what make our lives a little easier and a little more worthwhile. They come to rescue us even when we don't know we need rescue. Some come and you know their presences others do and you never know about their help or presences. Always get to know people before you let them take their blessings, they were bringing you to someone else. In life I have met multiple people like this, who are willing to go above and beyond for me and some I have not met, yet they have touched my life in some way. I am always grateful for them.

Going home was different this time. The person who was the foundation of our family was no more. The sadness we all felt was overwhelming. My mom was beside herself. My brother as well, was not himself. I, myself was not myself. It didn't matter though how I was feeling. Everyone was waiting on me to make decisions. I had never done any of these things before, my dad always managed everything with my mom. I had to subdue my emotions and do what needed to be done. Take care of my two babies. Care for my mom, my brother and his family too. This part of my life was a blur, I got everything done, but I don't know how. I had no real support from anyone. Everyone was dealing with this sad tragedy. I did not know how to handle my feelings. Friends and family reached out, but everyone knew me to always be so strong and independent, why would I need more support? I'm always the one doing the supporting. I would listen to my mom and my brother expressing their sadness, and I would internalize my own feelings.

I concentrate my time and energy on my family. Something that did affect me the most was when my dad had been in the hospital, I had called and asked to speak to him. I was told he could not speak at this time. I then asked if they could take the phone to him and if he could just hear me, but even that no one wanted to do. My requests have always been this way for others, never important. My dad was the only one who listened to what I was saying and would do his utmost to complete the things I asked. This was important to me, because I wanted him to know I was on my way home, and I wanted him to fight harder to stay for me to see him. This affected me and still affects me to this day. It didn't feel like a big request at the time and still doesn't at this time, but it was not done! Priorities, I always say I am in the details of everything I do for everyone, but no one can be in the details for me now that my dad is no more.

We came back to the USA and still I had no one to comfort me or tell me to just let things go and cry, vent, or anything. Everyone believed I was doing well. I used to cry in my car driving to work and back, this was my alone time. I tried to heal, to just live, but it felt like my heart and my mind were not truly connected. I was doing everything, but I was not me anymore. A huge part of me, died with my dad. He was the only person to love me unconditionally! How do you move on from this pain, I still do not really know. What I do know is that we learn to live with the pain as though it is part of us. We never get over losing a loved one, we live through it. This loss surpassed all sadness I have ever felt. To understand why I feel this loss this deeply, you must know the relationship my dad and I shared. We spoke every single day of our lives. No matter if I was in a different city for college or a different country, we spoke every day! I do speak with my mom daily as well but the connection my dad and I shared was priceless. It is true what they say about daddy's girls. My mom is my world and the bond we share is magnificent. My mom gives me the strength I need to continue, while instilling in me the key valves to live this life while nurturing my children in the ways of our God. My mom's knowledge surpasses her time on earth. Her experiences have taught me life lessons without experiencing them myself. She guides me to always be the person I want to be and always aim higher too.

The loss of my dad was sudden and shocked us. Mental breakdown is an understatement to what I experienced in life. I did not know whether I was doing anything right anymore. I second guessed myself all the time. The confident, self-assured, fearless, courageous, adventurous woman had disappeared. I did not recognize myself, physically or mentally. The realization that life would ever be the same again managed to push me into a greater depression. No one saw the depressed me, no one had any idea of what I was going through. I withdrew into myself. I tried not to be around people as much as possible. After going through three miscarriages and three extremely traumatizing pregnancies, where I and the babies I carried were at risk of losing our lives, and then losing the love of my life, this puts into prospective what really matters in one's life.

I fought through depression and heartache on my own. Life can be so crazy one minute and then be calm the next. I am not sure where I found the strength to start looking for healing, but I do know God is always the answer for me. God sends trails our way so we can appreciate the blessings we have. They are also to show us truly how robust we are. I concentrated on my kids and they in turn gave me the reason to push harder to get myself functioning normally. I was always a very hands-on mother, doing way too much with my kids. Has time passed and with the realization that I am only one person, and I cannot do it all, I started to minimize everything I was doing. I started to focus more on my health, cause if anything happened to me where would that leave my kids? I made myself a priority for a change, which helped me to start my healing journey.

My kids enjoy spending time with me chatting, and that helps immensely to help me just talk things out so to say. My oldest child is my pillar of strength. He truly takes on the role of the man in my life. My second born is my tender loving care child, always giving me tons of love and affection. And the baby, he reminds me so much of my dad in so many ways. In our culture we say when one dies another comes. This child could be my dad in spirit. He has the same zest for life and the same naturing spirit. I truly am grateful for the understanding and support through this healing journey. Self-healing has become very prominent on social media of late. Thankful to these media outlets for helping me with the tools I needed to start my healing. Thankful for learning and adapting to life. It is so important to have people in your life that will always have your back who will stand up for you when you can't stand up for yourself. Friends are formidable to have but when they are all busy with their lives and trust me life gets hectic when we all have kids and families to see too on top of jobs and life in general.

No one wants to burden anyone with their emotional baggage. I will say being so far away from my family and childhood friends makes things furthermore difficult. Cultures are so different as well. You can especially tell from being in a country where everyone is for and keeps to themselves. Growing up South African, everyone was remarkably close to each other. Cousins grew up like siblings. We visited each other regularly and we were always available for family. It could be this era, but this seems to not happen as often anymore even in South Africa, but it is even less here in the USA. It is extremely easy to feel lonely here. People do not socialize much and when they do it is noticeably light. People do not want to hear about your feelings or even take your feelings into consideration. If you are the type of person who is always considerate you will end up being taken advantage of. It seems like life has changed even more after 2020 and the craziness it brought after the virus. Mental health issues have drastically increased not just in the USA but in many other countries too.

You do not know how something is affecting you until someone points it out to you. My kids would say to me mom why are we not doing more interactive stuff like we used to do? I did not even realise my mind and body were literally just shutting down. Body pains gripped me, I could not walk without having pain in my legs and feet. I carried my stress in my shoulders which meant my neck was aways sore. I had a spinal leak after the epidural from my first child's delivery. The three cesarean sections tore my body apart and the mental toil from that itself was overwhelming. No one understood the pain I had, not even me. I could not really explain it. As time passed, I started to talk about what had happened to me during my pregnancies.

Most of the time, people probably thought I wanted sympathy from them, from me telling them my story. What they did not know was I wanted to vent but did not have someone to vent to who cared enough and who would listen. My self-consciousness was still present. My discernment made things harder. I could tell when someone genuinely cared to listen or when they did not. Juggling emotions and not being understood was the point I realized I needed to journal instead. I started writing down my feelings and because I did not want anyone to read them, I would throw them out afterwards, but I did get my feelings out. This helped me in this healing journey too. Sometimes we do need to find alternative means to express ourselves.
I started to feel more like myself again.

Travelling this world I have had the pleasure of meeting an array of people. Those to pick you up. Those who care about you more than how much they know you. Those who love, just who you are, with no limits to their love. Those who want to expose you to the extraordinary experiences they have explored and want nothing more than to share those experiences with you. Those who learn easier ways to do the mundane day to day activities, but who want to share those with you too. In being saturated with all these positive experiences, I have tried to do the same for those I meet along the way. I think back to something simple, a funny story now but so embarrassing when it happened. Walking around with toilet paper stuck to my shoe, thinking I looked so exceptionally cute and elegant, I walk back to my husband, having all eyes on me, thinking it was admiration, when in fact it was in pure jest at the fact that I was still attached to a roll of toilet paper. Laugher everywhere, and me so flabbergasted at the mere thought. Thankful to a kind soul, who swiped down to grab the paper off as I walked. Oh, how red my cheeks turned, when I realized what had happened. I was embarrassed at first, but then burst out laughing as well. A night to remember, eventful and fun. Realizing there are some who will watch you be in a pickle and just stand by, or even better, pull out their phones and record instead of helping. Go where your tribe is, those who will catch you if you fall, or even if you slipped a little. Life is full of positives and negatives, but one thing is for sure, life is meant to be lived, even if you trip over your own feet from time to time enjoy all the phenomenal things about this journey and about you!

Traveling has really opened my eyes to diverse ways of doing things. Different food, foods you may fancy, and foods you may not care for, but being respectful about it, is key. I have been exposing my kids to these from an early age. They used to watch a show, and, in this show, they always said, "you got to try new things cos it might taste good" and I have stuck with this way of thinking for my kids. Not only in trying new foods but in trying different things in life too. I am excited to say, they truly do try everything from our different travels so far, even my baby boy who is seven enjoys exploring the different taste sensation of our travel experiences. They know to never make a disgusting face, around servers or other people, but they can say in a pleasant way that they did not really fancy the food they tasted.

As a parent I find myself learning from my kids too. Kids have an amazing zest for life. This has been a remarkable journey of life with a magnitude of diverse experiences, but I would not change a thing. It takes going through the "bad" to appreciate the "good". In the end you are "you" because of who you were at one point or another and everything that happened to you. My kids always ask me mom if you could go back in time what would you change? I always say this or that, but in truth changing anything from our past would reshape who we are today.

Enjoy who you are and who you are becoming with the daily experiences. Leave the hurt on pages and take the pleasures. I am a devoted fan of dancing it off, always have been. I forgot for a moment what that does for one's body, mind, and soul. Try it, dance it out the next time you do not feel like yourself and see how it changes how you are feeling? Live the Alchemy that is you!

Mandy Douglas

South African born and raised, with her beliefs in Jesus first and foremost as her foundation. A homeschooling mom of three gorgeous boys together with her husband Michael. A medical professional, who has explored diverse facets of the medical field in a variety of countries and places. A passionate traveller who enjoys the beauty of our worlds culture and diversity. Influenced by her mom's unconditional love and her love of adventure and travel. Her mom encouraged her to spread her wings and fly across seas and reach for the sky. Fuelled with encouragement from her dad to be whoever she wanted to be. All while making her believe she could achieve anything she set her mind on. She enjoyed growing up with a brother who is like a best friend. A dynamic woman who continues to learn and grow. Her greatest passion is to ignite the flames of adventure in her kids, to explore our beautiful earth and beyond. To protect our earth as long as we can. Life motto, try any and everything at least once.

6

Being There Untold

"I don't hang as a portrait. I move as an ever-flowing stream."
Julie Cavaliere

A Reflection on Life

An adventure is only an adventure if you want to be on it, otherwise it is an arduous journey that treks from one tragedy to the next. Let me tell you of an arduous adventure. Trial. Tribulation. Cutting remark. Shunted sideways. Attempted annihilation. Voice silenced. They all fit the description. It is the overcoming that builds the character, solidifies the foundation and springboards into the future. Faith in the living God binds the journey into victory. How do I write the words to express the beauty and the love of God that enables and says I am worthy? He has me on a quest. His love builds up. It strengthens and defines, gives purpose, causes me to overcome. First, I must go through the fire. God projected within my mind a vision. A rod of pure, toughened virgin steel embedded within my spine. The top was splayed like a piece of soft timber pounded with a metal hammer. I voiced the air with rhetoric. What must I undergo to endure such pounding? Such brute force. I am hammered into the rock of Christ. I felt that I would enter the 'valley of the shadow of death' (Psalm 23: 4.) I must overcome me, rejection, ridicule, judgement, circumstance and torment by those familiar and those estranged. Division and lies. How is it that I am accused of stealing from my dead sister's house? It is not me. It is not within my nature. I only came to help! I am judged by the very thing that others could accomplish. Lies and Distrust. They are rancid.

God's love tears down that which is meant to be torn down and swept away. The anger, the pain, the lack of faith for change, the tears of desperation. I question myself. Does any love remain? Only God's. His love shapes that which is meant to be shaped. It sustains and preserves. My God is the potter who works the clay before making the bowl. He is the creating artist who created perfection. He creates beauty for ashes. He creates a path for the journey. The clay is thrown down, formed, fired and re-fired. Can you hear the 'ping'? He adds the perfect finish for the perfect collision. I am that which He is perfecting. I have been in the kiln. My life honed by fire. I am who I am because of this. Not ash. A phoenix rising from the ashes. An eagle soaring to great heights. I have collided with men who call themselves professional in their field who have deemed me not as great as they. I have collided with men in religion who think themselves God. Egotists. Narcissists. Psychopaths. All are ready to pull down that which they judge unworthy. They elevate ego. Their ancient patriarchal paths are relentless. You are a woman. You are not allowed to preach. You are not allowed to teach. Do not presume to give us a visionary word from the Lord.

Do they just dismiss the word of God and His intentional inclusion of the great women who overcame themselves and conquered others? What of Deborah and Ruth, Esther and Lydia, the honouring of women as mothers as they carry the seed for the next generation? My life is a journey of 'Here I am Lord, use me'. Let me speak of your treasures, your kingdom pearls, the richness of your word and the glory of your presence, the depths of your heart, the very essence of your creation. At what cost?

Life, you remind me of the Klimt portrait of Adele, the 'Golden Lady' with her pale skin and luxurious dark hair. Her beauty in the contrast. What draws the eye? Is it the mosaic that surrounds, or the gold of her cloth? The beauty is in the master's hands. God establishes the boundaries of life with pure gold. He illuminates. We reflect His glory. The defining line is drawn and we pursue its path. Roads paved with gold. Determined yet ever changing. Nuances and nanoparticles. Such is His transparent glory.

But she is only remembered for the gilt, her heart unseen; her heart broken and rebuilt for the world to admire. What strength of character lies within her depths? What has life pulled apart, rearranged and re-connected in another form that enable her strength in serenity? In truth, we can all be seen like that– the gilt glittering on the outside. The warm golden glow in the candlelight. Brilliance in the bounds of glory. The smile. The loving heart. The abundant embrace. The real adventure lies in how we get there.

Goliaths. Gigantic mountains that hinder the forward path of life at inconvenient times. They seem utterly insurmountable. They are the answers and triumphs. They cause us to change the way we change. They steer our paths into greatness as we press through. Strength. Resilience. The understanding of ourselves and others. We gain empowerment and wisdom wrought by God to mature us, to bring positive tension to our sphere of influence. Grow. Mature. Enlarge. Collide.

My life has been one of persistent mountain tops and valley experiences. The snow skier on the moguls. Thrown in at the deep end of life they cause me to grow rapidly, to overcome my doubts about me and the fear of mankind. Mr Disconnect (former husband) and I pastored a small country church that doubled in size within twelve months. *"Who is leading the worship?"* His reply, *"You are."* I am a flautist but did not consider my singing voice to be a worthy instrument to lead others into the presence of the most high God. A community hall, a microphone, an amplifier and perhaps a pianist. Sink or swim. Pray. Prepare. When God throws you out of the nest you soar if you will spread your wings. Don't look down. You are higher than you think. You soar on the thermals of the Holy Spirit. Your spirit and soul elevated. What a ride. Elation. Pure adrenalin success or not. Live and re-live the moment. Be humble. I do this again and again. Reflect. Improve. Change.

History of a Journey

I am proud of my working-class heritage. Underground coal mining was fraught with danger. Dad's friends were killed and some maimed. He survived the onslaught and worked with integrity. He understood the needs of the men he supervised. They all had each other's backs. In the hue of the head lamps 'crib' was eaten and euchre played. The sun only shone at the end of the shift. He grew up as one of seventeen children. He was strong of character and resilient. Three daughters and one son. Stable upbringing. He would fight fiercely if required to protect his family. I think I was his favourite. He loved my cheeky quirkiness without saying. A quiet, knowledgeable man. A deep thinker. When he spoke, you listened because you knew his words had relevance. *"Don't go down the creek. If it rains on those mountains (the ones we could see from the back veranda) it can cause a flash flood."* Indeed, it could. Too late. My siblings and the neighbourhood children spent many a weekend *"down the creek."* Rebellious. Pushing boundaries. Challenging thought. Danger. Exhilaration. Caught. Punishment. Tortuous. Four children sitting on the couch not allowed to speak. Death by silence. I was the loquacious one. Agony. Effective punishment. Used this on my own children.

My father wasn't much interested in what other people thought. My mother on the other hand was. Everything had to fit into the 'norms' of society. Not allowed to stand out. Not allowed to be me. I don't think I ever fit. I always felt different. The 'black sheep' of the family. I wrote with my left hand. Shame. I thought outside the box and made funny remarks. Can't cope with that. Squeeze. Struggle. Smother. The fear of man was instilled into my psyche. My mother, an intelligent, hard-working woman. Missed opportunities. Lived her life through her children. Our upbringing was dependable. Our parents loved us in their own non-demonstrative way as it was mostly then. Their lives driven by toil and regret.

You must experience the pitch black of an underground mine when all the lights are out. Your hand is in front of your face. You know because you put it there. You can feel its presence. You can't see it. You can't see beyond it. Encased. Enveloped by the intensity of the blackness. You are invisible. Yet you feel safe. You know your father is there beside you. He will lead the way out. His knowledgeable wisdom says, *"Face the direction of the fresh air flowing onto your face."* You follow its path. Holy Spirit wind blows. He guides. Leads. Refreshes. Revives. Finds a way out for us. Engage with His presence. By faith you are believing for the release. The correct path. The sunlight. Shards of light penetrate the darkness. I know where I am now. I see others on a similar journey. I have survived. I am injected into the light. A light so bright it illuminates my feet and lights my path (Ps 119:105.)

The Patriarchy

Perhaps I should name those mountains on which the pugilist stands. I don't see the need. The man at the top. It usually is a man. But not always. It's the 1990's and the patriarchy is endemic even in Pentecostalism. I am not the senior pastor nor his wife. I am the wife of the assistant pastor and thereby a non-entity. Although this role does not define me either side of Sunday. It brings liberty amongst the women only. I have three small children who I will not allow to be called 'PKs' (Pastor's Kids) nor to wear the burden of the label. They will not be unjustifiably judged.

I am a warrior woman, or so people say. True. I war in the prayer room. I fight for my family. I fight for the Truth as I know it. I fight for justice. I fight to strengthen others, to build resilience and depth of character. I am strong. I am well organised. I have a voice that speaks. Others listen. Or not.

And that is my downfall. I do things to a high standard. The patriarchy tells me it is not good enough. I do things much improved. The patriarchy tells me it is not good enough. I adjust, adapt, engage at a different level. The patriarchy tells me it is not good enough. *"You're Miss perfect,"* I hear Mr Disconnect say in his derisive tone. So much easier to put down others than to raise yourself up. Puffed-up. Proud. Dictatorial. European culture. Blame. Blame.

Love and laughter strengthen me to stand up for what is right. At some point I have been able to clearly set and express the boundaries in my life. At others I have been voiceless, suffocated by those around me who thought they had superior knowledge or a rite to mute the existence of others. The patriarchal, narcissistic behaviour that hinders and attempts to destroy. It frustrates life and ministry. My calling in God has gifted me with a prophetic ability to 'see' things very clearly and outwork systematic process. *"But can't you see?"* No, they won't. But will they listen? No, they don't.

Am I too intelligent? Too organised? Too competent? Too prophetic? Too discerning? Too sociable? NO! I am a woman! I am intelligent. I am organised. I am competent. I am prophetic. I am discerning. I am sociable. Why would you not listen? Mr Disconnect would say to others, *"Imagine how hard it is to live with a prophet!"* If you had listened to the words, heard the discernment in the voice, life would have been much different. We could have been settled, established, worked as a team. Equal. Built into one another's lives. Emotional energy spent on creating beauty. A life. Not merely existing.

Yet my ministry demands were exactly that. Why couldn't you see? Why wouldn't you see? I had to lead, decide, discern, plan, raise our children, speak into other's lives. My family first and church ministry as the lesser significance. I enjoyed my time in ministry, leading worship, a flautist, teaching biblical truths, impacting others with the supernatural power of God. Despite my inner turmoil, faithfulness was rewarded. Lives changed. My own children as grown men of faith. Courageous. Risktakers.

Your upbringing demanded men were at the top and women were to be controlled. *"I am the head of the home,"* you would say. *"Well act like it! Be the man God wants you to be, not the mess you have allowed yourself to wallow in. Set your boundaries."* All this screaming in my head. You tried to drag us down to your depths. Your words emotional blackmail. Pouting. No discussion. No agreement. Absence. You had a long moment that ended a marriage.

Women are there to be subservient, to be looked at. Beyond beauty the world sees nothing else. The battle begins. The sexism. The ageism. Wisdom with age is wasted on most men. The energy that could be used creatively to bring change, design, stimulate and impart, catapult others to heights is disdained. Amal Clooney. Highly intelligent, capable International Human Rights Lawyer. The media covered her 2017 speech to the United Nations[3]. Suddenly famous because of her husband, actor George Clooney. No other reason. It was him, not her, despite untiring accomplishments on a world stage. The Press fascinated with her fashion and elegance. The Bottega Veneta yellow dress. Her 'baby bump'. Humanitarian works and oratory against atrocities of ISIS vaporised. Did they comment on the men's suits and the coif of their hair? I read not.

---

[3] Schmidt, S. (2017) *A lawyer named Amal Clooney gave a powerful speech at the UN. Some only saw her baby bump.* Available at A lawyer named Amal Clooney gave a powerful speech at the U.N. Some only saw her baby bump. - The Washington Post. (Accessed: 25 March 2024.)

Arduous Adventure

I learnt to survive in life. Work hard. Be there. Do that. I reared three children solo within a marriage. Life became drudgery. I dug myself into a pit. A black abyss. No light. No escape. Jesus was my only answer, but I couldn't even call out to Him. I felt disempowered in life. Undervalued. Undermined. Under appreciated.

No joy, no laughter. Sadness and regret. A slave to the circumstance. I ran like a rat on an eternal treadmill. I had to get off. I needed to get off. But how? I voiced my concern to Mr Disconnect. I was mocked. Ridiculed. I had changed and I was not pleased with the change. I did not need to say anything of my plight. It was obvious to those close to me. I suffered a mental breakdown. Mr Disconnect said to me, *"It can't always be about you."* My response, *"It has to be, for now."* Where's the support from the one whom you need to love you and understand you, to have your back? No protection. No empathy. I was tossed to the wolves. I was exposed. Alone.

There is an assurance of God's faithfulness to keep His promises (2 Corinthians 1:20.) He had my back. My mind knew this. My heart could not receive it. I could not experience His strength nor protection. I doubted my faith, myself. I clung to hope. To change. A heart now encased. Deep walls of protection guarded against the world. The opposite to what Christ wanted. What was I going to do about my life situation? I struggled with the need for change. I wanted escape.

Mr Disconnect worked minimal hours. We were subsisting on government handouts. Totally unacceptable. I had a Science Degree. With three boys in Primary School, I gained a post graduate Diploma in Education. I would teach Science in secondary schools to earn a decent salary to support the growing needs of my family.

I was being verbally and physically abused by students at the State school in which I was employed. Oranges hurled at me across a playground. Spit balls in the back of my hair. Sworn at by gangs of youth who would gather around me to intimidate and bully. Senior Executive in denial. Blame the teachers. They can attract disciplinary action. Students uncontrollable. I was accused of inciting students against myself despite witnesses to the contrary. Life was a lose-lose situation. I did not or could not recognise the spiritual evil that was surrounding me. Life was enveloping me on all sides. I determined that action was required. Perhaps this was the beginning. Me reflecting on me. My purpose. My voice. I had to stand up and do something. Physical boundaries ignored. Set the spiritual boundary in prayer. I struggled with this. Remember,

I was cast aside by the one whom I needed to stand by my side. Do what you need to survive.

Frustration. Anger. Abuse. Lack of accountability given to students. Use what you have at hand. Set the boundary. Hold Senior Executive to account by their own policy. Fill out 'the pink form'. It was designed for students to access when, not if, but when they were bullied by other students. What negated me from using it to alter my plight? Nothing. The wording was broad. Submission compelled action. Resolution. How long do we put up with the behaviours of others? Why had I not set those boundaries beforehand? Perhaps I gave others too many chances. I set boundaries and was castigated. I recoiled. Position dictated. God's grace and love allow us to suffer for the gospel's sake just as Christ suffered. His mercy sets a boundary and says, *"No."* Not to the suffering. It allows the suffering that we might be overcomers. That is where the victory lies. That is where the strength lies. That is where our future lies.

Let me begin this journey of empowerment. I had to leave that school. By necessity I made the decision alone. I resigned. Verbal reprimand by Mr Disconnect. Money, money. However, such peace waylaid me. My choice. I knew I would get more work. Science teachers are always in demand. I walked straight into employment.

Why are we continually moving house? Is there no stability? Where did the money go? Why hasn't the rent and the school fees been paid? Where did all the money go? Voice crushed. Flippant retort. Children nearly expelled from school. You lost your job. You made us homeless so you could retreat to your mother. Why didn't you fight for us? You rented out our house. Three little boys. Your own family! You didn't care. We were nomads. Lost.

I came from a family who knew the value of hard work and its inherent and financial rewards. Parents born in the Great Depression, suffered WWII, who pushed through in adversity and built a life. Here I learnt perseverance. Strength. Integrity. I toiled for my own family emotionally, spiritually, domestically, financially. I ensured we had a church, community and friends. Mr Disconnect was jealous of my friendships. He did not, would not build any of his own. At the time I was the main breadwinner of the family. Sparks flew.

The church teaching by the older women was not to usurp the role of the husband. Afterall, he was the head of the house. What if he did not meet this assignment? What then? Who else is going to make the decisions and be there for everyone? Do you really want to know how to raise your children, build love, laughter, resilience, character into their lives? Do you want us to move forward?

I was supposed to encourage him, to tell him how wonderful he was and worship the ground he walked on. That is what he wanted. That is what was expected. Now that was a road too far. The burdens of everyday life placed upon my shoulders were heavy. Many of which I was not supposed to carry. I was incensed. Angry at such advice. I was caged. Different treadmill. Life is not meant to be a lonely association. Many years later I sought wise counsel. The agreement complete. Separation essential for my wellbeing. I asked him to leave. Divorce papers served.

The Collision

"I turn up and all hell breaks loose," I hear myself say. That is my reality. I have been through the fire. I am honed by the Maker. The purpose is set. The prophetic voice brings warfare. My hands trained for battle (Ps 144: 1.) The onslaught takes its toll. Providence re-locates me to a Christian School. *"It's your fault. It's all your fault."* The Executive Head of Student Wellbeing screams at me in a guttural voice. The students look on. My back against the rail. Cornered outside the lab. Goliath is towering over me. I am a woman. I am small. I am intelligent. I know my boundaries. I stare up into his eyes. They are wild. I recognise evil spewing vomit all over me. I silence my voice. I am empowered. I evade. I retreat. I know I am safe. I only came to teach for a term! *"Here I am."* God used me. Seeking God in the circumstance. Recovery, Healing and Illumination. The culture of the school exposed by light and truth. It repented. It too healed.

Wolves in sheep's clothing appear at times in our lives. Their sole purpose to intimidate and destroy. Have I not understood my calling in God? Have I not understood the journey? I had been prepared through fire, listening, teaching, training. I was not prepared for the suddenness of this onslaught. As I stand, the powers of darkness are challenged. Light and dark collide. I collided with them. Detonation. Explosion. Impact site destroyed. Release. Freedom. The course corrected. Physical vs spiritual. Good vs evil. The invisible has become visible, illuminated by the light of the world (John 8: 12.) It is exposed and I am vindicated. At what cost? Time to step up and speak out. That which is said and that which is out worked must be revealed.

My Godly gift is in the prophetic. Discernment in the now. Discernment for the future. My catch phrase, *"Don't you see?"* The answer is often, *"No"*. Others could not see what I saw, neither feel, hear, nor sense what I sensed. It is just who I am. Understand me. Take the time to listen in full and to the fullness of what is required to be exposed. The attack, "You *are too hard, unforgiving, you have no empathy, no mercy."* I had allowed any mercy to be driven out of me long ago. Judgement. Intimidation.

My family and church family were being attacked. The wolf was spreading gossip, rumour and accusation. He had to be stopped. Despite my warnings, no-one would stop him. We lost the battle and retreated to a place we should not have been. No more country church to pastor. An egotist who had his dream destroyed because of false humility. I felt like a voice crying in the wilderness. No wonder my childhood always felt so different. I was in a desert where people did not understand me. I needed watering but there was no-one there to water. I retreated to the invisible realm. I shut down. What was the point of speaking up?

Overcoming

So many questions. Am I running away? Am I hiding like Jonah only to find himself in the belly of the great fish ejected onto a beach? Did I want to be used of God? Was it self- preservation? Was it lack prayer or ineffective prayer? Was it unbelief in what God can do? Did I not allow God to work in the circumstance and took over His role? Perhaps that was the reality. I had a calling and God would get me back on my feet. He would set me on His path once again. The path on which I compromised my walk, where I allowed circumstance to rule. Repentance and forgiveness bring empowerment. Freedom. Joy. A corrected path.

I had been hurt too many times. Recognition is the first step of faith and healing. The second step, what am I going to do about it? Believers are called to be overcomers by the blood of the lamb and the power of their testimony (Revelation 12: 11.) I learnt how to overcome, how to set an effective boundary. Persevere. Sit at the feet of Jesus. Seek Him. Knock and He will open the door that leads to transformation. Praise, prayer, petition. Gather your friends, those who will encourage and uplift. They hold you up because you are valued. You value them. Listen to their voices.

I recognise the spiritual enemy. I find fulfilment in the discernment, the ministry that follows. I am walking my journey. I declare the goodness of God and His love for me over my life every day. It was a battle. It still is a battle. The battles become victories. I stand in who I am and who I am meant to be. I stand in my faith beliefs, the strength of my overcoming. I protect myself now with a different structure. Not with walls, but with freedom. I've walked out of the prison. I have a voice. I allow love to enter and be released. The mercy that once was, has been restored. It grows, matures and impacts. It is the Father heart of God.

I had to face my Goliaths. I needed healing. The Goliaths made a way for me to overcome. They exposed my flaws. They strengthened. I pressed into God.

Worshipped at His feet. Won the victory. Love guided, led and protected. Seek God alone. Wait in Him. Allow the Goliaths to be your solution. Govern them that way. Life. The joy of the Lord is now my strength. It wells up. It bubbles forth. My name means 'youthful spirit'. That is what I know.

I have known adversity in various forms. I have walked the arduous journey. The pounding of the hammer. I know how to wield the sword. I know how to overcome. I have a narrative. Many narratives. I encounter others amid their circumstance. I know myself now. I know my prophetic gift in God and its impact. I understand. I am not running away. I am at peace with who I am. I can love. Grace and mercy follow me. I speak truths, challenging others to rise. Heights before unseen.

Being Here - An Adventurous Journey

The pot cracked. Fragility accepted. Weakness strengthened. There is value in the imperfection. The 'Kintsukuroi'. Salvaged. Reclaimed. The purity of gold. Costly gold. Perfectly imperfect. Life has become a highway. Each road meandering into the shape of the roads of victory on which I walk. Roads on which I am seen. I don't hang as a portrait. I move as an ever-flowing stream. Liquid gold. The eye drawn to the fluidity of the static movement. I am at peace with myself. I know there is more perfecting to come. The fire will burn hot. The pot will crack again. The gold will run deep. I am ready for the refining. Golden scars. The reflection of God's glory. The resonant sound of the maker.

My greatest joy is family. Sons. Daughter. New generations. A grandmother. Treasured Friends. I have great capacity to love and enjoy uniqueness. I am strengthened daily by intentional love and assurance. I feel the value of life and the life-giver. The boundary set. The path illuminated. I am in a new garden. A new space. A new place. The sun shines. Blossoms burst forth. The satisfying, fragrant essence of life permeates the atmosphere. I am ready to dig and get my hands dirty. Plant new seed. Water new ground. I stand on a new platform. It allows me to write this story. The here and now are the new adventure and you are on it with me.

Julie Cavaliere

Julie is a gifted communicator and orator who speaks into the lives of others the wisdom and truths that emanate from lived experiences. Born at Cessnock in the Hunter Valley of NSW – the heart of coal and wine country – Julie was educated at Cessnock High School. She furthered her studies to obtain a Degree in Applied Science at Charles Sturt University and a Post Graduate Diploma in Education at the University of Newcastle. Working as an Environmental Officer in the Coal Industry, a Science teacher in Private and State School systems, an Assistant Pastor and a Board Director for a Not-For-Profit organisation housing and feeding the homeless has enabled access to and the building of relationships within varied cross sections of society. Julie has spoken at professional teaching events, preached in churches, led women's retreats and mentored young women. Julie lives in the Northern Beaches of Sydney. She has three sons, a daughter-in law and one grandchild. She enjoys live theatre, walking, swimming, reading, drinking great coffee, breakfasting at cafes and meandering aimlessly along the golden sands of the seashore.

Social media

LinkedIn: (24) Julie Cavaliere
Facebook: (20+) Facebook
Instagram: julie_cavaliere_

7

Holding On To Let Go

"Let go of how you want it to unfold or how you think it should unfold."
Nicole S. Farrell

What does that mean? Which is it? Hold on or let go?

Holding on to your faith and values so that you can let go of your stress or worry.

Holding on to your dreams so that you can let go of thinking current circumstances won't change.

Holding on to the promise of getting beauty for ashes so that you can let go of needing to try to figure out how something or some things will work out.

That's what it's all about. Life is a journey and how we choose to walk through it to our various figurative destinations will say a lot. It will impact us.

In life, we tend to think that we need to choose a side with everything, just like veganism or carnism; black or white; gluten-free or regular; plastic or biodegradable; meat or fish; bottled water or tap water; juice or soda. However, the older we get, the more we will realise that life's experiences aren't and can't always be 'this or that'. There are grey areas. There's colouring outside the lines.

It is said that trials were - stealthily so - designed to make us stronger. When experiencing trials, setbacks, disappointments and delays, we might feel weakened by life's curveballs sometimes, don't we? Depending on the circumstances, fear, doubt, exasperation, anger, frustration, sadness or anxiety might surface, compounding our already stressed-out minds. It might be difficult to give ourselves grace or to 'trust the process'. Things can seem to be too overwhelming.

Storms come. Imagine a woman immaculately dressed, hair perfectly coiffed, face well made up, walking through a blizzard. She might be looking beautiful but there is chaos around her. The coldness whips her exposed skin, snow is blowing swiftly against her face, the winds threaten to knock her over. Focusing on what's ahead of her is difficult because of everything that's coming at her.

Ah, the lessons of life. Apparently, we need them. I recall years ago as I was mentally battling about the consequences of a shocking revelation made by someone close to me, which would somehow impact our relationship, I questioned God. *"God, why this? Why did they have to do that? Why do I have to have this kind of experience? This just spoils everything."* I was hurt, angry, disappointed and confused. I had always said that I wanted to be a Motivational Speaker before that. So, as I fired questions and comments at God while I walked the town on errands, a still voice said, *"How do you want to motivate and inspire people without any experiences and if you don't overcome anything?"* The barrage of questions stopped abruptly. It was a humbling moment. My mind reeled. I couldn't exactly argue with that. It made sense.

Remembering episodes like that help me to take a deep breath and go again. Every situation has a solution, or at the very least, an expiration date. I've had times when I felt weak. I'm not referring to my physical strength but my mental, emotional and spiritual strength. There was a time when it seemed like for two years without fail, it was one problem after another. I was tired of having to navigate the maze of uncertainty and unforeseen circumstances.

We've got to hold on to our faith so that we can let go of our doubts, fears and creeping feelings. We cannot rely on our own understanding. A scripture says, *"Lean not unto your own understanding."* I'll be the first to say that that is certainly not the easiest thing to do! Unpleasant situations, betrayal, unforeseen circumstances, past trauma all contribute to us feeling triggered or compelled to write our own scripts. We forget that God is our mighty author.

When It Rains, It Pours

Years ago, I walked away from my corporate job, later enrolled in a course and started my business soon after. It's a long story as to how I got there but let's just say that I'd always wanted to be an entrepreneur and the time came when God instructed me to 'jump'! Did I jump? No. I kept procrastinating. I was making good money from my main jobs and freelance gigs, but I also had a high rent and the usual statutory bills. How could I leave such a secure arrangement and jump into the unknown?! Well, one by one, my clients left to go to other companies. Through no fault of mine. The economy was facing a downward slope and they wanted to go somewhere that they'd get more 'bang for their buck'. Still though… It was a huge hit to my income. Suddenly, funds got depleted and different choices had to be made.

As time went by, other freelance gigs began to dry up one by one. So, I was faced with a fraction of what I'd been earning. I had always been one who believed that no-one should put all their eggs in one basket but there I was with several baskets and they were bursting, threatening to destroy those eggs! Despite my best efforts too. It was then that I learnt that you can either be pitiful or powerful...but you CAN'T be both!

Footprints

Do you know the story, *"Footprints"* (or *"Footprints in The Sand"*), about one set of footprints? It's a popular piece where someone refers to dreaming about walking along the beach with God. At times, they saw two sets of footprints; other times, one set of footprints. They then deduced that at their saddest, most trying times, only one set of footprints was visible. The person asked God about it and God told them that the times where there was one set of footprints, it was when He was carrying the person.

How many times have you felt as if God was silent? As if He hadn't been listening to your pleas? As if He had abandoned you? As if nothing would change or seemed to be changing? I know I have. Now, I know He sees after me but yes, at times, I wondered why He wasn't answering my prayers, at all or fast enough. Boy, can we get impatient!

In my quiet moments, I realise or remember that He is always with me. Always! He carries me. He strengthens me. It might not feel that way at the time, but He is.

Waiting To Exhale

At times, I've gone through situations where I felt as if it was one unpleasant situation after another. Murphy's Law seemed to be in full effect. Delays seemed aggressively daunting. Breakthroughs appeared to be elusive.

One such experience was when I started my business. The business was two-tiered with Public Relations and Event Planning & Management services back then (I've since pivoted to Public Relations and Image Management.) I did the needful - registered my business, set up my social media presence and was consistent in advertising and marketing both online and offline. Weeks turned into months and not one call, not one booking. One day, I called my mother feeling emotional and told her that maybe I'd made a mistake going into business. Deep down in my heart, I knew that wasn't the case but at that moment, I felt as if I had made a dreadful mistake.

Yet, I continued to promote myself. Seven months later, my phone rang. That call came from the Director of a household-name international franchise and they wanted me to be their Communications Specialist and Publicist for a special project and campaign. They were my first major P.R client. After that stint, work began coming in, both from local and foreign clients. It was the breakthrough I'd been waiting on. My faith was tested. Oh, was it tested!

Pick Up Yourself, Dust Yourself Off

I've always joked that I allow myself one day to be 'all up in my feelings' and then I roll-up my sleeves and go again. However, there was this one time that I allowed myself almost one year. Yes, one year. I needed to decompress and recalibrate. So, I went on a semi-hiatus. I took the pressure off and got STILL. I sat in it. I honoured my feelings. I was honest with myself. Then, I took a deep breath and eased back into moving forward.

Was it a walk in the park? No. Partly because I'm accustomed to being in 'Go Mode', so being still was challenging but I knew that it was imperative. Rekindling that spark after the domino effect of challenges took numerous strikes of matches. Little by little, the inner fire was reignited. So, what can you do when you feel sucker-punched? Here are seven things that I'd suggest:

Give Yourself Grace: I'll be honest. I only learnt to do this within recent years. What does giving yourself grace mean? It means not harping on your mistakes, where you went wrong. It means not obsessing over what different path you could've taken. It means accepting that you did what you thought was best at one time or another. I'm not one to have regrets per sè (granted, I do have one that lurks at the back of my mind) but there has been times when I would think about the 'What Ifs'. Should I have made a different choice? What would things look like if I'd gone an alternative route?

However, I've learnt to give myself grace. I did what I did the best way I knew how. We can't know what we don't know. Does that make sense? And yes, sometimes we gamble, sometimes we know better but still go full throttle, but we live and learn. Right?

Sit In It: Honour your feelings. Whatever you're feeling, FEEL IT! Some people tend to condition themselves to be numb to things. They distract themselves from their emotions through chronic commitment to work, adopting vices, using humour or worse, using substances like illegal or prescription drugs (which they abuse) or having excessive alcohol consumption. If I were honest, I'd say at one point in my life, I was like that. I'd shut off my emotions and sometimes throw myself into my work. I'll tell you something though. You can't run from it. It will stay there and you'll have to deal with the root and/or symptoms.

Let Go, Let God: Give up the power. You won't ever be able to achieve what you want alone. This calls for accepting God's ways and timing. In His infinite wisdom, He knows best. Tell him what you want and allow Him to do what He chooses to do. Don't try to run ahead of Him, don't try to rush Him, don't try to help Him. Let go of how you want it to unfold or how you think it should unfold. Really, it's none of your business.

I tell friends that if they're going through a hard time and the words in prayer elude them, just say, *"I trust You, God."* ...even if they have to say it fifty times a day. He'll understand. He already knows your problems, but He wants to hear about it from you. He wants you to invite Him to help you, guide you, protect you, give you peace of mind.

Let go of how you expect - or want - Him to bring you solutions. We can be looking out for a pretty, varnished basket with a large bow, but God sends it in a brown paper bag!

Be Still: This one requires true grit! Grit to be still? Yes! If you're like me, you probably cultivated a habit of trying to solve things for yourself in years gone by. I was 'that girl'. I obsessed until I got my own answers and then did what I thought needed to be done. It took me many, many years before I understood not only how to be still but understood the benefit of being still! When you're still, you hear God better.

Go On About Your Business: Do your best and let God do the rest. Keep going forward. Keep making the effort to get things done. If it's a dream, breakthrough, or opportunity you're waiting on, live your life. Things will happen when they're supposed to happen. Be proactive.

Help Others: When you need help, sometimes that's the time to help someone else. Read that again. Take the focus off you at times. If someone has a need, step in and serve. Have you ever been fighting through your problems, but someone comes to you for comfort, advice, or help? Let me be honest. I've felt too tired dealing with some problem of mine, so dealing with someone else's problem drained me more just thinking about it. However, you know what? I still helped them. Now, I'm not saying to be someone's garbage truck or to not have boundaries. I'm just saying that sometimes being selfless is what we're called to do.

Concentrate On Your Dreams: Don't allow your experiences to cause you to stop believing in your dreams and goals. Over the years, I created a habit of visualising what I want every morning and every night. During a particularly bad period, well, challenging period, I found that I wasn't doing it as much. It hit me one day. That's when I realised that I was slipping. So, I got more INTENTIONAL. I would carve out time - several intervals a day at times - and visualise my dreams. I kept hope alive. I kept faith alive. I still believed.

Still Expect Good Things: Occasionally, it's easy to get distracted by all that's going on and you can become discouraged and disenchanted but we must stay expectant of good things and turnarounds. Change is inevitable. Still expect that promotion, those new contracts, the loan approval, the trips you want to take, your dream house, whatever it may be. I've learnt that we can't look at what's happening 'in the natural' because supernatural blessings will come our way.

Lessons Learnt, Missions Accomplished

I firmly believe that to overcome trials or to succeed (however we measure success), we need to embody a warrior spirit. We need to go to war. That can be in prayer, with intentional actions and/or releasing our battles to be fought by God.

Think of a boxer. He tries to get back up even if he or she feels dazed by the severe blows of the opponent. We might find ourselves stunned but we fight! We get up! We find resilience! No-one said it will be easy, but we find out that it was all worth it. Win, lose or draw.

One important thing we need to do as well is learn from our indiscretions. Always seek the lesson to be learnt. If not, we're going to circle that mountain until we get it! Ask yourself, *"What can this experience teach me?"*

I rely on my faith a lot. I think without it I'd be lost. In these times, that's probably not a popular thing to say but it's my truth and it will always be. Life is going to *"Checkmate!"* you occasionally but that doesn't mean you don't get to play again. Had it not been for the goodness of the Lord.

I know... Trials can make you feel as if you're in the ring with a younger Mike Tyson. The beating can be nothing short of brutal. The jabs might come fast and furious. You know what you need to think about despite that though? That no matter the outcome, you WON! Do you know why? Because you stayed in the ring. Because you stayed the course. Because you refused to give up. Because you chose faith over fear.

One of my favourite go-to lines is: STAY THE COURSE. Years ago, at a retreat, that came to me. It was before I began my entrepreneurial journey. It has become one of my silent motivators. Whenever it pops into my mind, it reminds me to pace myself like a marathoner. To focus on the goal and not the distance per sè.

As we continue to navigate through the twists and turns, let us not forget the power that we possess to conquer. Power is built over time. As it's said, every setback is a set-up for a comeback!

Nicole S Farrell

Nicole S. Farrell is a multi-faceted and multi-creative professional who, through her work in Image Consultancy and P.R Media, inspires change and creativity. However, change and creativity are constants within her own life. Known for her flair, dynamism, spirituality and cheerful nature, she tries to embrace life even with all of its twisted and rugged landscapes. One who is inclined to the notion of faith over fear, she has made some gambles throughout her life, and while some paid off in dividends, others failed miserably but she pushed through and carried on. A staunch believer of operating in one's purpose, she is mindful about what brings her peace of mind and joy and what inspires her to elevate. To her, a good laugh can provide some peace to the soul, even if for a moment.

Social Media

LinkedIn: Nicole S.J Farrell
Instagram & Threads: refinement_renaissance
Facebook: Refine Your Image With Nicole S. Farrell

8

The Mundane and Exhilarating Expedition of Life

"We all have a past and scars but that does not give anyone the right to throw daggers and create more nasty echoes!"
Michelle Jewlal

Introduction

Many great men have said many helpful things, in books, motivational videos, podcasts, poems, journals and movies - which only helps the ones that are willing and prepared to receive the wisdom to challenge themselves to push boundaries, change, evolve and grow into the greatest version of themselves. It is pointless to read self-help books on motivation and upliftment if you are not willing to put in the effort that will help you gravitate towards your goal, lean forward to grab that burning light that has been inside of you all this time. In my experience it does not have to be one huge impactful incident for one to change their path in life - for others like me the journey was on a path that I had to seek out for myself. A path that did not have many tracks or footprints, a pathway that has moulded and shape how things are in my life today.

Despite being well-informed on my circle of matters I have come to realise and not just pay lip service to the statement that we are not born perfect and perfection is an illusion. We all just wing it on this journey of life at least some of the time we know what we are doing and other times it flows. I have grown to glow brighter than the insufficiencies I suffered in my younger years. An enthusiastic young lady smiling with pleasant manners, well-groomed in her best rags, full of promise, humble, compassionate and driven. The courage, strength and perseverance to be who I am while contending with words from society on what and who I should be, imposing their norm of society branding.

Regardless of the external pressure I am still dynamic and unique. Climbed up the corporate ladder to CEO; confident, strong minded, forthright, legit and a passion for what I do. What you do and how you do it tells a greater tale than racking in the money. Everything takes care of itself when you lead from a place of experience and honesty. I have a knack of seeing opportunity in all situations including in the face of hardship. When I walk into the board meeting there are no airs or graces about me, the colleagues respect me and it is clearly visible. Meetings progresses with robust discussions and everyone has their say. Final decisions are based on solid contributions all round, resolution done - everyone is happy. Slapping on my CEO name badge is the last thing I do before I leave the house in the morning for work, it's part of my daily routine – *and I say to myself you have come a long way but there is still more work to be done.* The badge does not define me, my ethics do.

History

Many may profile me as middle child syndrome, I beg to differ!

The most interesting and fascinating thing about humans are we are loving, kind and caring. We are not born as an animal let alone a predator. By default, society is noble however judgements and discrimination has seeped in to spoil the landscape. Some people have evolved into vile and horrible human beings! And humanity at large feels the impact with more perspectives than that of a compass. And on that path of life's journey of evolving it is in this sphere your unique, rare and exclusive story emerges to help others. Our stories are told by our well-worn faces with the wrinkled lines and callus hands. Society defines us by the simple clothing we wear, the coy crooked smiles and by our warm and sensitive approach. The legacy we leave behind tells a story whether we go through life actively or passively. What we say yes or no to creates echoes for humanity.

I was born and raised in Stanger, a humble town in South Africa. My story is not just my story, I know that somewhere out there someone is looking for that beacon of hope. They are looking for that light in the darkness, that comfort from the storm, the glimmer of hope that things will get better, they are looking for you and me to tell our story authentically and unapologetically. Growing up under apartheid had its own unique challenges that people of colour face, this storyline topic is covered by many individuals including our late President Nelson Mandela. In addition to this we have the society or communities we were brought up in. My personal and intimate experience is not a tangible item that you can touch - my experience of how people made me feel and think, while growing up. I think to myself and downplay how bad it was – I comfort myself to say it was not so bad because we were none the wiser and we made do with whatever we had even if that was nothing at times - as a family we said we have us - this family, we accepted meagre as normal and was blind to reaching out for more.

Growing up we struggled with financial hardship. Being poor did not hurt as must as the scars that created the emotional pain - one can rise above the circumstances and change the narrative; however, shame is a different animal altogether - as you do not have control over the owners of those thoughts, rumours, gossip, hurtful words that adds more discomfort to the emotional self. It was survival regardless of the circumstances. This created more than just echoes for humanity. It created scars that will tarnish this species.

The illness of a few in society that served their hidden agendas of judgement and discrimination. The evil doers that made the choice to crush another, these were so called neighbours, friends and worse still some were family members. Individuals that one may have looked up to, only to be deflated with their snide contributions was a tough place to be. Other times people made it known we were poor, however the brightness of some shone brighter than those harsh or rude comments with their kind words you forget all about the hurt and pain and moved on, smiling with no care in the world. The defining moments in my life are when I realised that I wanted much more than life threw my way. I wrestled with the fact that I was born in the wrong family and I yearned for a perfect mother and father.

I hid my true emotions and tried to swim through life. As a child I found myself always smiling and not aware of what was going on around with a pure heart beating with love, joy and happiness while seeing people as true and honest until people around me started talking with their version or who they thought I was. It is just how people begin to label each other instead of lifting each other. Yes, the label that I was branded with started a long time ago. This cruel branding of my soul and life has left so many echoes in my life. My intention to write this chapter is to inform humanity how their actions and lack of actions impacts the young, old, rich and poor alike.

Family Life

My parents married when my mother was 16 years old and my dad 13 years her senior at almost 30. They had 3 children: 2 boys and me. My father was an honest, hardworking, intelligent and dedicated gentleman. He was a supervisor at a huge firm and got fired due to his subordinates' costly mistakes. In the 1970's this was seen as a huge blow in society and brought shame and disgrace on to our family. He did find a job at a local business that left him penniless after more than 30 years of dedicated service. The unfortunate reality is society does not stop to ponder when they throw sand in another person's food how this impacts them. Derailing a person to benefit yourself may give you a false lead in life however your actions will create a path for you.

The apartheid era was already hard and when someone was fired, they were somewhat doomed and deemed as not suitable for hire at big business or corporates, due to that stigma attached to a person. This situation put our family in a condemned situation. I lived the echoes of humanity and not everyone is conditioned to give unconditional love in this season. Then my mother rolled up her sleeves to keep everything going for the 13 years that dad was unemployed and had no stable income. During this time, we were left almost homeless - the local sheriff locked up the flat due to non-payment. We then stayed with a relative in KwaDlangweza and African township in Empangeni.

Mother then stepped in and worked tirelessly and further continued for more than 40 years. She did odd jobs for the neighbours, cleaning houses, hand washing clothes and cooking. She too became a wheeler and dealer of note, gifted, talented, intelligent and knowledgeable who found employment at reputable clothing factories. After about 13 years, once dad got a steady job, she took on other less intense jobs. She did variety of small work, sewing from home, crocheting and other unusual jobs such as hairdresser, selling confectionery for a local businessman (us kids went door to door for sales), counter sales, cook at a local café, worked for a catering company. She progressed and grew at any job she did in her earlier years, including assembling and servicing of big industrial sewing machines. During the machinist factory worker's days being young and impressionable, influences were everywhere and she was still in her prime youth years utilised some of her spare time to unwind going out with friends, fun filled days were prominent, of course dad did not mind her as they had their own understanding. The community did not understand our plight or know our story - and this gave her a poor status in the community. Nonetheless, the family functioned well and we all pulled through with the children of the family rising above all odds to reach success.

My Thread - Some Defining Moments

As far back as I can remember I was told we lived well as dad had a good job in a top firm. After he lost his job like some bad omen hit our family everything became difficult. Mother stepped in to work and support the family thus begins the life of hard knocks. We were never sent to school without our lunch sandwiches - anything in between 2 slices of bread was good. There were days we barely had enough food for supper, just sugar water or juice. We occasionally lived on welfare i.e. grocery and sometimes clothing donations and accepted hand me downs too. Sometimes my brother and I would collect beer bottles and take it to the local liquor store to collect the cash deposit to earn a bit of extra cash.

As children we were never demanding or difficult – we remain happy at home despite the financial challenges burdening us. Being a girl of this household was not easy - as I blossomed into my young teenage years – I noticed that most classmates (also neighbours) started to withdraw and only approached me for when they really needed some assistance and of course I am every willing to assist. I never understood it back then but with hindsight after a few years I got the brief that some of my 'friends' mums were scared to send their daughters to my place as they did not approve of the environment as my mother exploring her twenties created a different perspective and opinion in their minds. It was my mother's shadow that was cast onto me by society – a shadow that I worked very hard to dispel.

Have you ever heard the term *'fast girl'*? In the area where we grow up I was that girl with that label. 'Fast girl' could be described a promiscuous person, easily persuaded into e.g. kissing on the first date, or being an easy catch or loose in society. It was easier in high school to be friends with my brother and his team of guys as they were just one grade higher than me. They did not label me and they did not judge me as they saw me as I was. In fact they taught me a lot about who 'boys' where. While fighting off the 'fast girl' tag I was also fighting off many admirers and at some stage not even 16 years of age I began to attract families that saw me as a potential suitor for their sons (It was maybe a way for my parents to secure my future.) They came to our small flat to meet with my parents to talk about their proposal.

I did not want any of that I WANTED MORE FOR MYSELF AND FROM MY LIFE! And getting married and having children after I finished school was not in my vocabulary. I was already like a parent to my younger sibling. Having to step up from a young age, changing nappies, house chores, cooking, laundry, it was not the ideal, but it was done with passion. Keeping my experience real I would not lie I made mistakes too while growing up and at some time I did enjoy the extra attention from many teenage boys at school and the area where I grew up in and yes, I crushed on them too. While growing out of these awkward teenage years I kissed lots of frogs which got me into trouble at times and with a few teen crushes that left me heartbroken and shattered at times. With hindsight and even as a professional social worker all these teenage feelings, experiences, pushing boundaries etc, indicated to me that I was as ordinary as any other teen giving their parents a hard time.

My rebellious side was only a phase and soon I marched past that label, but the tag did not leave. The label fast girl lingered here and there sometimes. It was a phase and time in life where I was finding myself and knowing how far to push boundaries. Beside you always have the few from the community and so-called girlfriends who are 'haters' that won't let it go and that did not make things easier for me. Through a few blabbermouths and haters came smears campaigns about me being pregnant by some random boy from my area followed by abortion gossips and other insults and disgraceful untruths. I cannot recall anyone from my community that stood up for me and said to those gossipmongers - those are untrue stories in circulation. I was riddled with pain and the residue still echoes; every action has a reaction!

Plainly it was a very sad place to be, however it could never replace or come close to the feeling of being poor and destitute and somewhat isolated because you were not high up on the food chain. Without even much effort, thought or deliberation I used this difficult time to reinvent myself and add value and advantage. I ensured and entrusted to myself NOT to dabble in alcohol or drugs so that I would shake off this nasty marker to my name. I will be damned if any one person from that community or my high school peers can say that I had smoked a joint with them or a drink in some dingy corner – I thank God for the strength because no social ills touched me. At my high school reunion, I was not surprised when some peers learnt for the first time that I did not take alcohol nor did I smoke, they were confused because I was hanging around guy friends mostly and was a tomboy of note, hence they stereotyped with what they saw on the outside and believed what they wanted to believe. Some were even shocked to learn that to some extent I had a strong affinity for spiritual wellbeing, trying to find meaning in life. It was indeed a blessing in disguise as I stayed away from these social ills and all behaviour that came with it. I did this without much effort and the rewards have been a blessing my whole life through.

Emotional Scars

This tag followed me well into marriage. In the first 1 to 2 years people would enquire about my son, assuming I had married due to pregnancy. Suffice to say this caused significant frustration as this was not the case. This is how society can make or break an individual even when I worked so hard to change the circumstances of my life. The echoes from humanity haunted me regardless of my mammoth effort to turn the page! I was fortunate to have a family that understood I made mistakes and had made some poor decisions as a teen, but home was home with love. About five years after we were married while we were at an event in our home town of Richards Bay a wretched man walks up to us both and says the most diabolical thing ever to me *"hey your mother ..."* (statement too hurtful to mention), hubby was livid with anger but we were mature enough to know we did not need to defend any comments we just walk away with our integrity intact as my social upbringing and challenges faced in life were already known to hubby. My question is what did this man want to achieve by making such an inappropriate statement? Did he want a reaction from my hubby, or did he want to raise eyebrows? I will never know and nor do I want to know, I believe the wheel turns for everyone. We all have a past and scars and that does not give anyone the right to throw daggers and create more nasty echoes!

Dealing with my home life, teen crushes, teenage hormones and so many other challenges just made me into an even more rebellious teenager. I did everything my way and it went against my parents' advice. And on the flip side I knew I did not fit into the mould they wanted me to be in. I felt different, I was different and wanted considerably more from life in general. I did not want to get stuck in the 'Indian package or passage of life'; getting married, having children and being a housewife was the furthest thing from my mind. I had big dreams and big goals. I wanted to achieve what my parents did not achieve in their lifetime. I wanted a life whereby I was not going to be left wanting for anything. And I knew that I was the only one that is going to make strides for myself. I would get stuck in the newspapers and magazines. My mother would often say I was reading long before I got to school.

During visits to pharmacies and shops with free booklets and pamphlets, I would collect and read them all. I still recall in primary school some peers were irritated with me they even called me a know it all – it seems I always had an answer for everything, I cannot imagine now how annoying it may have been for them. Back at school I worked very hard with the limited resources, was an average achiever but always visible. I worked hard to be identified as prefect at both primary and secondary school level - it was a big honour and this spoke volumes of my character. As I did not have much of a home life like many of my peers, I immersed myself in participating in sport and excelled in school activities in general like netball, soccer, school plays, debates, needle craft, etc. I was not brilliant at sports however fared well enough not to be at the bottom. Sports gave me an escape temporarily from home life and it added more admirers to my already exhaustive list. Sports gave me the opportunity to be a winner for myself. In my own way, I as focusing on the principles of Hinduism.

Emotional Rollercoaster

Despite the distractions of many things happening in my teenage life I was secretly focusing on my life outside the family home. I wanted a new beginning and worked hard at school despite the many trials and misfortune a child could face, I did exceptionally well enough at standard 9 (now grade 11.) I used these marks at the year end to apply for bursaries while mother wanted me to be a nurse, father wanted me to be an accountant. What many may not know is that my field of passion was in medicine. I had done 5 handwritten applications for medical bursaries of which I received two positive responses of acceptance. The next step was to submit my matric results. In my matric year I did well enough to receive an exemption pass which resulted in both offers being available to me. With this I was unable to undertake these studies as my parents could not afford my travel to the associated universities.

Unable to attend university resulted in me feeling defeated. The echoes of the past still lingered and the prospect of getting married and having children was still NOT an option – I refuse to accept that I could not get into university because of finances, it did happen later in my life. I did not give up hope and more than 25 years later I sent myself to school and succeeded triumphantly. I was lucky to have my high school principal approach me it seemed he understood my background. He came to our home and said he had registered me to be a locum teacher and it's a start just for a short period but at least it will be some earnings, breakthrough at last. I did that for a month and then it was holidays, however, there was opportunities in a school in Richards Bay the following year. Not standing still I took a job at the local florist at the Stanger market for a short while. The florist had a vending cart at the bottom market section. I endured the tedious task daily of carrying dozens of pails of water to the bottom market and then carrying the flowers to set up in buckets. I would set up my little stall with much pride and joy. Selling flowers was the easy, how could someone resist my charm, smile and pleasant manners? I sold out almost daily and the boss lady was very happy with me. I was still however looking for a job that will help me and my family.

A New Season Begins

While at the florist I received a call from a family friend who were looking for someone fresh out of school without experience but must fit their criteria of having done accounting. And I had a matric exemption with high marks in accounting and I matched these easy criteria. I attended the interview in Richards Bay and went back to my job at the florist. I did not feel confident that I would get the job as there were other young girls well-spoken and lined up smartly dressed in their best apparel and here I was with a homemade dress and sandals, no heel, no handbag, no mobile phone, no make-up, just Plain Jane. I was pleasantly surprised when we received a call a few weeks later to say that I got the job. I was gob smacked with shock and excitement as the company was still in the stages of construction of the site and I was to start immediately. Just like many others yearning for better I too had to sacrifice the home life and make changes to take bold steps in life. For a young girl to start off from scratch with only a high school education the move was a life changing trek.

All around me there were changes while the country was moving into a new era of breakthrough and freedom, I too was changing my trajectory towards better prospects. With help from mother, I trekked to Richards Bay in 1994 with one small plastic packet of home sewn dresses. My heart filled with ambition for this new and exciting experience to learn, grown and earn money to help my family and achieve my goal of gaining a university education to better my circumstances and life. Mother arranged boarding and soon after my boss and his family assisted me to find my own place to live. They became my new family away from home, we had our ups and downs like any family would, however they treated me very well and supported me respectfully and wholeheartedly. I started with the business when it was being born and inherently, I learnt oodles of life's lessons, some aspects of protocols and etiquette and most prized learning was business acumen which I did not know will be valuable come 10 years later.

I got married in 1998 to a young man that was so besotted with love that he gave up his family inheritance just to be with the one he loves. We did not know this will be the first of many transgressions against the normal according to our families. While juggling many obstacles my Prince and I began life with nothing to our name, no financial inheritance from either side, no family support or motivation. We had intense discussions on the way forward in our life and we both agreed on a path more fulfilling than that of our current position. We both stepped into a path that neither family was prepared for. We lived together before getting married – and it was considered a distasteful and dishonourable move in the Indian communities. And at that time, I was considered by my soon to be in-laws as being of a low caste type which did not help us either. At that time, I was not the 'ideal girl' according to their standards, because I was independent, living by myself, was enrolled in a short business study, learning to drive a vehicle and started to look after my family - all with the little earnings I received and somehow that label also followed me miles away.

We began building our empire from a supermarket shelf packer and newspaper boy to being an accountant today and me from locum teacher and a flower shop girl to a CEO. It did not happen overnight. We had nothing to lose so the only way after we married was up. We prioritised education – the first for both our families. We decided not to start a family until after about 10 years of marriage. We were on a mission, a mission to change the narrative of our legacy and families. Nolen's journey of study was supported by his company. Mine on the other had was hindered with challenges. I completed a short course on business management which went well. Then followed up with a finance course which due to financial constraints I did not complete. I did not stop there, I registered for trainer the trainer and assessor courses and travelled regularly to Durban and this too fell short due to financial constraints. While we continued with our plans we were also saving for my studies. I registered at university for a BA Industrial Psychology.

Another challenge popped up, my parents needed assistance to purchase the council house they lived in, remembering how we were left homeless – I was not going to let their generational misfortune continue, I wanted to kill those elements dead in its track and with support from my hubby we stepped in. Just like everything on my journey I had to create a new pathway, I was getting good at it now. We offered the property to the sons, but neither one wanted to commit. We scraped the funds together to buy the house for my parents and the house was in our name. In addition, we signed another valuable and comforting agreement with my parents and it was to their benefit. The signed agreement allowed my parents to live there for as long as they need to, free of any charges, this meant no rental was being asked and we saw to the house maintenance etc. I did not want to go back to be destitute. With the delays for studying, I felt deflated but not defeated. On the other side married life continued as we were implementing our plan, studies, house, car, security and then family. During this time, we worked hard, we started our samosa side hustle in 1998. I juggled 3 jobs then just 2 jobs to push forward to contribute to our projects, plans and to rake up enough to study again. I joined LifeLine Zululand as a volunteer in 2000 and kept another part time job to supplement our income still focused on my studies.

We did not take time out for movies or date night, kept it to simple picnics and the beach. After a few years I registered for studies again and this time I did not even get through the front door as it was family time. My adorable baby girl decided she was not going to wait for our 10-year plan to materialise to be born and she was not waiting any longer. Then boom she chose her own birthdate to 30.12.2005. Studies went on hold for a bit, so did all other plans we had which included the new house we built from scratch. We managed to put up the structure and a kitchen with one room of furniture, subsequently, full furniture and finishings came about 8 years later. Still with zero help from family we both managed with a baby and me roving between jobs.

Nolen became the world's best dad and still is. I travelled a lot from the time our baby girl was 2 months old. Later, daddy was untouchable, ballet bag, ballet bun hairdo, shoes, make-up and homework. He was and still is an involved and supportive dad and husband. A few years passed and my visibility at LifeLine Zululand began to take on a life of its own, the quality of my work and the potential I displayed had been noticed and for me this was enough. With the support of the leadership and management I was able to work flexible and longer hours to cover for times I had to attend to family matters more especially a sick child, she was chronically unwell from birth until around age 8 years. Juggling was an art form by year 2, between doctors, hospitals, specialist, work and home life.

Somewhere in between my personal wellbeing was included – not much but it worked, it helped keep my head above water. There were nights that felt like it's never ending. We would go on for weeks at a time struggling to get her chronic asthma condition under control – as new parents we left no stone unturned in the pursuit of proper health management for our baby. Although I was flexible, dad had to pick up the reigns while I travelled. He did more than required, often going above and beyond, more than most men would. As the baby grew so did, we. We finally developed and worked out our own and unique style of parenting and it worked for us.

Back onto the work scene, I was instrumental and initiated and increased networking and market presence, creating brand awareness coupled with aligned implementation. Forging new corporate relationships, canvassing for support and rolling up my sleeves paid off as a slow but steady income stream was trickling in.

Starting from the ground up is a major advantage almost like a superpower in that it highlights the first-hand the experience and challenges faced by field workers, volunteers and others on the implementation level of the organogram. Starting at the bottom offers insight into making valuable contributions on policy and which is impactful. Studying was back in the picture, reviving my savings and moving towards my goals, was not easy, but it's something I had yearned for, it had to be done. I could accomplish a university degree; the BA degree took off. I had taken a sabbatical from LifeLine Zululand to study but stayed in touched on the volunteer side. Prior to my departure I ensure the sustainability and income generating initiative was up and running and it had generated adequate income to last at least 6 months if not more which gave the others taking over from me a positive foot to stand on before they start generating income. During my studies LifeLine Zululand requested I return to restructure their business as their company was failing. I agreed on the condition I continue my studies when the company recovered.

The organisation was not doing well financially, the landscape for non-profit and charity organisations was getting more and more challenging and some new strategies needed to be implemented. Having worked in the corporate and local government sectors and ad hoc employment experience it helped to support the organisation and thinking outside the box. The assessment, review, planning and strategizing took weeks and weeks turned into months and all because I love what I do. Within a blink of an eye new strategies were underway - reviving of networks and new engagements ensued. Time went by so quickly at LifeLine I lost track to completing my studies. I was unable to complete or get back to my degree, as the time frame for the degree had lapsed. At the same time, I was moving up the ranks making my mark in the organisation. I was fortunate to have started at the very bottom as a volunteer and more privileged to serve as a board member, training and development, projects, operations manager, deputy director.

A New Era Dawns

By 2015 at age 40 I was appointed as the Director for LifeLine Zululand. The appointment however was not as easy as the implementation of a succession plan. It had to be earned. I was told since I do not have a formal qualification as my history shows incomplete studies it did not look good for the organisation. I needed to acquire a formal qualification in line with my work and it had to be done on my own time and at my own cost. No one knew my background or my story. I have since started to wonder to myself what God has planned and willed for me was only being delayed because I needed to be emotionally, physically, mentally and spiritually ready for what was ahead of me. I was going to reach my goal; it was going to materialize as it is written for me. I accepted the challenge with gusto. With firm and unwavering support from hubby and baby girl and a few select friends and work colleagues I chartered this new territory.

I am reminded of a phase from the Bhagavad Gita, this phrase captured me when I was still young, that stuck with me for all my life and still holds strong in my mind, *"For one who has conquered his mind, a mind is best of friends, but for one who has failed to do so, a mind is the greatest enemy."* - Lord Krishna. I certainly believed in God's timing and plan for life and my studies. It was a very tiring, yet fulfilling and exciting. While keeping most of my studies away from family time, when it was homework time for little one – I too would get the supper going and sit with them and do my own homework. We would often crack jokes and laugh at the fact that at my age 43 I was going to school. Little did they know that at class I was the oldest and some other students were not pleased to have a senior or to some even a grandmother attend 'their' class. I was sometimes mocked at the same time can you ever image being mocked and still stand up tall with pride, joy and exuding confidence, it was breeze easy for me. They did not know my story and that was okay for me. What they also did not know that I was the director of a prominent organisation and that someday they would want to be employed by me.

I was a mature someone with a level head and knew what I wanted. I was in a more understanding space with myself and did not take responsibility for burdens that were not mine to bear. I excelled once again in all that I did with my studies. On the work front change and transformation was underway. The evidence of the work accomplished at LifeLine Zululand under my leadership spoke volumes that the university degree was not the reason for the milestones achieved. It was sheer unencumbered holistic natural leadership style accompanied by realistic strategies and out right everyday hard work that earned triumphant and unmatched results, propelling the organisation in being recognised as a Non-Profit Organisation (NPO) of choice and a trendsetter of note. I am tackling my new role with a holistic approach and attending to NPO challenges with innovation and creativity while remaining true to the mission and values.

How did I complete a full time 4-year degree with honours, no less than a few points short from a summa cum laude pass. At this age and stage in my life I feel they should have just given me an honorary degree. While being present at the office and making waves of positive changes to the organisation? The answer is simple – I trusted in God and his timing although it was not tangible - I had faith and then I did not stand still either, I had to also contribute and not just wait for God to write my exams or do my homework. Having also inherited an organisation that was on its knees meant I had to spend more time and effort at the office and dedicate time for studies too if I wanted to succeed as a director, it was like a sword of Damocles hanging over my head. I would come to work and then by 14h00 I would say I'm out for the day going to write my exam. Due to be being of a senior age and life experience and already flourishing career, I was able to glide through most of the modules passing with distinctions.

Moreover, I did not own a prescribed textbook, I had tons of pieces of pages on important stuff and the rest I was winging it. Somehow through some divine intercession I was able to retain information I learnt in class as well as through some internet videos. And if you ask me now, what I did last month on the third Tuesday at 10pm, I doubt I could remember even the slightest bit. I was so pumped up and eager, I never missed an opportunity to shine. There were never enough hours in a day and weekends were packed full of activities too and then some. I held my head high and remain humble and kept myself grounded and prioritised the different spheres of my life i.e. work, home and family. And just like that creating memories and experiences never to be repeated, the four years were up. Oh, did I mention I did fail one module - to the horror of my daughter, Leela-Rose 'mummy how could you fail and not just fail, how could you get 22%.' To this day I never lived that one down. And it became an inside joke for us at home now. Let me explain myself - I had two modules, the subject had an A and B module, well I studied and yes, I did study hard, in all the prioritizing and hectic schedules I studied for the A instead of B module. LOL moment when I got to the exam room, I was shocked and gasped, then silently laughed to myself, wrote what I could and waffled the rest, in 45 minutes I was done. Without any remorse I accepted that I will be rewriting the module.

I did score a distinction on the A module anyway. And then the supplementary exam for module B, I scored another distinction. In a nutshell, I completed my social worker's degree in 4 years with honours, while keeping a full-time demanding job and raising a family and fur babies too and bagging a few distinctions short of summa cum laude. It looked like a breeze and easy from the outside, it felt like an insurmountable hurdle from the inside. There were times I worked through the night and had maybe 1 or 2 hours of sleep and then back to the grind at work and dealing with a sick baby. There was no time for excuses. This was no easy feat taking over the organisation that was on its knees financially and today we handle a 30 million budget with more than 180 employees. I had to juggle family life and a variety of pets and see to my parents and then my studies. I studied very late at night after family time. I was not going to be an absent parent in the prime of my baby girl's life - from school recitals, hockey matches, orators, sports days, modelling, karate, ballet, I was her biggest cheerleader and supporter. During these tumultuous times filled with excitement and exhaustion I was still growing and growing into the most charming person, growing into an exceptional human being, grown to live and love the simple things in life.

The Echoes I Created

On 18th June 2019, just 10 days before my 21st Wedding Anniversary, my degree was conferred at a grand graduation ceremony in Durban International Convention Centre. The biggest achievement was having both my parents with me and it was a moment in time when they did not feel below the breadline and I know that they will never be left wanting ever again. I was the first in my family to go to university. The absolute bonus was having my husband and daughter there too, it was a defining moment in all our lives and would set a new legacy for the Jewlal's. It's not how fast you run the gauntlet of life - but how you finish the race you started. A moment etched in time never to be forgotten. I trust my journey gives you inspiration to leave your own echoes that will linger in humanity in a profound way.

My only advise for you is if you have a story to tell, TELL it whether you write it down, sing it in a song or shout, yell, or cry through it – even the quiet whispers count - GO ON TELL YOUR STORY let it ignite others to shine! We all are attached to our past that made us , it is who we are NOW and WE DO NOT HAVE TO STAY there, WE should not stop ourselves from growing, loving, living and exploring life more on what life has to offer - your life matters as it is and if you want to make your life better CHANGE YOUR STORY NOW , it will change your life!

We are all anchored by some element from our past - it has made an impact to last the rest of your life - yet you push past the hurt, blame, shame, anger, to be this beacon of hope and perseverance to others willing to run the gauntlet learn from your mistake and pay it forward. I'm not complicated, I'm unique. I'm from a house that had a Hindu Indian, Tamil speaking father, a mother that was adopted from a coloured family into a Christian Indian home. My parents married in the church and exchanged vows and rings and later they also had a Hindu Tamil ceremony. Essentially the household went to church and learnt about Christianity and went to the Hindu Temple as well. I was the only one in my family attracted to Hinduism from a young age and in Primary school I signed up for culture studies, learnt to speak, sing, read and write in vernacular.

At an early age I joined the different Hindu movements while growing up. (Hare Krishna movement and then later joined the Divine Life Society) all these in my own way, an effort towards rebranding myself from my past mistakes and the gossip, stereotype and judgements that followed me. I do not know if it worked, but what I do know is that I am grateful for having both religions and a mix of culture - I am reaping the benefits as we speak. I was not going to wait for society to come back to me to say, 'hey it's okay, you redeemed yourself, you on a clean slate now'. I just kept on pushing harder at everything that I did, failure was not going to be an option. On matriculating and not studying further, I asked my parent's permission to do missionary work - they refused point blank, they know my strong mind and will - and if I had gone, I was not coming back. What many did not know about me is that in my own way I was aligning myself to Hindu principles (Dharma, Ahimsa, Satya, Karma, Artha and Moksha to name a few) and some Christian values (such as peace, forbearance, joy, kindness and peace.) I wanted to be a compassionate and giving individual, I know very well I wanted to help people no matter age or race.

Lessons from my Life:

- We all make mistakes, never dwell there.
- Everybody lies, cheats, have hopes and dreams.
- All parents botch up themselves and their kids in some way or the other.
- We all have some sort of dysfunction in our families - there is nothing to be ashamed of.
- The reason we succeed: hardship makes a man humble and graceful and connected to God or higher order.
- Most happiness is based on some lies and yet we find it distinguishing and satisfying.
- Equip yourself with discernment to know the battles between the self and the ego.
- A hunter should not underestimate its prey… a wounded prey can be very dangerous.

Echoes of Humanity

Michelle Jewlal

1. Chief Executive Officer (CEO) - LifeLine Zululand.
2. Affiliated to LifeLine South Africa and LifeLine International.
3. 2024, Santam Women of the Future, Social Entrepreneur nominee.
4. 2023, Zululand Chamber of Commerce and Industry (ZCCI) - Business Excellence Award - Service Excellence Award in Community.
5. University of Zululand Ethics Committee, member Independent Community Representative (2020 - to current)
6. 2017, Business Women's Association (BWA) Zululand Region (affiliate to BWA National) Winner, Social Entrepreneurship category.
7. BWA Treasurer 2021 - 2023.
8. Zululand Welfare Social Services and Development Forum (ZWSSDF) committee member 2000 to date.
9. Master's degree in progress.
10. Pro-active and robust mum to Leela-Rose and our fur babies, dedicated wife to Nolen and caring daughter to my parents.
11. Community champion - provide free support, mentorship and coaching to Non-Profit Organisations and individuals requiring my skillset and guidance.

KwaZulu Natal, South Africa
035-7892472
Website: www.zululifeline.co.za

LifeLine Zululand located in Richards Bay, KwaZulu Natal, South Africa, and was established in 1987 by the late Mr Norman Midwood. LifeLine Zululand is a registered Non-Profit Organisation which renders free counselling and programmes to individuals and communities seeking its services, with the aim of promoting mental and emotional health for all. The organisation focuses on social behaviour change and works in the space of Gender Based Violence (GBV), HIV/AIDS, Youth and Community Outreach initiatives, including Men and Boys programmes. LifeLine Zululand is affiliated to LifeLine South Africa and LifeLine International.

9

A Lifetime of Resilience: Picking Up the Pieces

"You can do it, believe it or not. It is easier than you think if you can improve your situation by:
Just 1% every day - in one year you will transform 365 degrees.
Recovery, improvement and positive change requires Step 1 - YOU."
Patricia Anne Wilson - Cust

A Journey Through the Storm

As the days drift by, one sometimes is given the opportunity to look back at the past. There are happy memories and those not so happy. Lessons learned and experiences gained. Both friends and foes have added to the tapestry of life. When we are young, we are oblivious of the bruises that are yet to come our way - just enjoying the simple things and each day as it comes.

Circumstances often determine the path we take, the locations travelled and acquaintances made. Career decisions shape our life and lifestyle as well as those we associate with and shape the view we have on life.

I endured more than my fair share of hardships. I faced death as well as bidding farewell to loved ones whose absence left a void in my heart. Each loss had felt like a piece of my soul being torn away, but I had learned to carry on, finding solace in memories that danced like fireflies in the darkness.

Betrayal had been another bitter pill I had swallowed. Friends turned into foes, promises broken like fragile glass. Yet, I had refused to let bitterness consume me, choosing instead to forgive, not for their sake, but for my own peace of mind.

Divorce had left scars that ran deep, tearing apart the fabric of my family and leaving behind shards of broken dreams. From the ashes of my marriage I discovered a newfound independence, a strength I never knew I possessed.

The loss of my home had been a blow that had knocked the wind out of my sails. Forced to leave behind the familiar comforts of my abode, I had wandered like a nomad in my own land. But with each step I found refuge in the kindness of strangers, in the warmth of a smile and in the hope that whispered in the wind.

Abuse had cast a dark shadow over my past leaving scars that marred my skin and soul. But I refused to be defined by the horrors of my past, choosing instead to reclaim my voice, to stand tall in the face of adversity.

No matter what has happened in the past, it cannot be changed, only in the present can one strive for a better future. What has occurred in the past has shaken you to the core. How can you possibly go on after deaths, betrayal, divorce, loss of your home, lifesavings, job loss, businesses closure, surgery, abuse, near death experience - the list of tragedies is endless. Most of us have endured at least one if not more of the above unfortunately. Sorry to say I have endured all the above and somehow survived to tell the tale.

"Start over my darling. Be brave enough to find the life you want and courageous enough to choose it. Then start over and love yourself the way you were always meant to." - Madalyn Beck.

"Do not close the book when bad things happen in your life. Just turn the page and begin a new chapter." These words were often hurled my way, often with no consideration about what the stress and anxiety has done to my body or mind. From my lived experience let me encourage you not to live in a broken state. You are going to need stamina and clear thinking to tackle the beginnings of a new life wherever that may be. If you need professional help, seek it out. There are so many government and charitable agencies that can help. Don't delay. If you lack the capacity, then ask for assistance. Do not procrastinate your healing.

Lessons From My Experience:

- Be safe.
- If you lose your home, then find safe shelter immediately.
- Waiting lists are long for any type of accommodation whether it be social housing or rental.
- Seek woman's refuge shelters.
- Be proactive and do your research before you decide on any living arrangements.
- Once you are safe ensure you make rational decisions for your future.

Reach Out

Life is difficult, filled with hurdles. At some stage of life hard times will happen and support is not always guaranteed. To find a new path to your new season or world will take courage. You will never move forward unless you take the first step. Despite your age or circumstances, dig deep to create a better tomorrow. Seek advice if you feel overwhelmed and create a vision plan for where you like your life to land. Take baby steps if you need to but never stay stuck. Ensure you get up each day and move an inch forward towards your goal.

Remember

- You become a product of your association.
- You will become healthy if you surround yourself with healthy people.
- You will become happier if you mingle with joyful people.
- Success will find you if you include successful people in your circle.
- Your confidence grows when you associate with confident people.
- You will become generous when you surround yourself with charitable people.

Never go back to the situations or people that aided or caused your fall or who broke your heart. Forgive and move on. Always remember when you were at your lowest ebb, the people who helped you and forget the ones who pretended not to see a thing.

Gathering the Fragments

As I reflected on the chapters of my life I realize that picking up the pieces was not about erasing the pain or pretending it never existed. It was about acknowledging the brokenness and finding beauty in the cracks. One by one I began to gather the fragments of my shattered life. I found strength in love and in laughter. I found solace in the embrace of nature, in the simple pleasures of a sunrise painting the sky in hues of gold and crimson.

I sought healing in being an active Rotary member, in the melodies of music that spoke to my soul. I found purpose in helping others, in lending a listening ear or a helping hand to those in need and in fundraising for the Salvation Army.

Slowly but surely I began to rebuild. Each piece I picked up was a testament to my resilience, a reminder that no storm could break my spirit. And as I stitched the pieces of my life back together I realized that I was not just surviving but thriving.

It's Never Too Late to Reinvent Yourself

We cannot become what we want by staying the way we are. How can you possibly go on? Where to start? How to begin? How can I get back on my feet after all I have been through? The answer is within you. Like it or not you will always be judged by your appearance. However, focus on you, find that new job, look for accommodation, make the effort to apply for a loan, seek professional help and seek for a new partner if you prefer. Tackle the mundane and the stuff that steals your sleep.

Whatever you need to start over requires confidence in yourself. Always remember that you are number one priority and no one will champion to help restore your peace of mind like you. Take care of yourself and focus on destressing and work your way out of your past problems. You must get your act together.

Take a good look in the mirror and if it is not what like determine an achievable plan to improve your appearance. Be practical If you cannot afford costly spas or massages, take a long bubble bath or a long hot shower. Prioritise your selfcare and watch the tension slowly disappear. Then do something about your hair which has been neglected. If you cannot afford a salon, ask a friend to style and cut your hair or to colour your hair at home. Look in the mirror again and smile. Smiling is an antidepressant - it tricks the brain into thinking you are OK.

Remember you are not in competition with anyone - simply try to be better than yesterday. Nothing lifts your appearance more that clean neat clothes. New clothes are the beginning of the new you. Take a good look at what's in your wardrobe and sort out what is usable. If a belt or scarf will dress up what you have then keep what you can remodel and get rid of the old and tattered. It is amazing how the cleansing feeling makes way for a few new pieces to freshen up your look and energy. Simple but effective and long lasting. You can also opt to shop at charity shops that stock the latest trends and do not cost the earth. Get dressed to go out as it will boost your confidence and mood.

Embracing the Journey

As I closed my journal a sense of peace washed over me. Smile, you got this too my dear reader. I know from experience that your life will echo through humanity and paint it with vibrant colours. I know that my journey is far from over, that there would still be storms to weather and mountains to climb. But I also know that I am not alone, I have the strength and resilience to face whatever lay ahead.

With a smile on my lips and a glint of determination in my eyes, I will always step out into the world ready to embrace whatever the future holds. For I know that no matter how many pieces my life may shatter into I will always have the power to pick them up, one at a time. The new you will start to show through. Give yourself a pat on the back.

"There is nothing stronger than a broken person who has rebuilt themselves."
- Hannah Gadsby

You are a brave soul you are. Time to get up and face the world. Moving forward needs stamina. Your body has probably been sadly neglected, perhaps you gained or lost weight. You cannot reach your goal overnight. Remain focused and steadily move towards a healthier you. Just little by little you need to regain your strength. One day at a time, piece by piece. There are plenty of articles and books you can refer to. One little tip to start the ball rolling, never leave home without breakfast. If you have no time to have a proper breakfast before running for the bus then take a banana, apple, yogurt bar or a protein drink. This will stop the mid-morning cravings and save you both money and calories. Your mind will be clearer and your stamina will increase, helping you to make wiser decisions for the other meals of the day.

Never dwell on the past, remember how far you have come and what your goal is. Even on days that you can barely muster the strength to get out of bed, rise and believe in yourself. Wash away your tears and stand tall. Never given up as the sun will shine tomorrow and there will be better days ahead. Focus on the strength you gained and the life lessons that you learned. Be pleased with every small step you have made. The new you, confidently moving forward inch by inch.

Despite embracing semi-retirement, I embody resilience in every aspect of life. From navigating the complexities of my career to overcoming personal challenges, I have emerged stronger and more determined than ever. Even in the face of adversity, I maintain an unwavering spirit, drawing upon my experiences to fuel my passion for life. Whether it is pursuing new hobbies, volunteering in my community or enjoying moments of solitude, I approach each day with grace and resilience, proving that age is no barrier to strength and vitality. My journey serves as an inspiration to all who know me, a testament to the power of resilience in shaping a life of fulfillment and purpose and this will echo in humanity for eternity.

When things finally begin to improve
After so long of falling apart
It is the best feeling in the world
Be grateful and smile

Patricia Anne Wilson - Cust

Without university degrees I bravely strode into the outside world only armed with a home taught typing degree in 1963. Banking 1st/Advertising world/Marketing on and on for 15 years until I reached the pinnacle in the Corporate World, landing the position of Private Secretary to two of Australia's Wealthiest Men in Shopping Centre Development Worldwide.

Time to venture into my own Retail Outlets in Major Australian Shopping Centres (with a little help from my friends.) Believe it or not it lasted 28yrs, turning my Business into the longest lasting Independent store in Westfield's history at the time in 2003.

A big shift in my personal life leaded me into Event Planning/Implementation of my own Wedding/Function House on the Mid North Coast of NSW. A new career path yet again with the help of my advertising guru partner starting from zero to turning it into *"The Toast of the Coast"* which only lasted 7 years due to his untimely death. Unfortunate circumstances followed due to his passing I had to return to Sydney. Tail between my legs, looking for a new home, new career, at the ripe old age of 62. Enter once again into a new career of fashion.

Speaking from vast experience - we never know when fate is going to step in and turn our world upside down. Best advice; be prepared and hope for the best but prepare for the worst.

10

In His Hands

"When things are bad, remember, it will not always be this way."
Rebecca Dinoia

"I was born unwanted, growing up unwanted, so what's the difference now whether I am dead or alive?"

This was the question I asked God before I tried to commit suicide at the age of 17. My life has been a rollercoaster ride, taking me from the busy streets of Taipei to the peaceful suburbs of Sydney, from feeling hopeless to finding success in my personal and professional life.

I was born in Taipei, Taiwan, a country renowned for its beauty which was formerly called *"Formosa."* Both of my grandparents migrated from China after World War II when the Communist Party took over in 1950. Upon arriving in Taiwan, they were placed in mud brick houses along with other defence personnel and their families. These homes were hastily constructed as the government anticipated a return to China soon. My grandfathers worked tirelessly to provide for their families, while my grandmothers cared for the children.

My mother, like many young adults in the village, sought excitement and formed a gang out of boredom. They terrorized residents and shops, leading to frequent run-ins with the authorities. Amid this chaos, my mother fell pregnant with me and was advised to have an abortion but did not go through with it. She married my father, but as my mother later admitted, *"We were too young to know what love is."* Their way of resolving conflicts was through physical fights in the street and they divorced before I turned two and my father was given custody.

When I was a child, I was told that my mother was dead. Later, I found out that my father had refused my mother's requests to contact or see me. As a young child, I used to search every inch of the house, hoping to find a photo or something that indicated she was still alive. I held onto the feeling deep in my heart that she was still alive.

I still remember dreaming about someone standing at my bedroom door, in a long white robe with long hair, with a shining white face, so I could not see any facial features whenever I was sad or missed Mum. I told myself the reason I could not see the face was because I had never seen Mum and did not know what she looked like.

In primary school, just before Mother's Day, we would make carnations for our mothers. If your mother was still alive, you would make a red one and if your mother had passed away, you would make a white one.

Every year, I sat helplessly in the chair, surrounded by colourful craft materials, while my teacher repeatedly asked, *"So, what colour of carnations are you going to make?"*

I found myself unable to answer the question because no one had explained the concept of divorce to me and I wondered where she was. All I could rely on was my intuition telling me that my mother was still alive.

When I was 6 years old, my father remarried. His new wife did not want anyone to know about my dad's previous marriage and divorce, so I ended up being raised by my father's parents.

As a bus driver, my father would visit me once a month, but I had never been to the place where he and his new wife and children lived. Then one day my father decided to take me to a gathering with his new wife's family and friends. Just before leaving, my father took me aside and said, *"Whatever you do, do not call me father in front of anyone."*

At that moment, I realized I was a burden and I felt like a shameful secret that should have remained hidden.

At the tender age of 14, I received an unexpected phone call from a woman who claimed to be the sister of my primary school friend, requesting to meet. Her voice sounded urgent, so I agreed. Little did I know that this encounter would unravel a life-altering revelation. The woman disclosed that my long-presumed deceased mother was alive and residing in Sydney, Australia, with her new husband and three children. To my astonishment, she also handed me a letter from my mother. A whirlwind of emotions overcame me and I was left with a sickening feeling in my stomach. How could this be real? Such dramatic twists only occurred in movies, not in my ordinary life. I grappled with the truth of what I had been told all these years, feeling conflicted about whether to share this newfound knowledge with my father.

I managed to find my way home despite the overwhelming emotions I experienced. After my aunt discovered the letter, I had hidden, my father agreed to let me contact Mum.

It turned out before my mother left Taiwan, my grandmother on my father's side promised her that once I reached senior high school, my mother could contact me. Consequently, my mother wrote a letter and asked a friend to reach out to me.

After two years of correspondence, Mum arranged for me to move to Sydney.

Later, my mother shared that when she first arrived in Sydney, she joined a church women's group. With very limited English, she told the ladies about me and how she couldn't visit me due to cultural and legal barriers. One day, during a group prayer, someone told her that one day I would be brought to Australia by God.

For 14 years, my mother held onto that promise and prayed for me. In 1989, I arrived in Sydney and began a new life with her.

If I were writing a book, I might end it with, *"Then they lived happily ever after."* But the truth was far from that. After being separated from my mom for 14 years and being falsely told that she had passed away during most of my childhood, finding out the truth made me feel sick to my stomach. *"Go and live with your mom,"* my grandma said, *"and start a new life there."* Everything felt so unfamiliar; I just felt sick.

The taste of vomit still lingered in my mouth as I disembarked from the plane. I experienced motion sickness for the first time on the airplane and arrived in Sydney feeling unwell. I couldn't eat or drink and just wanted to leave.

During the time I lived with my mother, I faced challenges due to not speaking English and experiencing cultural shock. My mother, who was in her early thirties, had to navigate how to support a teenage daughter whom she had not raised.

There was no counselling or support for either me or Mum. I was reserved and did not want to talk much, so I kept many things to myself. My mom was often upset and I struggled to understand why. I could not handle that pressure, so one day, with the help of a youth worker from school, I ran away from home.

After staying in emergency youth accommodation for runaway teenagers, I moved to a permanent living situation after 3 months. In my new place, I had my own room and shared the house with three other teenagers, each with a unique story. Youth workers would visit us and we all had responsibilities to maintain the household.

I was still in high school at that time and I was feeling increasingly isolated. One evening, I prayed and contemplated why I existed, then tried to end my life. But that was not the end of my story. I lived in youth accommodation for about two years before marrying my husband in 1994. I was 20 years old then and we had three beautiful children soon after. For approximately 10 years, I stayed at home to care for our children and assisted my husband with his business. I thought that it would be like this for the rest of my life - raising our children until they grew up, witnessing their marriages, growing old and was just content with that.

After my husband's back injury forced him to close his business, we faced financial hardship for 8 months, relying on credit cards due to the loss of income. To overcome this challenge, I took on two jobs caring for elderly individuals and cleaning their homes etc. allowing us to manage our bills and support our family during this challenging time.

It was at one of the jobs that I was subjected to physical assault by the client's husband at their residence. I attempted to continue with my daily life as usual. However, I started experiencing symptoms of post-traumatic stress disorder (PTSD.) I endured frequent panic attacks and struggled to maintain focus. I witnessed myself deteriorating from someone who efficiently managed a business to someone who could barely manage simple tasks without feeling overwhelmed.

One day, I decided to take our second son, who was only about 11 or 12 at the time, to a busy shopping centre. However, we ended up getting lost in the maze of shops and corridors. As the overwhelming feeling of panic started to set in, I found myself pacing back and forth on the crowded street, trying to keep my composure. In that moment, my emotions screamed at me to go back home, while my rational mind warned that it was too risky to drive in such a state. It was as if my spirit was observing a heated battle between my emotions and logic, leaving me feeling completely torn and fragmented as a person.

I found it challenging to complete household chores and only had enough energy to prepare meals for my children. After each panic attack, I was left so drained that all I could do was sleep. Despite my efforts to maintain a sense of normalcy and continue working, I had to be admitted to the hospital.

I received treatment from a psychologist for about 2 years. During that time, I learned techniques to manage panic attacks. Hubby and I both went back to TAFE to study, completed a course and landed jobs as Sustainability

Assessor for Federal and State government programs. In this role, we helped the public and small businesses with energy reduction.

Toward the end of the state government program in 2013, I decided to start my own e-commerce business. Seeing there could be a demand for goat milk soap overseas, my original idea was to sell to that market. However, it proved to be more difficult than I expected, so husband suggested focusing on the Australian market first.

I was still worried about how I would cope after recovering from PTSD, so instead of setting long-term goals like most people in the business world, I decided to take small steps. My goal at that time was for the business to survive the next day.

We then started selling our products at the local markets and festivals, then at the expo and shopping Centre pop-ups. In 2018, I sought help from a Christian business coach to further grow our business. During one of the quarterly sessions, the business coach asked us to pray and seek a scripture as the foundation of our business. I remembered sitting in the hotel room and the scripture that I received was Psalm 23: 1-4:

"The Lord is my shepherd; I shall not want. He maketh me to lie down in green pastures: he leadeth me beside the still waters. He restoreth my soul: he leadeth me in the paths of righteousness for his name's sake. Yea, though I walk through the valley of the shadow of death, I will fear no evil: for thou art with me; thy rod and thy staff they comfort me."

At that time, I was busy building and preparing for our biggest business event. I was so busy that when my mum asked me to go out for a coffee, I told her my next availability was after three weeks' time.

I became enthusiastic about building a business and worked 15-17 hours a day, 7 days a week. Despite everyone advising me to slow down, I ignored their advice. Once, I received a $350 gift voucher and was told to go shopping, but all I could think about was the work I was missing and the emails waiting for me at the office.

A few months later, as I sat in the chair at the Westmead Cancer Centre, the weight of the doctor's words sunk in. They had just informed me that I might have a rare form of cancer. It felt surreal, as if it couldn't possibly be happening to me. Amidst the shock, a flood of questions raced through my mind. Could this really be cancer? What stage might it be in? How much time do I have left?

I also thought about all the birthdays, graduations, weddings that I would be missing.

After my initial meeting with the doctors, I had to undergo a set of tests and wait for the results. It was the most challenging time of my life. My husband and I decided not to tell our children until the test results returned. At our church, I did not ask for prayer publicly. Instead, I only mentioned it to a few church members and our pastors, so our children wouldn't find out.

During that month, I reevaluated my life more than ever before. from the initial shock to the sadness. Then I remembered the Psalm 23 verse I received earlier, which brought me peace. I came to terms with God – if I was healed from cancer, then God's name would be glorified through this miracle. If I did not make it and passed away, then I would be with the Lord in Heaven, in His loving arms. Either way, I would be a winner.

My heart was still pounding when I went back to get the results. When the doctor announced that they could not find any cancer cells, my emotion was like riding a roller coaster ride. This experience has motivated me to prioritize self-care and make conscious efforts to slow down and take better care of my body.

God has blessed us tremendously and since then, we have collaborated with some high-profile organizations and events, such as Miss World Australia, the Australian Chamber of Business Leaders' Annual Gala Dinner and the Australian Made logo certification.

I began working as a business advisor in 2016 and have assisted over 800 businesses, including sole traders, shop owners and professionals. I have also worked with inventors who utilized IoT and apps to launch or enhance their businesses.

In 2019, I took part in the Australian Export Trading Mission to Shanghai, China. In 2021, I was a finalist in David Koch's *"Back to Business"* competition. I served on the judging panels for The Stevie Awards for Women in Business in 2021 and the Asian Pacific Stevie Award in 2022. Also in 2022, we were honored to receive the Emerging Leader Altitude Award, followed by the KWE Business Excellence Award in 2023. In May 2023, we collaborated with IP Australia to produce an educational video highlighting the significance of business trademarking.

Since the day we got married, my husband has been my unwavering source of strength and my biggest cheerleader. Alongside my personal Savior, Jesus, I am certain that my life would have taken a different path without him by my side. As I stood to receive the Emerging Leader Altitude Award in 2022, I made sure to express my gratitude to my husband for always inspiring me to push past my self-doubt and reach for the highest heights.

As we have been blessed by God we feel compelled to give back. I have been mentoring and training the next generation of female entrepreneurs, sharing my expertise with social enterprise businesses. I have mentored students for Global Scope by Practera at Western Sydney University in Parramatta and participants in the Global Sister program.

In October 2022, I had the honour of being a panellist at a women's event, where I shared a part of my journey. After the event, two Spanish ladies approached me and one of them hugged me, expressing, *"Thank you for what you have shared. Because of that, I could see some hope today."*

When I first heard the comment from the Spanish women, I thought, *"Wow, only God can give people hope!"* However, as I pondered her words later, I looked back at all those years and asked God about the purpose of winning the awards, business opportunities, speaking engagements, PR, etc. both for myself and the business. I knew it was not just for me to feel good personally but served a greater purpose.

I realized that, as the Bible says in Luke 12:48, *"From everyone who has been given much, much will be demanded; and from the one who has been entrusted with much, much more will be asked."* God has given us gifts and talents and it is our responsibility to use and share them with others. We can keep them for ourselves or go out and make a difference in others' lives thirty, sixty, or hundred-fold.

So here I am. I was supposed to write an ending for my story, but I found I could not do that. Today, I had coffee with a gentleman to discuss business and mentioned my writer's block to him. He then said, *"Maybe you could not write the ending because you are still in the process of healing."*

As I drove back from the coffee catch-up, I reflected on many things, including my childhood. Despite suffering from a stutter at an early age, I loved to sing. In my early teenage years, I chose to be mute in hopes of gaining my father's attention. Accepting compliments was difficult because I did not believe I deserved them. I worked hard for achievements, hoping others would recognize my value and not forsake me.

I used to think it was just a part of my personality, but I realized that my reactions were a result of the trauma I experienced in the past. Reflecting on my life as I write this story has brought me to tears over my past because sometimes, I wish it had never happened. However, as I looked at the steps I have taken in the last ten years, I also became grateful for what I have today.

Without the love of Jesus, the support of my husband and my children, I do not know where I would be today. I do not have a magic wand and all I know is this: When things are bad, remember, it will not always be this way. This is not an ending but a journey and I need to take it one day at a time until the day I will be with the Lord.

Rebecca Dinoia

Rebecca arrived in Australia without knowing English, overcame personal challenges and started her own e-commerce business, Soap de Villa, in 2013. She has participated in various business competitions and won awards for her leadership. Rebecca has also mentored female entrepreneurs and collaborated with educational programs. Her achievements have made her an inspiration and positively impacted her community.

Rebecca Dinoia
Soap de Villa
soapdevilla.com.au
Rebecca Di Noia | LinkedIn
Winner of KWE Business Excellence Award 2023
Finalist of Business XCellence Award 2023
Winner of Emerging Leader award, The Altitude Award 2022
Finalist of 2021 Kochie Business Builder *"Back to Business"* competition
Nominee of 2016 Australian Ethic Business Award

11

I am ENOUGH

"I used to stand up for the children that were bullied, the outcasts, the single parent children, the ones from broken homes, as people loved to say."
Samantha De Kock

It was a period in my life where I felt happy and sad at the same time growing up was not easy being in a home of domestic violence and often being told by my dad that he wishes I was a boy was hard. Those words often resonate and somehow breathe life into your future. I was the only child to my parents.

A miracle is what they called me; my parents were not well to do neither did they have the finances to give me the life every child deserves. My mum worked hard as a machinist in a clothing factory while my dad consumed drugs and alcohol never keeping a job for more than 6 months. The decision was then taken by my maternal grandmother that I would be taken away from my parents and I would then live with my mum's brother.

Maybe my story is not so different from a lot of girls who have gone through similar challenges in life. What made me overcome and achieve in this life was my belief in my Lord and Saviour Jesus Christ. Memories all come flooding back at once and sometimes it feels like I am trying to keep my head above the water while I relive these moments in my life. The 1st time I was exposed to real violence was when I was 8 years old, my mum would fetch me on the weekends. Something I dreaded, I loved my mum and I wanted to spend time with her and my dad but the fear of my dad being under the influence of alcohol and drugs and then beating my mum up when she tried to prevent him from leaving just so that he would not get into any trouble.

It was a cloudy day a Friday afternoon like any other the birds seemed content while they sang in the language that God himself understands, the wind allowed the trees to sway as if they themselves were worshiping this great God. I guess I remember those things so well because it was the calm before the storm. I remember my mum taking me to the shop to buy me some goodies while my dad stood outside smoking weed. If my memory serves me right, he was always so happy when he smoked weed, he was a calm loving almost normal human being and if I am being honest, I preferred him smoking weed to drinking alcohol. I had some really found memories of my dad like the time he taught me how to hitchhike or the time he made me keep the weed in my pocket while the police searched for him. You may ask the question how these good memories are, you will see later as we continue.

So back to my mother who was buying me goodies, I walked around the store full of excitement pointing at something called a Zoo biscuit and I remember my mother saying that is too expensive to choose something else. While I looked at all the biscuits on the shelve my eyes remained on the Zoo Biscuits and the next thing, I remember is my dad saying to my mother buy her the biscuits she wants. I looked at him with appreciation but also fear as I knew this could lead to an argument.

My mum gave me this look that I was very familiar with, a look that made me feel like I was a burden and a problem. I felt that feeling many times in my life, the feeling of not being enough, almost like a regret that I even existed to them. While we walked to my parent's home that they rented I could see my dad looking a little weird like he needed alcohol and there was going to be a problem. We passed a liquor store and my dad went in my heart sank and the expression on my mum's face was of fear. I say under my breath I want to go back home to my uncle's house. My mum gives me a stare and then says *"You want me to get hiding because of you,"* for the life of me I could not understand why any woman would stay with her abuser.

Little did I know that the real trauma was about to begin, we passed a house and there were many puppies running around the yard. I stopped for a moment pulling my mum back while my dad walked a few steps behind us. *"That is a nice dog mummy can I have a dog"*, *"No you can't"* was her response. My mum and I continued walking, not looking back, until we reached their home. I looked back for a moment and could not see my dad. I asked my mum if she knew where he was and she gave me this look which I was very familiar with trouble was coming. My mum ran to the wardrobe looking through all the drawers and I asked what you are looking for. She said run quick and check all the drawers if you can see alcohol anywhere and give it to me.

I did as I was told and I looked under the bed for some reason and what do you know a bottle of Vodka wrapped in newspaper. I quickly gave it to my mum and she decided to throw the alcohol down the kitchen sink. Mummy do not do that! He is going to fight with you and just like that, the door opened and there stood my dad with a dog in his hand and a ribbon around its neck. My mum leaned over the sink with the bottle in her hand, suddenly the look of joy on my face for the dog turned to complete and utter fear when my dad slapped my mother so hard on her face that she fell to the ground.

While I held this puppy in my hand I screamed and within minutes what seemed like a beautiful peaceful day turned into a thunderstorm. The loud bangs and roaring winds drowned my screams for help, Daddy don't hit her, leave her alone I, screamed and he continued to beat her up booting her in her stomach. Picking her up as if she was a bag of potatoes and just tossing her around the floor. I tried to protect her with my little fragile body. I tried to hold onto her, my poor mother why did you put up with this abuse, why do you stay with him, why do you choose him over me. Those were the questions that went through my mind while I held my mother's helpless body.

There on the ground lay my mother. I feared she may be dead as she did not move, blood streaming down her face, her clothes torn and she just laid there. My dad never hit me, but I knew that from that day I had nothing but hatred for him. I felt pain unimaginable no 8-year-old child should ever be put through that, I looked at him and said what did you do daddy. He looked at me and for a second it felt like he was sorry, he picked my mother up, put her on the bed and walked out the door.

I knew exactly where he was going and I knew that this was going to be a long night. I ran to the main house trying to get help for my mum, but no one was home and it was dark and rainy I knew I had to get my mum out of that house before he got back.

I ran back into the house and tried to wake my mum up only to find that my dad out of nowhere had come back. He stole the dog and the owners wanted the dog back, they found out where he lived and they waited at the gate for the dog so they would not press charges if he returned the dog.

He grabbed the dog and he never looked back, I waited with tears streaming down my face not sure if it was for the dog or for the fact that my mum lay there motionless and I was scared.

My first encounter with God was that night I cried out and said God if you are real, I need you now.

I picked my mum's head up and tried to wake her up, she moaned in pain. I could see she was so ashamed that I was witnessing this. My mum always made excuses for my dad and I always saw bruises but never the beating, this was the 1st time. I helped my mum put on a gown and I said to her we must go now before he comes back. I held my mum while she had her arms around my neck. And she struggled to walk. I prayed that my dad would not come back or see us on the road while we got away.

I walked for what seemed to be forever and I felt strong and brave God had given me the strength and I said Jesus please send someone to help us, if you are real, please show me. A car stopped and the gentleman and what I assume was his family were in the car. He looked at me confused and asked if my mum was drunk, I quickly came to her defence and said "No, my dad was drunk and he beat her up and I need to get my mum to my uncle's house. I will give you money when we get there." The gentleman helped my mum into the car and I felt relived, I was not scared to go with them as I hitchhiked with my dad many times when my mum and he separated. For some reason she always took him back, she always chose him over me. We arrived at my uncle's house and I remember running down the driveway screaming for my aunty and she just held me in her arms, I felt safe and for a moment I forgot my mother was still in the car. The kind gentleman who I will never forget helped my mother into the house and explained to my uncle what had transpired. I told them everything was missing, no details, while they drove us home.

The kind gentleman refused money and I will never forget what he said to me. You are a brave girl and you will be a great somebody someday. God has great plans for you. Yes, the Lord did have plans for me you see in that moment in time I was forced to grow up. I was forced to become an adult way before my time, my mum stayed with my uncle for a few days but went back home to her abuser.

I did not want the weekend visits anymore I did not want to see my mum and dad. They broke me as a young girl. I made a promise to myself that if I ever had children, I would always protect them no matter what, I would always choose them. Months turned into years and every year I stayed in a different family member's home, new school, new friends, it was something I was familiar with. No stability I was to fend for myself working on weekends with my auntie's business. Leaving early in the morning and returning late at night. Selling TDK cassettes and T-Shirts using my life as a selling point my tragedy was earning me money. I had a diary and I recorded every detail of my life, I knew I was different from a young age. I knew that there was a story that I would one day need to tell that would be a survival guide for someone else.

I remember the prayer meetings that I would often go for with my aunt. I would see them crying and worshipping God. I would want that feeling that they seemed to be experiencing, I often yawned so tears would fall down my face. Until one day the Holy Spirit touched my heart and I remember it like it was yesterday.

Time passed and I had given my mum and dad another chance and I agreed to visit them. My dad seemed to be doing better. He decided to introduce me to his family and my mum often told me that my dad's family were dangerous like don't mess with them kind of people. She referred to my grandmother as a gangster, when I think about it now, I feel my grandmother was just an over possessive person, her family was everything. I remember the first time I met my dad's mum she was scary and big in stature. She picked me up in her arms and she said you look just like me.

They were not rich, they really struggled but they had so much love. I never experienced poverty until I visited my grandmother's home. I remember when I stayed over for the first time my mum packed toilet paper and toothpaste and food stuff.

When I got there my grandmother asked my mother you never buy cigarettes for her, that was the first time I saw a woman smoke. My granny was fierce and so strong she was such an amazing woman. I saw a shack on the outside of the house and I asked my granny who lives there? She said "your father. Whenever he leaves your mother he comes and stays there." I did not understand why my dad would have to sleep outside, but my dads' siblings stayed in the house. Let's just say I got my answer to my question very quickly my dad had taken me to visit a neighbour and just the sweetest lady she made black tea and jam bread and she said I know that you may not have eaten your granny is very poor but if you hungry come to me I will give you food.

Her son asked my dad to wash his car and he would pay him so that he could buy something to cook for me for supper. My dad left me at my grandmother's house and he went to wash the car, some time had passed and my dad did not come back. My uncle who drives the bus came inside the house and was screaming that my dad got locked up for stealing a radio from the policeman's car. This was the neighbour auntie son who offered my dad money to wash the car. I started to cry and I was scared, I wanted my mother and I cried for her.

These people were strangers at that time, this was my first visit staying over and I understood now what my mum meant. My grandmother was screaming and swearing I was in shock. She was becoming violent and it all made sense as this was my dad's behaviour. I was the eldest grandchild on my dad's side and I remember my cousin running into the house telling my granny that my father was in the back of the police van. All I saw was the entire family run onto the road. My granny just picked this policeman up by the collar and my cousin pulled me to the back of the police van. He opened the door and let my dad out. This was like a movie I was shocked, excited, scared. Everything was happening all at once.

I felt proud of my granny she defended her son this must mean she really loves him even though all her children were from different partners she loved my dad. The reason he slept outside was because he had a drinking problem, a drug problem and he would steal for his habits hence they put him out.

I returned home and my mum and dad lived together again for a little while until they had a fight, he beat her up to the extent that she wanted to kill herself. I must have been at the age of fourteen when my mum had poured paraffin all over herself and she was going to light the match. I stood there looking at my mother with utter disgust you chose this man and now you are so selfish that you are allowing me to witness this you wanting to end your life in front of me. I asked myself the question would I ever be enough, would I ever be enough for my mother or father. I remember screaming at my mother telling her to look at me, look at me, look at what you are doing to me. Do you not love me mummy, please don't light that match, please mummy.

Once again, I asked God if you are real, please stop my mother from killing herself suddenly my mother met my gaze and she put down the matches. Instead of running to her I ran out of the house, my life was never the same after that day. I began to hate my mum for so many things so many things that happened afterwards that made me to behave like a man instead of a woman.

I was no longer the one who needed protection, I was the protector. I remember becoming a bully in school. But in a good way I used to stand up for the children that were bullied, the outcasts, the single parent children, the ones from broken homes, as people loved to say.

My mum chose to reconcile with my dad and I stayed with them for a year and things seemed to be okay. My dad went to church, started a good job, gave up drinking alcohol and would just smoke weed. He seemed loving and caring towards my mum he worked with and provided for the family.

I did not have much, but I had my family together, I finally got a dog my best friend and my maternal grandmother lived with us she would never leave me alone with my parents. I was not the perfect angel I was rebellious and I guess I would often act out in disobedience as I grew older. My mum was very strict. She would often hit me first then ask questions and, in my mind, I often said that she could not stand up to my dad, but she had no issues hitting me for stupid things.

God bless her she tried her best I understand so much now that I am older and have children of my own. I remember an incident when my mum had given me money for school photos and I decided to bunk school with my friends and we used the money to buy snacks and watch movies at her home. I came home as normal as I had come from school only to see my mum was so angry. She asked where the school photos and I are said I lost the money while running on the school grounds.

She went on to say that I am a liar and I want to act like a big woman, she knew I bunked school.

And if that was not enough while I was walking home from my friend's house a boy that was in my class teased me often, he would comment on how poor I was and that my hair was oily and that I used cooking oil on my legs as lotion because we had no money.

In my defence he provoked me, so I took a beer bottle that was lying on the road and I cracked his head, he was not very happy that a girl hit him or that he needed stitches. My mother was furious because this guy's dad decided to come to my house while I was being reprimanded for bunking school because my friend's aunty decided to tell my mother. It seemed like my friend was not a good liar and I was the bad influence which I beg to defer as it was her that suggested we bunk school.

This guy's dad said some pretty nasty things to my mother that I could see hurt her as he called her a single mother and I had an absent father hence I behaved like a hooligan. He went on to say that my mother needs to pay the doctors' bills. He did not allow me to speak and explain why I did what I did, I was provoked and I was embarrassed and ashamed I did not choose my family. My mum just looked at me with disgust and when I tried to tell the uncle something she slapped me across the face.

The uncle left and my dad just got home, my mother noticed that my dad was not himself he looked like he consumed alcohol and I think when he slapped her for hitting me, she lost it. She took the belt and she hit me so badly. To the point that I was bleeding I sat there with no tears, just anger building up thinking in my mind she deserved everything my dad did for her she deserved it. Where was my mother when I was abused sexually and I told her who did it and she never believed me because it was her family? These memories and emotions came flooding back I could no longer feel the pain of her beating me, just memories of what I went through.

My hatred grew stronger to the point of wanting to just end my life. My dad left again and I was once again forced to go and live with another family member as my mother needed to find work again. It was in that moment that I decided that I wanted to end my life, I remember consuming my grandmother high blood pressure medication and her diabetes tablets. I must have taken about 40 pills. I packed all my clothes in a bin packet and I was walking on the road to my mum's sister's house she lived close by. My mother never stopped me from going, she did not know I took and overdosed, she just said to me as I walked out the door you are the biggest mistake of my life you just like your father.

I should have just died back then instead of her thinking about me and not killing herself. I am now forty-two years old and as I pen every word it seems like yesterday the memory is still so strong. I arrived at my auntie's house and I began frothing all I remember is my granny running outside and saying in Tamil what you took, I had a Litre of milk I am told and I began to vomit everything out.

Who knew the fate that would lie ahead for me and my mother in a couple of months' time. My mum and dad remained separated. She came to visit me at her brother's home and I on that day decided that I did not want to go to work the next day. I worked on weekends at a shoe shop and for some reason I made an excuse and said to my mum I will tell them my father died and I can't come to work. She went on to tell me that I must not tell lies and she began to preach to me. I did not pay much attention to her and went into the room. My cousin at that time was heavily pregnant with her third child and the phone rang and she answered the call.

She screamed for my mother and then fainted I ran into the lounge to see my mum screaming and crying that my dad died he was murdered and all I remember doing was running to the kitchen getting water throwing it on my cousin face and then locking myself in the bathroom. Not one tear rolled down my face and here was my mother screaming and crying for a man that caused her so much pain and suffering. I had to get ready to go to my grandmother's house with my mother and there was everyone crying and besides themselves telling me that I am the only remembrance that they have left of my dad.

I had to pick a casket and flowers and, in my mind, hundred things were taking place. I walked to the yard where my dad's body was found. Blood still on the ground, I remember the stories he told me about things he wanted to do with his life. I remember him sleeping outside like a beggar, I remember him beating up my mum and behaving like a monster. I never heard my dad say

I love you to me, I never heard him tell me that I am his baby girl. I know he was damaged and that he himself went through a lot that made him the man he became. My life was never the same again, I had to leave school to take care of my mum and myself and I had to become the provider. My life with my mother only began when my father died. And the rest is a story for another day.

I can tell you this much that there is a happy ending and that had it not been for God I would have ended up on the streets or worse. Jesus was my best friend he allowed me to experience many trials so that I was able to help others. I am now the founder of a non-profit organisation called **Jesus Christ Warriors *(JCW)*** we deal with gender-based violence against woman and children. I am a broker by profession. I am an ordained Pastor and I have received many awards and accolades here on earth. I am a mother of two beautiful children whom I adore and I am busy with my book - my memoir that will detail everything. This is just the beginning. There is so much, more in-between from then till now.

Thank you, Kelly Markey, for giving me this opportunity and allowing me to share my story!

I have finally taken the first step and I am so grateful to you.

A scripture I live by Jeremiah 29:11: For I know the plans I have for you, declares the Lord, plans to prosper you and not harm you, plans to give you hope and a future. I experienced this scripture in my life as a little girl and as I march on in adulthood, He stands true to his promise. His promises echo in my life and in humanity.

Samantha De Kock

She is a broker by profession. Senior pastor of Jesus Christ Warriors full gospel church. Founder of Jesus Christ Warriors non-profit organisation 236-983. Deals with gender-based violence against women and children. Samantha has won the award Influential Woman of the Year x 4. She also was the recipient of Woman of Wonder x 3. She is an outstanding humanitarian and community builder.

She graduated with a Diploma in Business Management. Samantha is an honoured mother of two and a wife to Ex Captain of South African Police Service, KZN Band Andrew B De Kock.

Follow on:
Facebook Samantha De Kock
Tik Tok @servantofGodsamantha
Email: jcwjesuschristwarriors@gmail.com

12

I Met a Man

One Woman's Journey to Discovering Marriage is not Her Greatest Achievement

"As long as we are running away from the essence of our being we will never experience true fulfilment, we will continue to place unrealistic expectations on inherently imperfect human beings, living in the residue of resentment and dashed hopes."
Rachel Biggar

John 4:29 (AMP) Come, see a man who told me all the things that I have done!" Can this be the Christ?

Man 1: My Daddy

Very much like most females who have a superlative relationship with their fathers, I think that there is absolutely no one on earth who will ever come close to him and any man who wants to be a part of my life must for certain meet his standards to a minimal degree; according to me they will most assuredly never touch the bar that he has set. He has many admirable characteristics, but there is one that I find myself relaying whenever I speak about him. A rather questionable characteristic that I have *"I am unable to deal with disappointment at all"* for context when I say *"At All"* my response to disappointment even as an adult can sometimes be likened to a child's reaction. A child who believes plans are never supposed to change; *"You said it and it's supposed to be exactly like you said!"* and any deviation results in the catastrophe of a broken heart, a temper tantrum, sulking and of course a tsunami of tears.

In spite of the numerous disillusionments I have experienced on my life journey, I still feel inclined to believe it shouldn't be happening to me and when it does befall me, I am visibly crushed to such a degree that I am incapable of facing the world for a few days. This reaction to disappointment which is frowned upon by many is on account of the remarkable man that my daddy is. My father is a man of his word and he has never once pledged to do something and not delivered, even if it was as simple as promising to buy me a McDonalds ice-cream. My dad has always had my back and he consistently shows up, but there is one condition He Never Negotiates God and the Standards of The Bible.

Proverbs 22:6 (AMP) Train up a child in the way he should go [teaching him to seek God's wisdom and will for his abilities and talents, even when he is old, he will not depart from it.

I Fell into the Church

Definition of Train: Teach (a person or animal) a particular skill or type of behaviour through practice and instruction over a period.

I was born to individuals who were not always sold-out to God, but the by the time I made my arrival on the planet the process of change had already begun in their lives, resulting in me opening my eyes in a world where my parents were called to be missionary pastors.

Now, you may have heard the colloquial phrase *"I fell into the church"* for many it's used for the purpose of emphasis, however in reference to my life it's the whole truth. I was already attending church while in my mother's womb. Growing up my life consisted largely of church and more church, every day of the week had a church programme that was mandatory. It often felt like I was ear marked to be the one! the one that would continue the preaching legacy my parents had started.

At the inception of Grade Eight I registered for a three-year Theology course that would run simultaneously to my high school studies, every Wednesday evening I attended a three-hour lecture. Mind you it is still something to brag about, I was the youngest ever to register for that degree programme. Keeping me on the straight and narrow seemed to be the reason for my parent's existence and that's no exaggeration!

An Example

When I was eighteen my cousin turned twenty-one. There was a huge party to celebrate her milestone. When the drinking and dancing started, my dad quickly whisked me away and off we went to the fun fair on the Durban beach front.

I was known as *"The Pastor's Child"* and with that title my future seemed paved out without any objections from me; I mean how can you object to: *"As long as your feet are under my table..."*

While most eighteen-year-olds were planning which university they would attend, that was the furthest thought from my mind. I was preparing to travel to Israel. Extra lessons and holiday classes were replaced with rehearsals, trips to workshops in Johannesburg and dreams of becoming the next Darlene Zschech. Yes, I was raised in the era of Darlene Zschech and Hillsong Australia, I knew all the songs, I even had clothing sewn exactly like the ones she wore on the live DVD recordings. The other day while moving house I found an item of clothing from that time in my life.

While reading this you may find yourself becoming a little enraging and wondering: *"Why didn't anyone smack her and bring her back to reality?"* Well, this was reality and I had a God given prophecy to substantiate it.

Definition of Prophecy - a prediction of what will happen in the future.

At the age of fourteen, in June of 1996 at a Youth Camp held in Pietermaritzburg Natal. I received a prophecy and based on this prophecy everything I was doing was catapulting me into the direction of seeing its manifestation.

The Prophecy:
I see you standing on a stage.
Filled with large crowds of people.
Behind you are flags of every nation.

The Wheels Come Off

The Israel adventure came to an end, I returned to the small town of Richards Bay in KwaZulu Natal South Africa and now what? There was no great voice from heaven while I was doing what God had called me to do, I was not discovered, there were no signs of stages or great crowds in my foreseeable future. I was still the same *"church Rachel", "The Pastors Child"* only now without any future. In this moment I felt robbed, I felt like my parents, the church and God had stolen the beauty of a *"Real Life"* from me and I was determined to play catch up.

With the notion that I was bamboozled into moulding my life after a woman on a DVD and living a life void of excitement, I began a new chapter one that would leave me unrecognisable to my parents, my family and anyone who had known me for the last eighteen years. Partying, clubbing, drinking, smoking, drugs and on more nights than I can remember not coming home was the identity I now owned. While rarely being of a completely sober mind and in my elaborate undertakings to recapture what I assumed was purloined from me I got involved with a man eleven years my senior.

My Stop Sign

January 2003, I remember it like it was yesterday because in that moment the confines of a corporate bathroom cubicle began to feel like the prison cell of a twenty-year-old female who was sentenced to life imprisonment without parole. It was Boxing day of December 2002, while my aunts and cousins waited for me to return so we could attend a church dance, I was on my knees with my head in a porcelain bowl throwing up from having yet again taking too many ecstasy pills. This time it felt different, I had never ever experienced an overdose in this manner before. Being the never say die party girl, I brushed it off; the next morning I did my walk of shame through my granny's home and life went back to my definition of normal.

A new year rolled around I was back at work; however, I was just not feeling like myself physically. As I went through a mental list of all the things that could be wrong with me, I felt my stomach drop. Could it be? There was that one thing that as Christian girls we vowed to keep sacred until marriage, I signed the card and even wore the promise ring. Regardless of the vow I had made, my insatiable obsession to reclaim what I deluded myself to believe I was deprived of led me to a moment where I betrayed my values, abandoned my standards, traded myself respect, sacrificed my integrity giving all of me to a man I had only known for a few months. Now at the age of twenty while my mother was planning a Twenty First party, everything had **STOPPED** for me! I was contemplating whether I should abort the child that was now growing inside me.

Man 2

He was totally exhilarated with the news of being a father and couldn't wait to make the announcement to his family. I on the other hand was living a real-life nightmare, trying to predict all the ways it could turn out once I told my parents. I was the ex-head girl of my high school, the Pastors daughter, I had gone to Israel to do what God had called me to do and now I was pregnant with a bastard child. One can only hide a pregnancy for so long and the inevitable had to happen, I told my parents. The disappointment was thick enough to cut, the resolve however was non-negotiable. I was to marry the father of my unborn child saving the family from shame while giving my child the blessing of a complete and loving family. Everyone's expectations met, my life restored by Christ, my mind sober and my vision clear.

For the first time since meeting the father of my child I saw the real man I had agreed to marry. He had never dabbled in drug use; alcohol, going out on a Friday night and not knowing when to come coming home were his favourite companions.

While I had made a complete life transformation this was not a propensity to which he was inclined, culminating in the accelerated degradation of the relationship. By the time my son was eight months old I had already filed for divorce twice, which my dad had managed to talk me out of. I had reached the end of my rope; I was exhausted and was done compromising my worth. I filed for divorce and followed through. Twenty-One, divorced, independent and a single mother to a little boy aged one.

Man 3

Restored to life preceding *"The Wheels Coming Off"* and two years single; I thought it was time to try my hand at a relationship again. Convinced that it would be the perfect one, for the simple reason that this time around I was doing it with God on my side. Living in a small town where everyone knew everybody's business made starting a new relationship challenging. No mother wanted their son associated with *"damaged goods"* like me. Thanks to the advancement of technology and the creation of Mxit.

I met the man who ticked all the boxes according to me with the main one being his walk with Christ and a desire to be entrenched in *"A Church Lifestyle"* A whirlwind cyber connection began. It was set in motion in June, by September he had made the long drive to KwaZulu Natal to meet me in person, October saw us engaged, me leaving my job in Richards Bay relocating without much planning to Johannesburg South Africa and June of the following year we were married.

Our relationship was like a page torn out of a fairy-tale; we had two beautiful children together, we established a thriving business, travelled the world, lived in luxury, but above we were solid in the word of God and Godly principles.

One day after two years of smothered suspicions, being led to believe I was insecure and imagining occurrences; the moment I dreaded arrived. It felt like my oxygen had been turned off, my world as I had known it for ten years was caving in around me. This was not supposed to happen! Not Again! we were in right standing with God! he was completing Bible school and everything seemed perfect on the surface.

I was not about to add another failed marriage to my name, I persuaded myself that reconciliation was possible. We had three different marriage counsellors each with their own set of marriage restitution skills, I convinced him that if we branded ourselves with each other names it would symbolise our eternal commitment to one another and if it were not for the fact that I was medically unable to bare more children I would have suggested the tried and failed method of *"a new baby will definitely bring us closer."* Amidst all the things I was doing to restore what was broken, internally I was shattered and one morning while sitting at my desk I had a stroke.

Waking up to a new reality: certain parts of my memory had been affected, I would need rehabilitation to re-learn how to speak with the possibility of my speech never being fully restored and I would need to be institutionalised for the treatment of clinical depression.

This all still seemed insufficient to open my eyes to the truth, that the curtain call was made on marriage number two and it was time to walk away. Until my psychologist called my then husband in and uttered these words *"Against my better judgement and my code of conduct I need to tell you that if she doesn't leave you while she is alive, she will leave you dead, this relationship will kill her!"*

I returned home a bitter, angry woman I wanted someone to pay for what I had experienced and what was happening to me. I was disappointed with God to my core. I wanted my husband to pay for what he had done to me, I wanted him to feel the same pain I was feeling, I wanted him to experience the excruciating anguish of rejection and I would feel not an ounce of remorse for the path that I would choose moving forward.

Fuelled by bitterness, disappointment, the residue of rejection, a million questions about what I had done wrong to inspire his misguided decisions. Still dealing with panic attacks, bouts of amnesia and paranoia of it happening again **(A leopard never changes its spots ringing in my head.)** One morning only months after being discharged from a Psychiatric hospital, I found a new house to rent, I decided with absolutely no announcement that it was time to leave. Taking just my clothes and a bed I had bought for my eldest son; the chapter of marriage number two had reached its conclusion.

Two marriages, two divorces, three children from two different men, the residue of infidelity, chronic depression, chronic anxiety and epilepsy too. It was acrimonious!

Man 4

I regained consciousness after another one of his episodes to the words *"Die Bitch"* written on the bedroom wall in my blood. That sums up the eight-month nightmare of being married to the man I label as *"The Muslim man."*

After the wrenching heart break of a ten-year relationship that I thought had God's stamp of approval, I wanted absolutely nothing to do with God. In my state of rebellion, I denounced Christ, I destroyed everything that was associated with Christianity, I isolated myself from my family, I became a devote Muslim and I married *"The Muslim Man"* without telling a single representative from my family - they discovered I was married via social media.

My dad refused to accept my decision, he believed that I would once again be restored to my rightful position in The Kingdom of God, he was not prepared to stop fighting for my soul. He sent out a voice note to men and women of the Christian faith asking them to pray because a soldier in Gods army was lost. James 5:16 (KJV) says "The effectual fervent prayer of a righteous man; availeth much."

A Father's Answered Prayer

It was a Sunday morning I was awoken by a voice saying, *"Wake Up, get ready for church!"* I didn't question, I woke up and got dressed. I hadn't the faintest idea where I was going but I drove led by The Holy Spirit. Arriving at a church I had never seen before; I recall the door of the hall had a huge hole in it. While in conversation with God I said: *"Now why would you bring me to a church that can't afford to fix a hole in the door!"* In my continued negotiation with God, I recollect saying *"I would only stay in church if the church felt like my church back home, the people better be friendly!"* I walked into the church I was very late the people at the door were warm and welcoming. I was seated in the balcony Praise and worship was already done; the Pastor was coming up to preach. Great consternation overwhelmed me as the Pastor started speaking in Afrikaans most of his sermon was arrayed with various Afrikaans jokes and phrases between his very rapid English. That was it!!! this could not be the church for me, the only Afrikaans I knew was what I learnt at school, without any consideration for my feelings, God had other plans in mind. This church was to become my place of refuge, my space for restoration, my incubator for the manifestation of Gods plan for my life, the atmosphere in which the lover of my soul would re-introduce Himself to me.

After months of being known as *"The Crying Lady"* by fellow congregants total healing was very apparent, spirituality, emotionally, Mentally and above all Physically. Through constant counselling, mentorship and Spiritual guidance from the shepherd of the house I was now walking in my destiny with visible signs:

- Preaching the Gospel on a Christian Radio station that can be listened to all over the world

- Appearing on Christian television, the proud creator of my very own YouTube Channel, a personal blog, seven years of relationship status: SINGLE and not feeling incomplete or the uncontrollable urge to rush into another relationship.

Despite my harrowing relationship experiences I determined that I would not permit myself to subscribe to the school of thought that *"All Men are Dogs"* I still had faith in love, I still wanted to get married again, grow old with some who loves me and honours my God calling. At this juncture in my life, I was asked on multiple occasions why I had turned down numerous suitors, why I was not going on dates or putting myself out there? My response was the same every time without hesitation: *"scripture says: He who finds a wife, not she who finds a husband. My plan is to continue doing what God's will is for my life and when he who should find me discovers me, he will find me working on me, fulfilling my God given purpose and then journey alongside me towards a common God Goal."* Amos 3:3 (KJV.)

Can two walk together, except they be agreed?

Man 5

While immersed in bettering myself, advancing my career and focused on Gods work, when I least expected it, my now fiancé made his gentle entrance into my life. Bringing with him some much-needed relief from the storms I was facing in that season. In the five years preceding our confluence I had been retrenched from a good paying job, lost my home, my children had to live with their dad on a full-time basis and after almost having to live in my car I was able to rent a one room out house in which you couldn't even swing a cat around.

Funny Story, I never saw him coming! He has a well-manicured grey beard; he is always donned in a tailored suit and was caring. Which easily creates the impression of an old man. During our business interactions, I assumed that he was as old as my father.

The awe-inspiring thing about all of this is amidst the absence of material acquisitions, I was at peace, I was content, *"I was living my best life!"* I was doing all the things I loved - Radio, television, content creation, preaching and my foundation was solid in the understanding of my salvation.

For the first time in a long time, I was not chasing anything or anyone, neither was I trying to prove my worth or validate the call that God has placed on my life.

For a while I deliberated with the concept that many would speculate my acceptance of his pursuit could be awarded to me being weary of struggling and just needing someone to look after me. After realising that society would always have an opinion to which they are entitled I quickly pushed that thought to the back of my mind, choosing to focus on the fact that I had come this far and survived not because of any human man and I would continue to achieve all that is predestined for me with or without a man by my side. With this foundation established on the inside of me I turned my attention to how God was showing His love for me in human form through the man He allowed to cross paths with me while I was doing what I was created for.

Whilst penning this chapter I had an *"ah ha"* moment: *"No matter how far we may assume we have journeyed away from something; it in no way means that it has journey away from us."* I had concluded that after seven years of being single, preceded by my vast experience of failed marriages my tendency to engage in love relationships on fast forward was a thing of the past, but I found rewind being the position in which this relationship was playing out. We met in September by October he asked my dad for my hand in marriage and plans were being made to be wed in March.

Between October and March there were numerous revelations that placed us in a position to assess our compatibility, our belief structures as well as our readiness for re-marriage. Valuing both ourselves, Gods purpose in our lives, our children and our families we agreed to put marriage on the back burner. Choosing to prioritise the process, savouring the meander of discovering each other and above all embracing the actuality that true fulfilment isn't discovered in another imperfect human being or in one more marriage.

This relationship is a blend of match made in heaven, the tendency for repetitive behaviour, the residue of past relationships and much back and forth. It has also placed me in a position to have moments where I can pat myself on the back while reflecting on how I have grown, how I am able to pause, how I am able to realise my value as well as the value of another human being.

I still bare my father's surname, I do not have a wedding ring on my finger, I don't have the bragging rights to say, *"My husband"* and with all my many hang ups, the things that get under his skin and our constant difference of opinion I cannot undoubtedly say that marriage number four is a certainty.

Married three times, divorced three times and the one I am with currently is not my husband!

Man 6

Through every chapter of my husband experiences there has been only one constant, there has been only one who has never left, one who had never disappointed me, one who has never rejected me, one who always stood on the sidelines waiting, yearning for my return and no matter how many times I rejected Him, He never gave up on me. At every crash and burn He was there on standby with a way of escape.

Very much like Gomer in **Hosea 3:1-3** I was prostituting myself to worldly living, different religions and many lovers, but God was always willing to take me back because he had already bought me with His Son's blood on the Cross of Calvary. My life is the epitome of **John 4: 8** *"for you have had five husbands and you aren't even married to the man you're living with now. You certainly spoke the truth!"*

Like the women at the well, I was in search of gratification in the arms of error-prone men. Brain washing myself to accept that marriage would quench the thirst deep within my soul, yet my parchedness was not for libation of natural origin. John 4:14 (AMP) *"But whoever drinks the water that I give him will never be thirsty again. But the water that I give him will become in him a spring of water [satisfying his thirst for God] welling up [flowing, bubbling within him] to eternal life."*

The realisation: That the God space can never be occupied by an earthly husband, that the call of God on ones live can never be traded for fickle human love or earthly pleasures it will never be sufficient.

The woman at the well never experienced true satisfaction or wholeness until she drank of the water that Jesus had to offer. Until I removed the labels I had placed on God, until I stopped blaming Him for the consequences of my decisions and until I accepted His love for me without coercion from my earthly father I would continue to add to my inventory of failed marriages.

For generations society has led us to believe that our greatest accomplishment is marriage, I dare to propose to you: *"That if one does not find true fulfilment first in the giver of eternal life, marriage may just become your death sentence sucking the life out of you thereby drawing you away from accomplishing your God given purpose on the planet."* (Zoë which means life that is real and genuine, a life active and vigorous, devoted to God, Life that comes directly from God. Abundantly or Perissos means over and above, more than is necessary, superadded.) Lemuel Baker, Ph. D.

The ultimate reason for the creation of the human race was to commune with God and our purpose for living is to fulfil the instruction given in Mark 16:15. As long as we are running away from the essence of our being we will never experience true fulfilment, we will continue to place unrealistic expectations on inherently imperfect human beings, living in the residue of resentment and dashed hopes. Perhaps like me you've been searching; you've been hurt and greatly disappointed. Come meet a man who told me all about myself, a man who offered me living water so that I will never thirst again.

While my story to becoming Mrs is still being written, my story of being fulfilled has already been concluded Jeremiah 1:5 (AMP)*"Before I formed you in the womb I knew you [and approved of you as My chosen instrument] and before you were born I consecrated you [to Myself as My own]; I have appointed you as a prophet to the nations."*

Reference
- Google's English dictionary provided by Oxford Languages
- Amplified Bible and King James Bible

Echoes of Humanity

Rachel Biggar

With unflinching honesty and vulnerability, Rachel Erica Biggar, affectionately known as Lady Ray, makes a triumphant debut as a published author. Her writing is infused with tenacity and courage, drawn from her personal experiences. Hailing from South Africa, Lady Ray is a trailblazer in the broadcasting industry and a pioneering female entrepreneur. Through her gift of preaching and teaching, she offers a beacon of hope to many, inspiring others with her remarkable journey of growth, resilience and transformation. Her life is a testament to the human spirit's capacity for overcoming adversity and emerging stronger, making her a powerful voice for hope and inspiration.

Facebook　　　　　　　　Instagram　　　　　　　　LinkedIn

Contact
You Tube: //youtube.com/c/LetsGetRealWithLadyRay
Blog: //rachel4984.wixsite.com/website
Tik Tok: //vm.tiktok.com/ZMNMPvvhe/

13

Faith in the Fire

"Adversity often signifies that we are on the right path, affirming that our efforts are making a profound impact. In the face of challenges, it becomes apparent that we are fulfilling our purpose and advancing God's kingdom, serving as beacons of light and agents of change."
Fideliz Cruz

The Lord Is Close to the Broken Hearted

Let me take you back to 2022. A year that changed everything for me. You know, I always thought things like this only happened to other people, or in the movies, but never to me. Life was good—no, scratch that, it was great and almost perfect. I was living the dream, surrounded by a loving family, incredible friends and a fulfilling career as a Christian life and business coach. Everything was looking up and thriving.

Looking back now, I realise it was like a sudden storm on a perfectly sunny day. One moment everything was fine and the next, I was blindsided by something that shook me to my core. I will not dive into the specific details of what exactly happened; that is not what is important. What matters is the effect it had on me and how it led me down a path I never thought I would walk - depression.

This incident, entirely beyond my control, left me feeling worthless and inadequate. Each day, I grappled with deep sadness, sometimes mingled with anger and self-pity. There was this overwhelming sense of shame—how could someone like me, a Christian life coach, find herself in such a dark place? Shouldn't I have had all the answers to manage life's challenges? What would others think of me now? Could I even muster the confidence to show up as I once did, knowing I felt so low and unworthy?

I also faced disappointment and frustration. Here I was, with so many exciting opportunities on the horizon, forced to set them aside because I could not focus, my emotions were in turmoil and even my health was suffering. I had to decline incredible offers and put a hold on numerous plans—all because of this one incident that seemed to have knocked the wind out of my sails.

Now, let me tell you, feeling negative about a situation is not exactly my default mode. As a Christian life coach, positivity and empowerment are practically woven into my DNA. I thrive on lifting others guiding them through life's challenges and being that beacon of encouragement in a sometimes-dim world. But this time, it felt like blow after blow and this one incident was the final straw that sent me tumbling to the ground. Depression is a sneaky little beast. It slithers in when you least expect it, whispering lies of worthlessness and hopelessness until you cannot distinguish up from down anymore.

I will never forget the day when I hit rock bottom. It felt like a miracle just to muster the energy to reach out to one of my dearest friends and utter those three words: *"I give up."* I was on the brink of admitting defeat, ready to abandon everything because I could not see a single reason to keep going.

Let me tell you about my friend - she is remarkable. Refusing to let me surrender without a fight, she insisted I see a doctor that very day because she could sense that something was not right. Thank God for friends like her, because when you are caught in the throes of it all, sometimes you do not even realise that you are sinking into depression.

It is often easy for those who have not experienced depression to offer well-intentioned but misguided advice like "Just snap out of it" or "Just pray about it." But having walked this path, I can tell you that depression is not something you can shake off. It is rooted in a chemical imbalance in the brain, affecting not just your emotions but your overall well-being too.

Deep down, I knew I needed help, but it was like a battle raging inside my head. On one side, the voices of despair urged me to succumb to the darkness, to let it swallow me whole. But on the other side, there was a still, small voice—a voice of hope and faith—that urged me to fight back, to seek help and to believe that things could get better. And so, with trembling hands and a heavy heart, I decided to fight. I sought medical help, started medication and reached out to my closest family and friends for support. And let me tell you, that decision marked the first step on the long road toward healing.

"If your heart is broken, you will find God right there"; if you are kicked in the gut, He will help you catch your breath. Disciples so often get into trouble; still, God is there every time. *"He is your bodyguard, shielding every bone; not even a finger gets broken."* - Psalm 34:18 (MSG)

I clung to the promises of God - I was so desperate to get out of this depression that I prayed and said to God that I was holding on by a thread, please do not let me go.

Healing is a Journey But Be Open for a Miracle

Healing is indeed a journey - one that does not happen overnight. It is like rediscovering how to walk, learning to trust again after enduring immense pain. I found myself surrounded by walls I had built to shield myself from further hurt, closing off my heart to dreams and people alike, thinking it was the best way to protect myself. I wrestled with anger towards God, unable to hide it from Him. I poured out my frustrations and disappointments in prayer, questioning why such pain had happened to me despite my efforts to stay faithful and serve Him in every aspect of my life and business.

Amid my daily walks and prayers, as I continued to voice my grievances to God, He spoke to me in a still, small voice. *"Fideliz,"* He said, *"don't forget who the real enemy is. We are on the same side."* His words pierced through my heart and tears streamed down my face. I realised then that I had lost sight of the true enemy, allowing him to infiltrate my thoughts and convince me that God was against me. At that moment, I repented and asked for forgiveness, renouncing the spirit of depression. As if a heavy cloud had lifted, I felt a weightlessness wash over me, the sky was now clear again.

"The thief cometh not, but for to steal and to kill and to destroy: I come that they might have life and that they might have it more abundantly." John 10:10 (KJV.) *"If my people, which are called by my name, shall humble themselves and pray and seek my face and turn from their wicked ways; then will I hear from heaven and will forgive their sin and will heal their land."* 2 chronicles 7:14 (KJV)

At that moment I resolved that enough was enough - I refused to be intimidated by the enemy and my circumstances any longer. While what had transpired was beyond my control, I recognised that I still held power over my actions. I could choose to respond to my situation instead of merely reacting to it.

Undoubtedly, the road ahead would not be easy. Reopening my heart and rebuilding trust would require effort. Yet, deep in my heart, I held onto the belief that God would not forsake me. He had never failed me before, even amidst past hurts and trials. Why would He abandon me now? I regretted having entertained the enemy's lies. I asked God for forgiveness and I asked

Him for His wisdom and strength to navigate what I was going through, surrendering all my pain and disappointments to Him.

At first, I thought that overcoming depression would be a lengthy process, especially while relying on medication. However, as soon as I decided to trust God, I sensed a shift. The need for medication gradually went away and things began to change. Each day, I felt a bit lighter, a bit stronger, as if the weight of it all was slowly lifting from my shoulders, one burden at a time. What I once thought would require years of recovery miraculously occurred in just over a year. I never imagined I would be back to being myself again - I can only say this was a miracle.

Divine healing transcends the limitations of human understanding and God's power knows no bounds. Trust in His ability to turn your pain into purpose and your sorrow into joy.

Heavenly Reminders and Lessons Learned

When going through challenging dark times, remember this:

1. God is not against you. He is for you.

I wrestled with the thought that I had somehow invited the hardship upon myself. I searched for answers, questioning my actions, but God gently reminded me of a verse in Matthew 5:45 that speaks of rain falling on both the just and the unjust, emphasising the inherent unpredictability of life's trials. Sometimes, adversity strikes indiscriminately, neither orchestrated by the enemy nor ordained by the Lord but part of life's ebb and flow. Nevertheless, the Word of God reminds us to remain vigilant against the schemes of the enemy, urging us to put on the full Armour of God as outlined in Ephesians 6:10-18 to prepare ourselves for such times. As 1 Peter 5:8 warns, we are called to be sober and vigilant, recognising that the adversary prowls like a roaring lion, seeking whom he may devour.

It is also important to understand that adversity can also arise because the enemy perceives a threat to what God is accomplishing through us. If the enemy were not threatened by our impact, he would not be targeting us. Our very existence poses a challenge to his dark work.

When I faced this incident, I sensed that I was in a season of significant impact within the Kingdom of God. Being a Christian Life and Business Coach is not just a career path or business. For me, it is a divine calling to serve. At that time, I was blessed to serve hundreds of women, empowering them to break free from poverty through God-aligned businesses that nurtured their families, enriched their communities and glorified God. Witnessing lives transformed and souls saved, even amidst our coaching sessions, underscored the enemy's relentless pursuit to stop God's work in my life.

Adversity often signifies that we are on the right path, affirming that our efforts are making a profound impact. In the face of challenges, it becomes apparent that we are fulfilling our purpose and advancing God's kingdom, serving as beacons of light and agents of change.

"For our struggle is not against flesh and blood, but against the rulers, against the authorities, against the powers of this dark world and the spiritual forces of evil in the heavenly realms." - Ephesians 6:12 (NIV)

2. You Will Come Out Gold

Gold is refined by fire, as Peter talks about in the Bible (1 Peter 1:7.) The trials we face are not meant to break us down; they are meant to build us up. They are God's way of purifying us, getting rid of all the things that no longer serve us and making us stronger.

I know you would agree with me when I say that tough times can be life's greatest teachers. Experiences give us wisdom; they build in us resilience and deeper faith. So, even though it might feel like you are walking through the fire, keep your head up. Because on the other side, you are coming out shining proof of God's faithfulness and His power to turn things around for good.

When you put your trust in God, victory is a sure thing. Life might throw you into some fiery trials, but when you remain steadfast and trust God, you are not going to get scorched. Remember Shadrach, Meshach and Abednego? They walked out of that blazing furnace without a scratch, thanks to God's protection around them.

It used to be all about *"what happened to me,"* but now it is more about *"what happened for me."* Even though the enemy meant it for harm, God turned it around for good and He's still working through it! Through the lessons I have learned, I have become an even better Christian life coach. Now, I can connect with my clients on a deeper level, especially if they are going through depression. I can understand what they are going through and guide them on their journey toward healing.

"And we know that all things work together for good to them that love God, to them who are the called according to his purpose." Romans 8:28 (KJV)

3. God Will Give You Double For Your Trouble

Because of what I had gone through, it made me realise it was time to make changes. I was not just trying to get back to who I used to be - I was ready to grow and challenge myself to be more of the woman that God has called me to be. And why shouldn't I? After everything I had been through, it only made sense that I would come out stronger than before.

Now, as I reflect on where I am today, I am amazed by how far I have come. I have not only reclaimed what I had to set aside during my battle with depression but surpassed it in ways I never imagined possible. For instance, in my business, I am now earning triple what I did when I was struggling. And being a part of this book? It is a testament to God's faithfulness and His ability to turn my pain into purpose.

God's healing touch has not only restored me but has reignited my childlike faith in both life and business, creating space for His abundant blessings to flow. Physically, I have never felt better—I have made lifestyle changes that have led to a healthier, happier me. And our family? We have experienced blessings upon blessings. We now reside in a beautiful home, four times the size of our old apartment and my husband has seen incredible professional growth, being promoted three times in just two years. And to top it off, our daughter is thriving academically, excelling in her studies. But the most fulfilling aspect of our journey is seeing the spiritual growth within our family. We attend church together every Sunday, united in our service to the Lord.

Reflecting on all of this brings tears to my eyes. Despite the darkness that once threatened to consume me, God has brought me through to a place of abundance, joy and purpose. He has given me double for my trouble, turning my trials into triumphs and my sorrows into songs of praise.

Let me remind you that God's promise to give you double for your trouble is not just a dream - it is a solid truth rooted in His character! Throughout the Bible, we see countless examples of God turning situations around for His people, blessing them amid their trials. Take Job for instance. He faced unimaginable losses - his wealth, his health and even his loved ones. Yet, in the end, God restored to him double what he had lost. Job 42:10 says, *"After Job had prayed for his friends, the Lord restored his fortunes and gave him twice as much as he had before."*

Then there's Joseph. He endured betrayal by his brothers, slavery and imprisonment, yet God had a plan for him. Joseph rose to a position of great authority in Egypt, second only to Pharaoh. In Genesis 50:20, Joseph acknowledges God's hand in his trials, saying, *"You intended to harm me, but God intended it for good to accomplish what is now being done, the saving of many lives."*

Even the Israelites experienced this principle firsthand. After years of bondage in Egypt, they were freed by God's mighty hand. Not only did He deliver them from slavery, but He also led them to a land flowing with milk and honey - land of abundance and blessing.

These examples remind us that God is not limited by our circumstances. What may seem like insurmountable trouble to us is an opportunity for God to display His power and faithfulness. So, when you find yourself facing challenges, hold onto the promise that God is working behind the scenes to bring about blessings beyond what you can imagine. He will give you double for your trouble

"In all these things, we are more than conquerors through him who loved us." Romans 8:37 (NIV)

As I close this chapter, I want to leave you with a truth that has resonated within my soul: victory over depression is not about our strength or willpower—it is about the redeeming feature of Jesus Christ. In despair, it can be easy to feel isolated and alone, but I assure you, you are not alone in your struggles. Many of us have walked through the shadows of depression, but through faith in Jesus, we have found the path to victory. Hang in there even if it is by a thread just like I did! God will not let you go.

Let me leave you with a promise of God - a proclamation of God's unshakable love and compassion for each and every one of us: *"He heals the brokenhearted and binds up their wounds"* Psalm 147:3. No matter how deep the pain, God can heal every broken heart and cover every pain. He is our peace amid the storm, our joy amid sorrow and our hope amid despair. So, as you journey forward, may you cling to the truth that God's love for you knows no bounds. May you find comfort in His presence, strength in His promises and hope in His unfailing grace. May you be encouraged by the reminder that no matter what you face, you do not face it alone. God is with you, guiding you through the darkness and into the light of His love.

With Love and Prayers,
Coach Fideliz
Award Winning Christian Life and Business Coach

Fideliz Cruz

Fideliz Cruz is a skilled strategic and empowering leader. A Certified Life Coach, with a passion for cultivating real connections within communities. She has over 14 years of experience in managing her business and community network focused on educating & coaching women across all levels of their personal and professional development.

Fideliz is the founder of Kingdom Women Entrepreneurs Academy where she helps Christian women launch, build and scale their God-given business. KWE community has been created to add value and serve Christian women to grow their business and, in their faith, walk, hosting their annual KWE Business Conference and KWE Academy Awards Gala which honours Christian businesses making an impact in their sphere of influence.

Fideliz' focus on delivering high-quality functional educational program outcomes is reflected in a portfolio of written work including the Amazon best-selling book, *"Your Divine Assignment"* and industry awards including an International Coach of the year award (Beautiful You Coaching Academy 2018-2019 Awards) and People's Choice, Business Coach of the Year Award (Ausmumpreneur People's Choice Awards.) She is also a finalist for 2023 Local Business Awards for Outstanding Professional Services.

Fideliz has helped numerous businesses with their business launch strategy cultivating their brand & growing their brand online visibility over the years. Fideliz Cruz is a visionary, who loves seeing women rise in leadership in any aspect of their lives, using their gifts and talents to build a business & life that honours God, as they walk in their God-given calling.

Fideliz runs a few bespoke workshops in Sydney one of which is the Vision Casting Workshop that aims to help women create their Personal Life Vision and kick-start their journey towards their dreams. Fideliz has been a guest contributor for both Sandigan Radio, Tagumpay Radio (Filipino Community

Radio) & SBS. Her work has been featured in magazines such as EHM, YMAG & Inspired COACH, Philtimes, to name a few.

Contact
fidelizcruz.com
kingdomwomenentrepreneurs.com

14

You are the Key

"Life is a series of locks and keys. The association to "keys" is about identifying locks or problems. When a lock is revealed, the way to unlock it, is to be the key or the solution."
Janice Morris

Introduction

Life is a series of negotiations and choices. But sometimes you don't have a choice, until you do. While waiting for the moment, up-skill yourself. Study. Learn. Be ready for when opportunity presents itself. Life is not about luck. My chapter is about looking into oneself to craft a key to open a lock and move forward. Being true to your core values and standing up for others when they can't stand up for themselves. This is my journey to writing a book for educators to help children in childcare. The obstacles I've faced, my drive to keep going and why putting on my big girl pants to be brave enough to see it through has been challenging.

Purpose - Identifying the Lock

I have been in the service of customers most of my life. Always going above and beyond to over deliver clients expectations. Liaising with clients, hearing their needs, respecting their choices, guiding them through the process and celebrating the result. But a shift in me happened when the clients were only 0-6 years old and cannot speak up for themselves. The children are obviously too young to read. They are vulnerable in the hands of others. The children are obviously too young to read. The only way to help them that I could see, was to help the educators. The lock is, too many Educators are stressed and tired from the workload. Endless amounts of reports to write that must link to other reports or learning frameworks to validate their purpose. The emotional roll-a-coaster of the fun times, the sad times supporting emotional children, juggling colleagues and parents demands while staying within the safety of the laws and the regulations and always upholding a quality standard. It is a lot of pressure.

I wasn't choosing to become an author of a book. I was compiling ten years of acquired learning and experience to put in the hands of Educators. To give educators a mentor to have in their pocket to ease their learning journey and reduce the weight of anxiety that falls upon so many. The aim is to empower educators with knowledge of their role quickly making them more confident and happier in every day they are with the children in their care. The result is to have happy, confident and well-balanced children nationwide. Every part of myself, my experience and acquired knowledge has gone into crafting this book. The book's title is, *"An Educator's Handbook."* An outline of an Educators role to empower them to enhance children's lives. But I did not start strong.

Low Self-Esteem - Personal Lock

Feeling heavy from diminishing self-esteem from closing our businesses of eight years, I was somewhat looking forward to turning up to work in someone else's business. Going back to being an employee was both simple and hard. The simple part was not bearing the heavy load of running a business. Having to think about ordering stock, orchestrating the instalment of another garden, keeping up with trends, keeping the books, juggling the kids needs and everything else that goes along with running a business, I was exhausted.

The real estate agency our business paid rent to invited me to come to work for them. I was excited. When I did the real estate course, my experience and approach to customer service led the others in the class. Unfortunately, the real estate office I went into had young self-empowered, ego fronting sales agents that made me wince at the thought of applying their tacky ways to get a contract. I was there for six months and got a contract within my first three months, my way. Staying true to myself and applying my high-quality customer service skills was hard with the pressure on me to conform. It left me crying. I was weak from the sadness of closing our business and needed nurturing. I couldn't stay but I couldn't leave because I had a financial noose around my neck. Every day I stayed, I cried. I had to leave. But how to resign without looking like an emotional fool?

I drove into the back carpark, unloaded all their *"for sale"* signs, walked in normally and sat at my desk. I sent my boss an email, stacked their mobile phone with the office keys and my business cards neatly and walked out. I didn't say a word. By the time the owner read the email I was gone and he had no way of getting in contact with me. Relief !

Entering childcare was a strangle choice from anything I had done before. In some ways it felt like a step down from running my own business, adding to my diminishing self-esteem. When you are of 50 years with a lot of experience and accomplishments behind you, it would be nice to keep stepping up in your career. But I was damaged.

When announcing myself as an Educator I felt I was being pitied by others, even strangers for working so hard for little income in return. I noticed not being invited to events due to their expectation that we couldn't afford it. Even during Covid every working sector was recognised for their gallant bravery to keep the country moving, except the childcare Educators. On all the lists of appreciation, Educators were not mentioned. Forgotten.

Transition - Finding the Key

Going from being dependable to being dependent I started as an educator in childcare with a lot of apprehension but with a sense of fun and light heartedness. I felt my role was to keep the children safe and happy while guiding and teaching them. The centre had no uniform, so I wore bright coloured tops, sparkly earrings and a big smile. It felt good to relax and be among good hearted people. The staff were friendly and the children were inquisitive of me.

Despite feeling pitied by society, in the role I was laughing daily, feeling bright, using my creativeness and being appreciated. I didn't have to sell anything to anyone anymore. I didn't have to work weekends. There were many personal rewarding benefits being in the industry of caring for and educating children. My spirits began to lift.

For the first few weeks I'd sit and colour in looking up to see a new moving landscape of busy children around me. I would wonder to myself, *"What am I doing here?"* This is so different from anything I have done before. My clients are now 0-6 years old. I really knew nothing about the role and relied heavily on my teammates. Studying helped me understand my role but the process of learning lagged behind the daily demands of the role.

The childcare sector needed a road map. After ten years as an Educator and new staff were starting still with little guidance. No solution in sight. I thought, *"I can't just leave the industry knowing as much as I do, not without doing something to help make a difference."* I realised; no-one knew what to do.

The children can't fix the problems, yet they are the ones that cope, silently. I saw experienced staff still feel helpless and stressed. New staff anxiously learning their intense role and for many, the role proving far larger and more difficult than they expected. The expectations that it will just come naturally is unfair. Unions were fighting for pay and conditions and another body was fighting for family fee relief. No-one was considering how the pressure on the educators to divide time between what must be done to provide care while doing what needs to be done to meet the administration requirements was affecting the children.

Childcare in Australia cares and educates for 45% of children aged under 5 years. *"In the March quarter 2022, 48% of 0-5-year-olds (883,510 children)."*

Reference
https://www.aihw.gov.au/reports/australias-welfare/childcare-and-early-childhoodeducation#How%20many%20children%20are%20in%20child%20care?

The centre I worked in prioritised the children's needs. It had its own troubles and educators left. But they surprisingly returned upset from witnessing things that were outside of the Laws, Regulations and National Quality Standards. It became clearer that the Sector of Childcare needed help quickly including instilling a culture of professionalism.

Key - Epiphany

I handed in 4 weeks' notice to resign after ten years of having a ball of a time as an Educator. A ball of fun, laughter, spontaneity, friendships, trust, creativity and joy. All tightly wound up with mental pressure, emotional stress and tension. Standing in the playground, typically surrounded by a throng of wooden and rainbow-coloured toys, children's laugher in the air, the hum of the afternoon plane flying overhead with hundreds of people returning from another holiday and feeling numb knowing that the next educator was walking into the same vacuum of mental and emotional stress. As I stood there feeling bewildered, quietly shaking my head squinting my eyes in silent disgust wondering *how* the wheel of hope for change keeps turning, rolling down the same path of endless angst with no new path in sight.

My Epiphany was, *"I need to advocate for the children."* This is when I decided to craft a key to help the children in Childcare. If I can hand the next educator all my knowledge and experience in one lump of info to give them confidence in their role from the week they start, it will flow into their care for the children. This is what I must do. I researched and asked amongst my colleagues and on social media chat forums if they had read a book when they started that helped them in their role. Nothing. There was nothing out there. My drive to see the book finished, published and in the hands of educators was powered by a cry for change in the sector of education for the youngest of our people. A problem that was locked by the unknowing of how to create a key was rife within the sector.

Disapproval - Lock From Doubt

I was keen to get writing knowing how much such a resource was needed and I started to talk about my idea of writing a book. I surprised a lot of people. I had support and encouragement from those in the industry. But I was also confronted with *"Why will someone read your book? You don't hold a degree. You don't have the qualifications to validate why someone would buy your book."* These comments were not about the content but about me. And then there was this, *"You won't make much money, don't bother."*

Feeling hurt and low, I tussled with this disapproval for a while. I looked to other professional people to ask if I needed qualifications to qualify being an author? The feedback was very supportive, *"just get to it and don't worry about what others are saying."* I re-set and thought, *"people are just going to have to look beyond my qualification and see all the value the book will bring."* I couldn't give up on the kids.

Powering Forward - Action is the Key

During the 4 weeks leading up to my final day, I picked up a pen and started writing. Making note after note as memories and lived experiences came to mind. My years of learning began flowing out of me. I couldn't write fast enough. Colleagues were giving me ideas and telling me their experiences. My notes turned into pages then chapters. I added charts and quick tips, references and resources that I and my colleagues used in our work, bringing it all together to pile into one amazing handbook. The handbook is loaded with more than ten years of knowledge and experiences as if to be putting a mentor in every educators pocket. The book will fill the gap between starting in the role and finishing the studies. It's not to replace their valuable studies for their qualification but to deliver information in an easy to read and digest form that can accompany their studies. The underlying intention of the book is for it to be a game changer. It will unveil the complex role of the educator and expose the volumes of knowledge an educator must learn and apply in their daily practice. It will give respect to educators; just as other professionals have respect. This is exciting!

I was becoming a writer on a journey to be an author. The thought of becoming an author was quite overwhelming so I avoided thinking about having a new title as I tapped my laptop keys. The book is not and never has been about me. It has always been to make a difference in the lives of children through their Educators. The children's wellbeing was my purpose and my drive.

The Map Is Not the Territory - Locks and Blocks

Even though I had been an Educator for ten years I still had to learn a lot more to write the book. Thinking about the whole of the book was overwhelming. I had to stop myself from thinking about the big picture and let the chapters form one by one. A saying would come to me, *"If you want to build a house, you lay one brick at a time."*

With so much to learn, I began to realise an entire library could be filled only with what an educator needs to know and still there would be more to learn. How is one person expected to know so much? There are doctors specialising in one area of health. Teachers specialising in one or two subjects. Educators must know many facets of child psychology, various approaches of teaching to meet learning types, be excellent communicators, report writers, know and work to the laws and regulations, maintain quality standards, know a lot of First Aid all while staying alert to maintain a high level of supervision, be spontaneous when needed, be fun and know a tremendous amount of children interest topics.

And then there is working with others. I realised I will have to write about how to manage thoughts when working with people who don't see things as you do. People who have had, for example, a strict upbringing and try to apply those strict tactics in childcare where is just not acceptable. But how is a new employee going to know that being strict is not acceptable? People working closely together can experience bullying, exclusion, unmotivated people of low work ethic so, how do you stay in line with the standards without outing yourself? Part two of the book is about personal care and wellbeing to cultivate a professional industry culture. Lessons from Life Coaching to be accountable for your actions and have courage to stay true to oneself will be included. There were days when I was tapping away on my laptop when self-doubt would fill me. Can I really do this? Procrastination over capability to write was a huge steeler of time. Friends would ask, *"How is it going?"* I would always say "fine" when I should have been saying "slow". As I wrote chapters, I'd send them off to colleagues to check. I needed the reassurance. I had to get it right. My journey of writing teased out the best parts of me. I learnt from my mum how to keep hoping for the best. What I also learnt is hoping is not action. Being actively researching and typing is the only way to complete the book.

Leaning into Me - Key Finding Self Belief

Everyone has a tool kit. A tool kit is everything learnt through life's lessons of successes and failures. A bounty of accomplishments compliments you have been paid, achievements and anything that picks you up to refill the void of disbelief in oneself. In these moments, I would reach into my tool kit. I would reflect on successful days at the nursery, the award I won for Innovation, the many designs that made customers happy, the parents who thanked me for caring for their children, my husband and our children. I know I can muster up the drive and courage and take charge. I've done it before. It's in my tool kit. A huge element of my truth is when I became a mum. Becoming a mum was an instant rise to CEO - Chief Executive Officer of one precious little human wellbeing. It is definitely a WOW moment of realising your need to be dependable, responsible, present and accountable. It is a form of having your own business, because like a business, the buck stops with you.

Elizabeth was born by caesarean section. The very next morning when I woke, she wasn't next to me. My maternal instincts were, where is she, is she safe? Has she been taken? When I was in my teens, Indigenous Australians were still having their children taken from them and single women thought to be an unsuitable parent, would be persuaded to give up their baby. I wanted to go to her, they said she was in the nursery and I must stay in bed and rest. I got out of bed and walked the hospital hall only hours after having a caesarean like a 90-year-old with osteoporosis, all bent over holding my stapled belly, looking into the nursery. They brought my daughter to me.

Our son, Jethro arrived 3 years later. A born musician. A creator and producer of music and lyrics. He has his own business and leading an adventurous life. Watching his disciplines he embodies to follow his path blows my mind and helps me to follow mine. Raising two children was a precious time. While they were young, I painted and sold my painted craft at markets. I was my own boss in business. My husband, like my dad, held a steady 40 hour a week job. His stable income granted us approval to purchase our first home.

Remembering all that I have been capable of gave me courage to keep writing, even when I felt it was way over my head. My mother taught me how to run a business while my father demonstrated discipline and conformity by working a 40-hour week. My dad was still a boy when he had to leave school at fourteen to support his family. He had a passion for learning and every fortnight borrowed a stack of books from the local library. He empowered himself to learn, which I believe is why I also look for solutions to any problem that blocks my way.

Travelling by myself was also interesting to finding me. Before I met my husband, I flew to Nepal all by myself. I had a stopover in Thailand where we had to wait inside the airport. I stood near to a pole with a small backpack on my front and a larger backpack on my back. I had to stand near a pole because I was so laden with backpacks if someone bumped into me, I'd fall to the ground and wouldn't be able to get back up. I was travelling not long after the release of Nicole Kidman's movie *"Bangkok Hilton"*. My dad was so scared for me and when I returned, as soon as he saw me, I could see the relief fall out of him that I was home safe.

Trekking through the Annapurna Range with a sherpa and a group of strangers, I knew the only person responsible for me, really, was me. It was amazing standing on the top of a mountain that took all day to climb up only to see the Himalayan ranges towering above me. The contrast of people from 1st world Australia to 3rd world Nepal was grounding. Definite evidence of true happiness lying within oneself. Delighting in simple pleasures without the distraction of possessions or conformity. I met a lovely happy and bright 14-year-old Nepalese girl in Pokhera who needed a uniform to go to school. When I got back to Thamel where I was staying, I took a trip to Katmandu city and purchased some school uniform fabric plus a few other school items and posted them out to her. I still have her heartwarming letter she wrote me back in 1990.

I returned to Australia with an abundance of gratitude for my parents choosing Australia to raise their family in. Yet with resentment to my fancy furnished room with a view of the Sydney Harbour Bridge from a charming terrace window located in Neutral Bay. With only a short walk down to North Sydney swimming pool where I'd stroll to on Sunday mornings and swim 20 laps, then sit in a glass booth on the edge of the harbour with white sailed yachts skimming by while I read my book. Back to this indulgent life after seeing many an aged person sleeping on piles of rubbish to feel the warmth of the decaying matter beneath them was perspective altering. Appreciation, gratitude crossed with resentment and bewilderment of how two lands on one earth can be so different.

Conclusion - Keys to Locks

I feel it is a privilege to care and educate other people's children. There are so many precious moments parents sadly miss due to their need to work. Yet with so many children of various cultures, parenting styles, learning differences, levels of ability, individual and emotional needs, an educator is like a detective identifying locks to craft individual keys to form connections for teaching and forming relationships. Learning through experience takes time. To hand someone the knowledge in the beginning of their career, it can only make a difference to their understanding of how their interaction plays a part in the shaping of every child. This early know how will extend to children having brighter days in care. Stepping up to become the key for change will be worth every hurdle. Keep your eyes on the direction you have set your goals to go in. Follow your path and every step you take towards it, the goals get a little closer. You too can be a key for change.

Janice Morris

I'm the daughter of Scottish parents loved and raised with three siblings in the Western suburbs of Sydney Australia. I left the local public school at year 10. I am inquisitive and love to learn, yet don't hold a passion for reading. I'm a creative soul. A hand's on learner. My husband and I married after we had been together for twenty-seven years. We have two lovely children and three precious grandchildren. Life is great on the Central Coast of NSW where we live today. I'm a daughter, sister, wife, mother, mother-in-law and now a grandmother becoming an author.

I don't balk at studying. I've achieved a certificate or diploma in every decade of my life from age 17. Secretarial studies, Horticulture, Real Estate, Early Childhood Education and Care, Life Coaching, CBT, NLP and Mindfulness and TAE, Trainer & Assessor and many short courses along the way. I have been an employee, a business owner and employer and a sub-contractor. My work history is a series of taking on new challenges. Using my acquired knowledge and building on my skills and experience through a variety of vocations. In my opinion and experience it's never too late for new beginnings. We all have transferrable skills.

I'm a happy person and I delight in seeing others happy too. Designing for clients to give them their dream kitchen, garden, or swimming pool and bringing them to fruition is a wonderful gift to have. A highlight was winning an award from the Plant Hire Association for *"Innovation"* of a commercial scape planting. I had architects chasing me asking where they could purchase pots I had personally designed and had manufactured for clients.

Secretarial Studies gave me the valuable skills of how to organise the paperwork side of running a business. With my husband we owned and operated a retail Garden nursery, art gallery, cafe and landscape design business for eight years. I have also co-owned a school readiness and tutoring service for children 3 to 12 year old. Going back to being an employee to become an educator in Childcare took some adjusting to get used to answering to others. Before I left childcare I studied my TAE and now I am a Trainer and Assessor for adult learning. I am writing a book and have always had an online side hustle. I did not pursue Life Coaching as a career but I do apply the lessons every day and strategies for personal care are included in by book for educators.

I am so incredibly grateful to be included in this Anthology and sincerely hope the authors here inspire you to live your life well, make good choices and pay it forward where you can.

15

Breaking Through Old Paradigms: Thriving Amid Chaos

*"I glimpsed the light on the other side - a faint glimmer of possibility. What awaited me there? Perhaps not riches or fame, but something more profound: **freedom**. Freedom from self-imposed limitations, from the shackles of doubt and self-defeating paradigms."*

Dr Stephanie Fletcher - Lartey

The story I am about to share is about my journey through a challenging period of my life and how I was able to overcome negative paradigms and break through the chaos, to a new purposeful life. In this story, I share how chaos became fodder for an unquenchable fire to see change and to manifest purpose and I hope it inspires you to make a bold step towards your dreams.

Introduction to 'The Chaos'

In January 2023, I enrolled my then 5-year-old son into Year One at our local primary school. He was very excited to begin his new life at a new school. However, after the first day I got my first phone call from the school's principal. My son was very unsettled and according to the reports he appeared to be having a panic attack. This was the beginning of a journey that would lead to my son being diagnosed with attention deficit hyperactivity disorder (ADHD.)

We had recently returned from overseas where I worked for a year as an advisor to the government of a small country in the Pacific, providing technical advice and support for their COVID-19 response. We had arrived at the start of the year and during the middle of a State of Emergency, with a heavy curfew in progress, which lasted several months. This meant that only essential services were available, including health, with schools being suspended until further notice. As a result, my young child remained isolated at home with his nanny for nearly five months before he was able to attend school with other children, when classes resumed in June of that year.

The international school he attended was within walking distance of my office. However, it was not long before I began to receive complaints about how unsettled he was and that he was not only distracted but was also a source of distraction for other children during their lessons. It was reported that he had made several attempts to leave the school to 'find his mommy who was working nearby'. At the end of the year, my husband and I made the difficult decision that I would bring my son back home to Australia, so we could get professional help to determine what was happening to him.

So here we were, surrounded by our family and friends, but the issues we had faced overseas had now escalated to another level, exacerbated by this new school environment. I was getting a phone call from school about my son nearly every other day.

In addition to my son's health challenges, I was also dealing with my own personal issues. Firstly, I had started to doubt myself about the decision to return home. I am usually a person who makes sure I am at peace with decisions before I make a move. However, this move was made under much stress and a sense of uncertainty remained about whether I had made the right decision to prematurely give up on my job, working as a COVID-19 advisor, to return home. This role was indeed a level of self-actualisation in my journey as an Epidemiologist: an important professional achievement. To underscore the level of achievement and the recognition I received for my work, the organisation had even offered to extend my employment with the opportunity to work remotely and then move to my dream location overseas, to help me manage the situation. However, I had reluctantly turned down the offer.

Amid all the chaos caused by COVID-19, my son's health not the least of the issues I faced, I made the difficult decision to walk away from the career opportunity. I had felt at the time that this was a decision that I needed to make for my own sanity and for my son's sake. I did not want to wake up one morning in the future to realise that I had neglected these critical needs to chase after a dream. The dream was not able to give me life and align with my values. In the moment, I believed the reasons were compelling and I felt that I had made the right decision at the time. However, several weeks later as the pressure mounted, I began to question myself about whether I had made the right decision.

The decision to walk away from such a promising opportunity can be incredibly difficult. In my case, I had to weigh several factors, including personal well-being, family considerations and long-term fulfilment. While the opportunity to work as an Epidemiologist for the world's premier international health organisation was a dream come true, there were other important things I needed to consider:

1. As a professional woman, (and many of you can relate to this), my personal struggles were affecting my ability to embrace this professional opportunity. It's essential to recognise when our mental or emotional health needs attention and in my case, both my child and I needed the space to focus on our wellbeing.

2. Balancing career aspirations with family needs can be a delicate act. In my situation, I had to consider how my decision would affect those closest to me. As an Epidemiologist, I understand the importance of family support. I knew that if I trusted God to handle this challenge He would grant me the grace to redeem the time I was investing in my child's wellbeing.

3. In my coaching training, there is a concept of testing the dream. Is my dream worthy of me? One of the five principles of testing the dream is to determine whether it fits within my values. While the position I was offered held immense promise, I had to reflect on whether it aligned with my long-term goals and values. Sometimes, what seems like an enviable position may not lead to lasting satisfaction. I was uncomfortable at the thought of sacrificing my child's wellbeing for career progress. I concluded that the answer to my question was no: choosing the new job did not align with my values.

4. Our intuition often guides us, even when logic points in a different direction. If something didn't feel right, I had to trust that inner sense and make the tough call.

I had chosen to prioritize my well-being and personal life over professional advancement. It was not an easy decision, all things been equal. However, I still believe that because of the honest motive of my heart, this difficult period and the difficult decisions I had to make allowed me to find a different path - one that felt more authentic and fulfilling.

Notwithstanding, this was by no means the end of my internal struggles. After a while, I realised that I was feeling some resentment towards some of my family members and some in my social circles. Now, before you judge me, hear me out. The people around me seemed oblivious to the chaos going on in my life. They all seemed to be so happy that I had returned home; oblivious to the great price I had paid and the ensuing turmoil in my emotions. No one seemed to care about how torn I was between giving up on the endless possibilities associated with my 'dream' job nor understood how I had put on my big girl pants, a big bright smile and covered the pain behind the uplifting lyrics of new songs. The fact that, from how I saw it, they were all very happy that I had walked away from something so important to me, so they could have me at their 'beck and call', was a source of resentment. I was even angry with myself for not speaking out or not standing up and finding another way out that would let me keep the things I so much desired. The thing is this: money was not an issue for me on the International Consultant salary I was earning. But I lacked the emotional support I needed to navigate the challenges from that distance and without the emotional support required, the most practical solution for me and the child was to return to Australia.

Upon my return to Australia, I could only find a job that was paying me less than 50% of what I earned in my consultancy role (based on the managerial salaries at that time.) The financial realities in Australia including a monthly rise in interest rate, would begin to add to the stress and the strain on my finances as well.

My son was diagnosed with attention deficit hyperactivity disorder (ADHD.) One evening as I drove into the car park of my church before Friday prayers, my son's school principal called (again), to make another complaint. My 5-year-old son had been suspended from school earlier that day, charged with 'violent behaviour' because he had hit another child who had provoked him. My cup which was already full, ran over.

As a worship leader, I can use my voice and my song to heal myself. It is something I have practised for many years. My songs have taken me through many battles, many struggles, many failures. But that night, my mind found it difficult to focus on singing. Even while I was on the stage with the microphone in my hand, all I could see was just my sweet child being turned into a monster by a system. My head felt like it was attached to another body and my vision was blurred. I barely made it through the service and I was thankful that I was only doing backing vocals that night. At the end of the service, I ran to my pastor and asked him to pray for me and I felt the cloud lifted.

The stress of it all was taking a toll on my health and it was evident in my waistline. I had gained weight and my blood sugar and cholesterol levels were out of control. One day as I was doing my regular check-up, my General Practitioner said to me; *"If you don't do something about this now then you will regret it. The weight is taking its toll on your health."* I began to think of all the attempts I had made to lose weight. The weight loss meal plans, the injections, the medication and nothing had really worked, or the prices were prohibitive to maintain the regimen. Tried walking, aches and pains, gym –

and personal trainer – lost 1kg in 3 months! Nothing I tried had worked. But that was about to change.

Throw Me a Lifeline and Draw a Line in the Sand

Finding the right help for my son to manage his challenges was not easy. Behavioural specialist, occupational therapist and psychologist all had extensive wait lists. It was a bit shocking to realise how busy these professionals were. The amount of money to consult with one of these professionals was also another shock. It was difficult to find someone to assess my child and I was being pressured by the school to get an assessment and a diagnosis - time will not permit me to describe what I believe were the motives behind this and the resulting stress it caused me. It was during one of my own visits to see my General Practitioner that she was once again, a source of inspiration and information. She told me about a special program at one of the universities that specialised in childhood behavioural studies. I had submitted an expression of interest several months earlier, but they too had a long waiting list for about a year or more before we could get an assessment. As I began to drown in the search for alternative programs, I unexpectedly received a call from the university's program indicating that they had found a space and would prioritise my son for an assessment. I am pausing here for a praise break because this was literally a miracle!

I am happy and grateful that we passed the eligibility assessment and thus began our journey through family therapy, obtaining professional, unbiased support to help us understand, navigate and manage my son's behavioural challenges. I am also grateful that this service did not cost us more than the time we invested in weekly meetings with the specialist and the energy and time we needed for implementing the recommendations over the therapy period. As my husband and I participated in the program, we learned a lot about our child's needs and how our own behaviours needed to be adjusted to support his recovery. By the end of the program, the positive impact on the child and us as parents was amazing.

The experience with my son in family therapy had also helped me realised that I needed to prioritise self-care and it had motivated me to take better care of myself. It was one cold winter morning later that year, I drew the proverbial line in the sand and decided it was time to also focus on my health. I decided that I was going to take back control of my own life. Too many things were dictating how I was feeling, how much money I had or spent, how my health was progressing and I seemed to be like a puppet on the strings of some unknown opponent's stage. But I had had enough. I was determined to take back control of my own life.

Serendipitously, I woke up one day and was browsing through my Facebook page. I came across a promotional video that was discussing weight loss and the struggles middle-aged woman face with batting the bulge. My interest was piqued as the video presented an angle I had not heard before. Basically, they addressed issues about how the body stores and burns fat and busted some myths about weight loss. Before you knew it, I had bought their weight loss program and a personal nutrition coach to go with it. I hadn't planned to do this. But there was a deep longing in my soul from a place of a greater deserving – I deserved to feel comfortable in my own body and I was the only one who had to power to act. I knew that I deserved more than this miserable life I was living and I felt like a good place to begin was to work on my physical health. So, with a physical activity solution tailored for me, I was willing to try losing weight one more time. Soon, I bought a yoga mat and started my three months weight loss program via an app on my phone. All the self-doubt and the arguing about how I would find time to do this seemed to vanish. The nutrition coached tailored a meal plan for me based on my dietary needs and I was off to a shaky start.

Tackling Old Paradigms Head On

The hardest part was to make the first step. Although I wanted to lose weight, my mind was telling me all the reasons why I could not make it work. I convinced myself that many of the foods on the meal plan were either out of season or not available. Then, I was wondering when I would find time to exercise, considering my already busy life. What if I had to cook two different dinners, where would I find time for that? And what if I did not lose any weight just like all the other times before? What if I had just been scammed into giving away my hard earn US$150 that was well needed elsewhere? I have never considered myself a negative person. I am a glass half-full kind of person – or so I thought. No one could have prepared me for the number of negative thoughts that clouded my mind, as I was finding even more new 'what ifs?' than I had ever imagined. Fear bounded me and I was panicking. Franklin D. Roosevelt's famous quote *"There's nothing to fear but fear itself"* emphasizes that fear can be more harmful than the actual threat.

The Rewards of Perseverance

"Courage is the most important of all the virtues because without courage, you can't practice any other virtue." - Maya Angelou.

Amid all the fears, my courage burst forth. I am not sure where I got the strength from, but a determination arose deep inside to take control of my life and I was going to start by giving my weight loss journey a chance. After the first day of approximately 25 minutes of rigorous exercise in the comfort of my living room, I was convinced that I could do this. Yes, I was sore afterwards and could barely climb the stairs at work, but I felt something: a flicker of a flame, rising inside of me. Afterall, I had much skin in the game. There was no turning back now. If there was no time, I would make it. After a few days of trying, I realised that the 'after-work' work-out would not work well for my evenings, so I decided that I would just have to wake up 30 minutes earlier and do my work-out before my day began. This turned out to be a perfect solution.

As the days went by, I worked out my meal planning and bought two scales: one for my kitchen and one for my bathroom. There was something about having a scale in my house. I am not sure whether it was the scientist or the researcher in me, but the scales ignited a new fire. I was going to put them to use in support of my cause. In the first week, I lost 3 kilograms (6.6 pounds.) My scales became like cheer leaders in those initial days. I had been afraid to test my weight, but I was on a new mission and I needed to see the smallest gains which became a source of motivation.

I began to feel better about my body image. I was full of energy and I was motivated. On my rest days, I would go for a brisk walk or do a bit of high intensity run-walk training. I realised that when I did this, I lost more weight in that week. Before you know it, three months had passed, along with 15 kilograms from my body weight and several dress sizes: just like that! And this is a good place for another praise break!

From the Darkness into the Light

My perseverance through my weight loss journey continued. I was determined to maintain the gains as best as I could and had included an evening walk or run on my rest days. There is a small park close to my home that has a concreted walkway that connects two sides of our community. The walkway which is about 350 metres long is lined heavily on one side with eucalyptus (gum) trees and was less dense on the other side, but there were no streetlights.

Late one evening, I wanted to increase my step count to achieve my daily goal. I could take the long way around along the street, but I realised that, if I could take a shortcut through the park, it would add the extra distance I needed without me needing to go all the way around. But I was afraid of the dark and the moon was hidden behind the clouds that night. As I stood there contemplating, the alley stretched before me - a narrow corridor swallowed by shadows. The darkness swallowed up the walkway, whispering secrets of fear and uncertainty. My heart raced, each beat echoing my hesitation. But something inside me shifted that night - a resolve, a spark of defiance. I picked up a sturdy stick from the fallen branches at the park.

I stepped forward, my footsteps muffled against the concrete pavement. The air thickened, suffocating, yet I pressed on. The alleyway seemed to narrow, its shadows closing in like the jaws of a beast. The trees looked daunting and I could feel my heart in my chest beating like an erratic drummer. Fear gnawed at my insides, urging me to turn back - to retreat to the safety of well-lit streets. But I had grown tired of safety. Tired of tiptoeing around my own existence, tiptoeing around my dreams. So, I ran. Against the odds, against the darkness, against the very fabric of my fears. I ran like a gazelle being chased by a lion. My now fit and agile body flew down the pathway like a teenage athlete, going for gold.

As my sneakers pounded the ground, I felt it - the barrier of fear splintering. It wasn't a grand explosion, no lightning bolts or triumphant fanfare. Instead, it crumbled quietly, like old parchment yielding to time. The fear that had held me captive - fear of failure, rejection, giving up on my dreams, the unknown - dissolved into dust.

I glimpsed the light on the other side - a faint glimmer of possibility. What awaited me there? Perhaps not riches or fame, but something more profound: **freedom**. Freedom from self-imposed limitations, from the shackles of doubt and self-defeating paradigms.

Lessons in the Darkness

My journey through the dark alleyway was to increase my step count towards my daily goal. The breakthrough I had experienced that night was unexpected and I there are three vital lessons we could take away from the experience:

Fear Is a Mirage: Fear thrives in the shadows, but it's often an illusion. We imagine monsters lurking, but when we face them head-on, they lose their power. Fear is a storyteller, weaving tales of catastrophe. Yet, when we step into the narrative, we realize it's just ink on paper.

Courage Is a Muscle: Like any muscle, courage strengthens with use. That night, my legs carried me forward and my heart followed suit. Each step was a bicep curl for my spirit. I flexed my courage until it no longer trembled.

Life Lies Beyond Comfort: Safety is a cocoon, warm and familiar. But transformation happens in discomfort. To break through, we must embrace the chill of uncertainty, the sting of vulnerability.

From Lack to Abundance

And so, I emerged on the other side - breathless, a gasping, triumphant soul. The alley spat me out into the very familiar streetlight lit roadway. The world hadn't changed, but I had. I could feel Spirit inside of me saying, you have broken through to a new level tonight: nothing can stop you now. I carried the night's revelation like a lantern, illuminating my path.

The experienced through the darkness had helped me to realise that my life had shifted. I faced fears headlong - pitching ideas, asking for help, pursuing passions and gave birth to various projects that are now strategically helping to unveil a greater purpose and fuelling my passion as I pursue a more deserving dream. The abundance I sought wasn't mere material wealth; it was the richness of experience, the currency of growth.

As you read my story, may I encourage you to ask yourself what awaits you beyond your own dark alley? What fears will you sprint through, leaving them in your wake? Remember, the barrier is fragile and courage is your chisel. Chip away and discover the abundance that lies just beyond. And don't worry if they show up tomorrow. Just keep being intentional in your thinking: focus on the dream you want to achieve and keep chiselling away at that fear with positive life-giving thoughts.

A Mindset Shift

The greatest lesson I have learned from these experiences is that God cannot use you publicly until you've gotten victory privately. My ability to help my son through a very challenging period, maintain my mental health and lose and maintaining a healthier weight, were all connected to a strategic shift in my mindset and becoming more intentional.

Ephesians 4:17-18, *"You must no longer walk as the Gentiles do, in the futility of their minds. They are darkened in their understanding, alienated from the life of God because of the ignorance that is in them, due to their hardness of heart."* Basically, negative mindset and thoughts separate us from the life we are created to live! In Romans 12:2 Apostle Paul admonished Christians not to be conformed to this world, but to be converted or transformed by the renewing of their minds. Paul must have had a revelation of the potential that exists within our minds. A mindset shift plays a crucial role in recognising fears and self-sabotage and becoming more intentional in the way we think. This helps in creating a *"vibrational match"* or an attraction that aligns us with the divine plans and attracts the kind of energy that we produce. I see this as an alignment with divine purpose. In my difficult experiences, I began to change the way I saw the challenges and personal health issues. This then led to a feeling that I was able to not only find solutions and overcome but also that everything around me began to align with my purpose and calling. This was all part of a greater purpose to assist me to live out the purpose that God has lovingly designed for me.

As I took some time to reflect on the experiences I had over the year, I also realised several other things had happened as a ripple effect of the actions I had taken. My actions had not only impacted my life, but there was a domino effect happening around me.

Very soon after I started my weight loss journey, my family had begun to pay attention. My husband and children were enjoying the healthy meals I prepared. I no longer needed to worry about preparing separate meals because everyone in my household enjoyed the creative healthy meals. People outside were also taking notice: at church, at work, in the supermarket, on the street, just about everywhere I went. People were making positive comments. I mean, I had my own little lunch time fan club at work.

One of my teenage daughters who was usually buried behind a computer screen in her bedroom, had started to take long walks. No one had asked her to. She just got up and started walking (just like mum!.) People who had not spoken to me were suddenly stopping for a chat and asking for weight loss recommendations. Everywhere I went I was making meaningful and impactful connections. Whatever was happening inside of me was attracting people to me in a good way. I was being invited to speak or perform in unusual places; purposeful connections were producing good results. The mindset shift and associated weight loss journey had triggered and opened a portal to attract new positive vibrations in my life and these were producing amazing results.

The Ripple Effect

Indeed, my determination to purposefully decide and act and the lessons from that moonlit alley rippled through my life, touching every area of my life. Let me share how:

Career: At work, most people would possibly describe me as a fearless leader and an exemplary worker. Work was my outlet and I was good at hiding behind my professional success. However, I noticed a more pronounced desire to fulfil another part of my calling. There was an overwhelming feeling now more than ever that I wanted to coach and mentor people. I had been strategizing about this for a while. But I now felt like I clearly understood the process that was required to get from the place of discontent and longing to a place of dreaming and fulfilment. The fear of failure would sometimes appear, but it no longer had the power to paralyse me into inaction.

Wealth Beyond Money: I began to realise that many of my previous failed business attempts were a result of my negative vibrations linked to an inability to see past my fears. I also realised that my focus needed to shift from just money and to look instead at wealth. My creativity flowed like a river. Investment opportunities and wealth creation began to materialise like I had never seen before. My career benefited from all the new energy which spilled over and infused greater innovation into my work.

Impact Over Comfort: My story was not glamorous, but it taught me that legacy isn't built in comfort zones but etched in moments of courage. After months of hesitation about starting a podcast, I finally went online and recorded my first episode. My podcast schedule is booked up for up to two months ahead with authors and other people who desire to speak on my platform. I hosted regular workshops and webinars to mentor others, shared my story and encouraged them to break barriers. My son experienced and witnessed this transformation. His struggles became our shared canvas. He saw fear crumble, purpose emerge and abundance bloom. His resilience fuelled mine and I was better able to support him on his own recovery journey.

In the end, the revelation at the end of the dark alleyway was not a solitary event; it was both a reaction and a catalyst. It set off a chain reaction - a symphony of choices, relationships and growth, revealed in the blooming and abundant fruit I produced. Whatever your own chaos or struggle may look like, I encourage you to consider that external success is applause; personal growth is the sunrise within. Setbacks aren't roadblocks; they're invitations - to resilience, authenticity and wisdom. So, dear reader, when life presents you with lemons, squeeze them into your cup and make lemonade. The flavour is exquisite.

Conclusion

As I explored and reflected on my experiences with my son's ADHD diagnosis and my own struggles with my weight, here are a few things that I learned in the process that I'd like to share:

Belief and Perception: Your mindset shapes your beliefs and perceptions. When you shift from a negative or limiting mindset to a positive and expansive one, you alter your energetic frequency. Imagine your mind as a radio dial: negative thoughts tune you to a lower frequency, while positive thoughts elevate you.

Law of Attraction: The law of attraction suggests that like attracts like. When you focus on positive thoughts, you emit a corresponding energy. If you believe good things are coming your way, your sense of expectation will drive you into actions, then you will begin to identify opportunities and synchronicities more readily.

Emotional State: Your emotions produce powerful energy vibrations. When you feel joy, gratitude, or love, your vibration rises. The opposite is also true so be careful to nurture the positive emotions. Be intentional about shifting your emotions. An easy and effective way to do this is to practice gratitude, forgiveness, cultivate positive feelings and dream about success.

Thought Patterns: Self-doubt, fear, or a scarcity mindset are negative thought patterns which naturally lower your emotional vibration. It is important to understand that everyone can have these negative feelings but you must identify and stop these negative patterns from taking hold. Quickly replace them with empowering thoughts. Helpful ways to rewire your thinking includes gratitude, affirmations, mindfulness and meditation.

Alignment with Goals: A mindset shift aligns your thoughts, emotions and actions with your goals. Once these are in alignment, you become a magnet for opportunities and positive experiences.

A Sense of Worthiness and Deserving: The way you see yourself affects your vibration. It is important to build a dream that is deserving of you. If you see the dream that gives you life, aligns with your values and is worth going after, then as you begin to see this, by faith, you begin to attract the dream and the abundance associated with it. Be intentional about cultivating self-love and recognize your God-given value and worth.

Faith and Trust: Faith involves trust, belief and reliance on God.it is not just an intellectual assent; it's an active and intentional response to God's promises and truth. Genuine faith requires a renewed mind. Romans 12:2: *"Do not be conformed to this world, but be transformed by the renewal of your mind, that by testing you may discern what is the will of God, what is good and acceptable and perfect."* A renewed mind involves the process of shape our thinking and worldview through transformation of our thought patterns, perspectives and understanding that is anchored on God's truth. The goal is to go beyond an outward behaviour change but to a deep transformation of our inner being. This inadvertently results in a paradoxical detachment from what is seen to that which is unseen, because of the trust that things are unfolding perfectly – even if there is no immediate evidence that something has changed.

Please be mindful that this is not about some magical vibrations or a new age philosophy. This is about taking hold or control of your thoughts and renewing the way you think. It is about aligning your thoughts, emotions and actions toward positive internal frequency, which emits a corresponding positive vibration that results in external positive shifts in your experiences. In her video titled *"The Extravagant Mind - The Power of Intention"*, Dr. Cindy Trimm describes it like this: *"You are actually one of God's greatest expressions of His brilliance and His intelligence and not only that; He gives you as a gift to humanity and so you are here during this time during this generation and with these inflection points because of what you are individually carrying for pushing humanity forward and bringing solutions to world problems."*

Dr Stephanie Fletcher-Lartey

Dr Stephanie Mahalia Fletcher-Lartey, epitomises the personhood of an overcomer. Born in a rural district in the northern part of Jamaica, she has excelled academically and professionally and is a successful entrepreneur. Dr Fletcher-Lartey, has distinguished herself as a servant leader throughout her more than 27 years of professional life. She has been privileged to serve in numerous professional roles internationally, where she is known throughout the field of public health for her excellent spirit and can-do attitude.

Stephanie is a devout Christian, who operates as a prophetic intercessor and is an ordained minister serving as Executive Pastor at the Destiny Impact Worship Centre, in Australia. She is multi-talented and uses here gifts as an astute entrepreneur, Life Coach and spiritual advisor, providing leadership and strategic advice to professionals, ministry leaders and businesses. She is also a singer and songwriter who has recorded multiple songs available on all music streaming platforms. Stephanie has authored the book, The Professional Believer's Guide: Principles to Help Christian Believers Thrive in The Marketplace.

Stephanie started her career as a Public Health Inspector in 1997 and quickly rose through the ranks. She completed a Master of Public Health with Distinction from the University of the West Indies in 2007 and was later appointed as Regional Environmental Health Officer by the Northeast Regional Health Authority. She soon afterwards won a scholarship from the University of Technology Sydney, Australia where she successfully completed the Doctor of Philosophy Degree (Epidemiology) in 2013.

She is an Epidemiologist specialising in emergency preparedness and response and has worked on the frontlines coordinating the COVID-19 Response in the Caribbean, Australia and more recently, in the Solomon

Islands on behalf of the World Health Organization. She works as the Senior Research and Evaluation Manager at Western Sydney Local Health District.

Stephanie's professional excellence has been recognised through various local and international awards including the Jamaican Governor General's Youth in Excellence Award in 2007 and Sanofi Pasteur Research Excellence Award in 2020. She has published more than fifty articles and book chapters in peer-reviewed journals.

16

Yesterday's Scars are Tomorrows Seeds

"Persecution produces persistence and perseverance."
Conelia Harry

Introduction

After falling pregnant at age 16 I was convinced my life was over. My dreams, goals and future aspirations all crushed by one poor choice: engaging in unprotected sex. While sexual education was taught at school and I was quite aware of where 'babies came from', all the knowledge and information did stop me from entering a relationship and falling for the love trap. This one act I found would dramatically alter my future and have a ripple effect on the rest of my life. The embarrassment and shame unleashed on my family, coupled with the hurt and disappointment I served my parents through this one act of disobedience, left me with many sleepless nights and permanent regret.

As a child myself, I was forced to grow up in a flash with the pressure to raise another human weighing heavy while juggling motherhood and continuing with my high school career. With the stigma of being a teenage parent hanging over my head and the immense pressure to now over-achieve to hopefully eradicate the shame and embarrassment, I was unknowingly pushed into beast mode to excel.

This was one of my early recollections of taking a bad situation and working hard to turn things around. And this experience saw me draw strength from a painful period in my life, take the hurtful comments, words, doom and gloom spoken over my life and channel it into fuel to push me to my next level of completing my high schooling. My goal was geared towards tertiary studies and securing a better future for my son and hopefully the family I would one day create.

It was during this season of my life that I learned to value the importance of having a good support system. There were other young mothers at the time who did not have support and fell by the wayside with no one to motivate, encourage and give them a helping hand.

Thankfully, my mother did not believe in giving up and hailing from a hard upbringing made her the strongest woman I knew. She lost her dad at a young age, having to leave school in her early teens, she became the breadwinner of her home - a family of six. She valued education and ensured all her younger siblings completed their matriculation in order to pursue trade and professional careers. Education was always at the top of her agenda, so I did not have an option but to return to school, juggling motherhood and finding my new identity as a teenager with a mountain of adult responsibilities.

During the critical times of exams the extended family and friends all chipping in to lend a hand to help and lighten the load. In this instance our families were the 'village' that helped raise my son.

While 2002 felt like the end, it was in fact just the beginning of a new life filled with unconventional choices that needed to be made to forge ahead with more purpose and passion to prove the naysayers wrong and dispel the myths that said teenage moms' lives would never amount to much.

There were of course those who spoke much negativity over my life and this, unbeknownst to me then, propelled and pushed me to go after everything with such zeal to excel, become an overachiever and by default become a people-pleaser as I attempted to redirect the mistakes of my past to a brighter future. My only option was to succeed and I ended my matric year with a merit exemption, distinction and overall good results ensuring I was able to gain tertiary acceptance.

During that time one act of kindness by my high school principal would change the course and destiny of my life forever. I was blessed to have a support system at school as well as teachers and a simple symbol of acknowledgment - a Christmas card received via post from my high school principal wishing me well on completion of my matric and all the best for my future, would bolster me into the next chapter of my life with a renewed energy and zeal to chase after my dream. I felt special that someone other than my parents had seen some greatness within me, believed in my potential and was in my corner, rooting for my success. She had over 1000 children under her watch every year, but she took time to send me a handwritten letter. Her thoughtful gesture made me feel seen, that my life had value and that I could go on and be the best version of myself despite my mistakes. Miss King never gave up hope, continued to motivate me through high school and always had a kind and gentle word of encouragement despite the choices I had made.

A few years later, I would be employed at our local community newspaper, Zululand Observer, as a reporter and continue my relationship with my high school principal, reporting on highlights at the school, their projects and programs and assisting wherever possible.

While one poor choice could have resulted in devasting outcomes, through the intervention of a support system and network of people who had my best interests at heart, a catastrophe in my life was averted. I was redirected on a new path, eliminating fear, anxiety, discouragement, embarrassment and shame and turning a mess into a message by becoming an advocate for change and promoting awareness on social ills and teenage pregnancies. Just because I am a statistic of teenage pregnancy does not mean I cannot advocate for it.

I am encouraged by the life of Sarah Jakes Roberts' (35) - a renowned author, speaker, pastor and media personality who was also a teenage mom, falling pregnant at 13. The daughter of American pastor and author, Bishop T.D. Jakes went on to change the course of her destiny. She did not allow the mistakes of her past to dictate her future and is now globally recognized for her empowering messages and leadership role in ministry. I am a firm believer in the scripture from the Bible (Jeremiah 29.11.) *"For I know the plans I have for you,"* declares the LORD, *"plans to prosper you and not to harm you, plans to give you hope and a future."* We all have the choice of changing the direction of our lives, even after our mistakes and poor choices – we can rise from the ashes and for a new path for our lives.

Determination Despite the Odds

Landing my first full-time job shortly after turning 21 years old in 2006. I had no journalism knowledge, work experience, or any idea of what being a news reporter entailed. I passed my interview process sealing the deal with my strengths as a people's person and a high level of curiosity. I was an avid entrepreneur having lived with parents who were always trying new ventures and businesses to supplement their incomes. Working was nothing new for me as I maintained part time jobs throughout high school. In high school, I sold hamburgers and crunchie biscuits and helped my parents in their tuck shop in addition to selling vegetables, clothing, or any other goods on weekends at the local taxi rank.

I can without a doubt say that the journalism job chose me because I had no plans for a career in the media industry, but I found it effortless to unearth stories, make contacts and write across all beats from human interest, accidents, crime, education, entertainment, social and hard news. The job keeps you on an emotional rollercoaster and not every day is the same. So, it can go from heartwarming and life-changing stories of persistence and celebrations to heartbreak, trauma, destruction and the tyrant of natural and man-made disasters.

In my earlier years, I dreaded accident scenes - the trauma, tragedy and uncertainty with life and death hanging in the balance often made me anxious, nervous and well up with emotions. Attending well over 100 collision scenes, two remain etched in my mind owing to the gruesome and tragic nature of the incidents. The first scene involving a taxi and bakkie (small van) returning from an Easter weekend religious retreat and homeward bound on a Sunday afternoon left my mind on overdrive for weeks. Vehicles mangled and wreckage scattered across the four-lane highway was coupled with victims being ejected from the vehicles and many lifeless bodies still trapped inside the taxi. Combing the scene from a distance, thoughts of the victims, their lives and their families flash through your mind as you try to make sense of their final moments before their untimely deaths. While you do not know the victims, as a mother my heart would ache for the family members who would soon come to learn of their relative's untimely departure. No matter how many accident scenes I attend, one never gets used to staring death in the face. Open-ended questions hang in the balance as you try to connect the dots leading up to the collision, what transpired, the contributing factors and what could have been done to avert such a situation.

You are then forced to take stock of your own life, your family and what you would do if this were a family member. A thousand scenarios unfold in my mind before I sit down to put the story and narrative together for publication. Attending these scenes opened my mind to a whole new world of being more cautious, alert and always striving to be on guard.

From the onset my job brought an immense, heightened sense of awareness of the real workings of the world and society, how valuable life was and how every decision and choice had a ripple effect, whether good or bad. Not only did it open me up to new experiences and information, but it also gave me a greater sense of appreciation. It could have been my turning point and where my increased faith was bolstered.

A few years later in 2013 I would encounter another incident, but this one would cut straight to the bone as it involved a family that were from our local church. Our family had returned from church and we were preparing lunch together when I received a call about an accident nearby. I left to the scene with my younger sister giving me company. The wrecked vehicle looked like one of our church family's car's. Minutes later our worst nightmare was confirmed when family members arrived on scene and identified their relatives - a family of four as well as their neighbours two children who had perished in the collision with a water tanker truck. The emotional intensity, trauma, grief and sheer unbelief being unpacked during that time was unbearable as loved ones and congregation members learnt of the devasting news.

That night my mind just kept racing and was on overdrive. Reporting for work the next day was so exhausting as we walked into a deadline day with a major story to unravel. A counselling and debriefing session was organised for that afternoon to unpack my experience. I did not feel the need for it, as I felt okay and had never had trauma debriefing or counselling after any of the accident scenes before. This would be a turning point in my life and I would realise the importance and vital role that counselling and therapy play in one's emotional state and well-being.

I always had the belief that therapy was for other communities because growing up in a mixed race community, receiving help was always seen as a sign of weakness and it was taboo to speak about your feelings without being seen as a weakling. While reluctant, my sister and another work colleague joined in for the group counselling session. After unpacking the experience, my emotions and sharing the ordeal with the counsellor, I felt an immense release, my energy was restored and the weight had certainly been lifted from my shoulders. I had a newfound respect for counselling, what it entailed, its importance in society, benefits and how community members could benefit from this service that had a lasting impact on my life. This was my first personal encounter with Lifeline Zululand who provided free counselling. And it was the start of my association with the organisation. While I had reported on their programs before, now I had a personal encounter with their service. I went on to share their services with anyone who emotional support or could benefit from their programs.

In 2016, I had the opportunity to enrol in the Lifeline Personal Growth Course and Basic Counselling Course and I found it added immense value to my personal development. It afforded me an opportunity to volunteer and serve at the organisation, be part of their GBV and rape awareness programs and work the counselling crisis line. I began advocating for people to turn to counselling in times of crisis or to deal with life challenges.

Over the past 18 years, my job as a journalist has opened my life to so many new experiences, learning opportunities, growth and avenues to break through my cultural barriers and give me a window into different communities, lifestyles and status levels and to be open to different perspectives.

As I covered a multitude of different stories, I always found a way to extend a helping hand by sharing the details of Lifeline's counselling line when I interviewed victims of crime, trauma, death, suicide, life challenges, or who just needed someone to talk to through their times of crisis.

In addition, my career in journalism has given me the opportunity to serve my community and humanity by highlighting topics and issues affecting everyday citizens, bringing awareness to different causes, raising support for non-profit organizations and worthy causes and using the platform of the media to make a difference in the lives of people.

A decade later, I would never have imagined that I would be serving as a board member at Lifeline Zululand in 2023, as well as on the national board of Lifeline South Africa, to promote their work and services.

Community Service and Development

Entering the third decade of my life with a new baby on my arm, in 2015 I found myself in a relaxed era, now settled in my career as a community journalist, enjoying my part-time side hustle as a health and beauty agent for the direct selling company Sh'zen and serving as a committee member for two community projects. Yet I still felt there was more I could offer in my service to humanity, community involvement and paying it forward to the next generation. Community service and involvement changed the narrative and pathway of my life's goals. So, when a work colleague and friend shared her heart's desire and dream to start a youth project, I was the first to latch on and run with her vision.

Lynette Dunn, a passionate and dynamic young mother, has walked a similar journey to mine as a teenage mom and threading through life challenges also overcame a hurdle of setbacks to build her career in finance, human resource management, community activism and continuing to study and create a safe and thriving life for her family.

In 2016, I joined her organisation called Gentle Touch Foundation (GTF) and over a 5-year period, we worked as a team to educate, empower and mentor young boys and girls from a suburb called Aquadene in Richards Bay, Kwazulu Natal Province, South Africa.

GTF focused on community outreach and life skills programs targeting school-going children and we rolled out several programs for young children focusing on awareness of teenage pregnancies, abstaining from sex, good morals, anti-bullying, discipline, health and hygiene, substance awareness and educating on careers. Children were also encouraged to support charity projects, take care of the environment and spread kindness.

On a monthly basis, we organised events, tours and excursions to expose the children to new experiences, visit different areas, integrate, relate and have exposure to other communities. Children also engaged in economic empowerment ventures where children attended baking classes to learn a skill to start their own small businesses and recycling projects to earn incomes.

In addition, children supported several charity initiatives: CANSA walks, beach clean-ups, volunteering at animal shelters and children's orphanages, collecting food and clothing for the homeless and destitute and paying it forward to make a difference in the community by helping pensioners with chores around their homes. They were encouraged to start their own vegetable gardens at home and in their schools, to be their brother's keepers and to advocate for anti-bullying campaigns.

Being involved with GTF until the COVID-19 pandemic struck in 2020 was a tremendous blessing in my life and we reached and impacted the lives of over 100 children in the Richards Bay and Empangeni areas. During the pandemic, GTF rallied up support from local businesses for grocery and bread drives delivering parcels to families that were struck with unemployment, including senior citizens, orphans and child-led households.

My two children who are now grown, Alister (21) and Lacon (9), at the time benefitted from the programs and exposure, being active participants and supporters of all my community work involvement. My eldest son who was a teenager at the time, helped with the younger children and was very hands-on with the fundraisers and campaigns for anti-gender-based violence and rape. He was also my right-hand support and he helped me execute my tasks.

During that five-year period, our family weekends and school holidays were jam-packed with GTF events. The GTF Dress A Matric (Grade 12) learner program was another highlight, as the community got involved by donating ball gowns and suits that were given to learners in need. This helped families who could not afford the costs of the matric dance.

While the project aimed at helping disadvantaged learners attend their matric dance in grand style by providing them with dresses, hair and nails, make-up and shoes, we used the platform to promote awareness on the dangers of the blesser/blesse phenomenon, teenage pregnancies and drugs. The children involved in the programs took away knowledge and experiences and we believe it helped them develop into caring and compassionate citizens of society, paying it forward as they continued to serve and help others. The aim was to instil the spirit of Ubuntu in our youth and community and build a culture of selfless service, taking care of other's needs, giving and serving humanity.

In a generation where technology has overtaken our younger generation and removed human interaction, it was heartwarming to see youngsters come together and go back to basics, build relationships and friendships, be there for others, offer a lending hand through their community efforts and bring about social change in society.

Catalyst for New Potential

The pandemic pushed me toward new potential. The first case of COVID-19 was reported in South Africa on March 5, 2020 and it coincided with my mother's renal failure diagnosis and an ensuing decline in health until her death five months later.

While navigating a new normal with the national lockdown, working from home, COVID-19 cases increasing, fatalities on the rise; offering support to my mother during her hospital stay was challenging as visitors were limited.

Being in the hospital, the one thing that brings comfort is visits from family, friends and associates. It was a difficult time for the family and we spent more time together outside the clinic, hospital, or doctor's room waiting for my mother to receive treatment. We had a new appreciation for what we had previously taken for granted, with rules, regulations, limitations and curfews now restricting our every move.

My mother fought a good fight, loved people and battled with the fact of not being able to have human contact, physical support, hugs and the bonds of family within her reach and touch. Family rallied behind and the importance of having a support system made all the difference in times of grief. This was a time where I witnessed firsthand the importance of counselling, as all one could do during this time was offer an ear with no literal shoulder to cry on or a physical embrace to console those dealing with the loss of a loved one.

Counselling was in high demand and awareness of emotional wellness and mental health was in full force as the community battled to cope under the lockdown, struck with COVID-19, the fear of death and losing loved ones at an alarmingly high rate. It was vital to have support systems in place as deaths in families were occurring daily and members were not being afforded enough time to grieve. It was a charged and traumatic time for all and the uncertainties of life were a reality with people being buried or cremated daily.

I too leaned into my support networks to maintain strength as I navigated new territory without the pillar of our family, my mom. She was the first loved one we lost in our family and grief was all new to us. My mother had lost her father at the age of 17 and I couldn't imagine how she went through life so positive and zealous with 40 years of living with the pain of losing her father. She had resilience and passion for life and never showed us her pain.

I struggle to think how oblivious I was to her pain every time her father's death date, birthday, Father's Day and every special holiday passed. It never occurred to me to ask about her feelings as I had never known my grandfather or even experienced the loss of someone close to me. Pushing my own grief on the back burner, the gaping whole my mother's passing left was evident as the helping hand, I had with my kids was now gone. I had to juggle all my roles of wife, mother, work employee, sister and friend without her support. I had relied on her for everything and my daily routine revolved around seeing her daily as we lived on the same street, just a 2-minute walk away. Life had radically transformed overnight and a song, a flower, the weather, or a scent would send tears streaming down my face.

I began thinking more about my life, my spirituality and the afterlife. Now eternity mattered to me because there was someone on the other side I was anxiously waiting to see. I found myself pouring more into my faith and prayer life and seeking a more meaningful life, wanting to transform, be a positive influence for my family and make a meaningful contribution to society, especially as life was so precious as we watched people lose their lives to the raging COVID-19 virus. During the pandemic, I picked up high blood pressure (BP) and nurses advised me to relook at my diet and include exercise to manage this chronic ailment. I believed I was too young to have BP in my mid-thirties and began increasing my efforts around exercise and improving my nutrition.

With a mission ahead, I worked daily and throughout 2022 to make lifestyle changes, set small fitness goals, enrolled in personal growth courses and read all the self-help and motivation resources I could to recondition my mind for a new path in life. The power of a positive mindset should never be underestimated, coupled with small actions to bring about meaningful long-term changes. Reinventing myself and using social media to share my journey of wellness and fitness and encourage others to make health a priority, many women were motivated to start improving their lives too. Daily, I shared my routines and disciplines and how small daily actions had yielded massive results over a sustained period. Conversations and networks began around the subject of making lifestyle changes instead of quick fixes that did not last. After a year of commitment I had lost 26 kg and continued to maintain this loss of weight.

The transformation of a new body, mindset and energy broadened my horizons to new experiences, hobbies and a whole different way of enjoying being more active and enjoying the outdoors. The success stories that followed were incredible, with women not only gaining their health back but also their confidence and self-worth and challenging themselves to go after their dreams.

It was remarkable how sharing my story inspired others and all they needed was to see another woman doing it to give them momentum to try again. The victory in restoring my health through nutrition and exercise, increasing my fitness level and eradicating the high blood pressure was extended to my community of women who took the lead to make changes in their lives and have remarkable changes in their health too.

We created a tribe and network of women who remained in contact via WhatsApp and continued to support each other and have someone to lean on and a support system that helped everyone continue on their path to living life to the fullest and in optimal health.

While still enjoying the perks of a newly transformed body and newfound confidence, energy and zeal for life, I became a victim of cyberbullying. My Facebook account was hacked; fraudsters were creating fake profiles with my pictures by the dozen daily and despite efforts to block and report them, more continued to pop up. They began contacting my family, friends, work colleagues and associates by WhatsApp and Facebook Messenger, spreading rumours of infidelity and accusations of promiscuous behaviour, followed by stalking, death threats and calls and texts of intimidation.

Despite the onslaught of hate speech and accusations to tarnish my character and reputation, I continued unphased and unshaken in my efforts and continued to give my best to my work and the community projects I was involved in. I was not going to allow the chaos happening around me to get inside of me and affect my emotional state or dampen my spirits. My business continued to thrive and my work productivity increased as I pushed myself deeper into my work to escape the drama that was unravelling in my life. This drama was causing havoc in my marriage, my home and work environment due to false allegations.

I deleted my social media accounts; however, the cyberbullying continued as the trolls created fake profiles to continue their slandering and attacks on my name. In addition, they began writing on my friends and family's Facebook pages as well, tormenting them. I erased all my social media accounts and it was like I never existed on social media, as everything had been completely erased and my 14-year social presence was gone in an instant. At the time, I did not think about all the memories I would lose which were stored on the internet because I just wanted my cyberbullying nightmare to end.

I had opened criminal cases with the police fearing for my life, beefed up security and kept movements to a minimum as stalkers said they were watching my every move. I lived in fear and even suffered spates of anxiety and panic attacks owing to the constant calls, messages and harassment on my private number as well as at the office. It affected my work as stalkers jammed our switchboard with non-stop calls. I could not market or promote my direct selling business via social media and my social life came to an instant halt as I refrained from interactions with others in any public places for safety reasons.

My world had plummeted into a negative downward spiral of self-doubt. Constant calls and messages alerting me to my name were being blasted all over social media. It was exhausting being the talk of the town, but I continued to maintain my routines and disciplines where I could and leaned into my family support and church community networks for strength. Being isolated from everything and everyone pushed me to a closer walk with God. He was the only one I could pour my heart into and share my deepest fears with.

The cyberbullying had destroyed some of my relationships and showed me who were real friends were and I am grateful to have the support of a handful of friends who are now family who I continue to navigate the storms of life with. The first few months of anger and rage turned to empathy and compassion because whoever was orchestrating such mayhem and discord in my life through such vile, vulgar and horrendous acts of defamation and derogatory allegations and rumours was really in a terrible mental and heart space. For them to work so tiresomely day and night for months on end to destroy my life, they had to be really suffering and doing all this behind a mask. Their animosity showed their lack of integrity. I felt pity for them and prayed a lot for them. Knowing that vengeance is the Lord's and I had no control over the situation; I was not about to commit my resources or time to finding out who this was, so I continued with my life, work and everything else I was committed to.

This was a sideshow and distraction in my life and I began to change my perspective on the matter and use my time for self-development, prayer and living a more meaningful and impactful life. I went back to the basics of my life and it was good to release all the public obligations and social engagements and take time out. Pushing on despite the challenges, thanks to the support of family and real friends, my fear, doubt and unbelief subsided and as the months went by, the grip of fear loosened as I began lashing back at my stalkers, wearing them down with my positivity and prayers for them and their families.

The character assassination attempts went on for 11 months before ending abruptly in February 2024 with no closure or explanation and even now I still have no explanation of who was behind the ordeal. I found encouragement in the word of God (Ecclesiastes 3:17.) *"I said in my heart, God will judge the righteous and the wicked, for there is a time for every matter and for every work. I said to myself, In due season, God will judge everyone, both good and bad, for all their deeds."* I left the process to take its due course and for my accusers to wear themselves out.

I took the experience as a learning curve as it moulded me into a stronger woman. Dealing with adversity, false accusations and rumours spread to tarnish my reputation and bring my character into disrepute only helped me to grow thicker skin, push harder and intensify my efforts to make my mark in society.

The slandering and accusations did nothing to my reputation but instead increased my social media following and brought more attention to my brand and the causes for which I supported and advocated for, such as emotional wellness and mental health. I was able to share my cyberbullying experience and how my faith in God, counselling and therapy had helped me to daily unpack my feelings, fears and emotions and set me back on track to deal with life and continue to maintain a balanced life.

I began weekly counselling in 2020 after my mum's passing and it has continued to date. It has helped me grow as an individual and deal with life challenges as they arise without bottling or storing up my emotions until they explode. Being able to check myself and do self-introspection on a regular basis allows me to take stock of my life, where I am at and how I plan to move forward with my goals and aspirations.

Every Cloud Has a Silver Lining

Despite what life has thrown at me over the years, my faith, my family, my support network and my passion and desire to make a difference by sharing my experiences and offering support give me the fuel and momentum to never give up, no matter the situation. I might need time to rest, reset and refocus, but quitting is never an option because, with God, all things are possible.

My journey to advocate for communities to equip themselves with emotional intelligence and to build emotional wellness and mental health awareness continues. In my work capacity, I built many networks and relationships while reporting on stories and uncovering their programs, projects and ideas, which led to the most creative contributions, meaningful impact on humanity and making a difference in communities.

It has always been an honour to hear people's life journeys, translate them into stories and see how the Zululand business community and individuals come on board with their financial generosity and support to bring projects of change to life. I take my role as a news reporter seriously and saw the impact of how an article could rally support and help organizations and their staff rise above their challenges and grow and succeed.

We have numerous success stories in our community and many unsung heroes who we had the privilege of profiling their journeys and bringing awareness to their causes, leading to others being inspired to follow their dreams and make their mark in the world through worthy causes. For me, supporting organizations through my work brings me immense job satisfaction and shows how paying it forward generation by generation can leave a lasting and meaningful contribution to society.

Conelia Harry

I am an agent of change using my career as a journalist to impact society, promote awareness of social ills, support communities through charity efforts, and empower women to financial freedom by entrepreneurship. I am a board member for Lifeline Zululand and Lifeline South Africa as well as serve on religious, school and community organisation committees.

Contact
Facebook: Connie Conelia Esmeral
Instagram: c_shzen_diva
LinkedIn: Conelia Esmeral

17

The Resetting of Humanity Towards Victory Through Proven Social Change Practices

"Hope without Action is like Fire Without Fuel."
Nadene Joy

"The Biggest Catalyst Towards Positive Change starts with YOU and What You Choose to Become to Move Towards and Act on Starting Today."

Social Change and Why It Matters

Change is constant and everywhere you look in societies and communities globally you will find some sort of societal change underway. To better understand where we are going, we need to understand where we are at and what has shaped us from our past to understand where we are going in the future.

Firstly, let's start by discussing the definition of social change which is defined by sociologists as alterations in the basic structures of society or as a group. Overall, social change and more specifically an area of social change termed *"structural functionalism,"* (1) should serve the best interests of society, with the goal of maintaining equilibrium and balance within the social system. From this perspective, social change occurs when society needs to maintain stability and continue to function efficiently. It resists the idea that conflict or revolution should be used to bring about change. Fundamentally, changes in social institutions will only occur to ensure those institutions continue to fulfill their main purposes.

On the other hand, according to Conflict Theory, social change occurs suddenly when conflict arises, upending the status flow. Conflict theory considers social problems within a society to be a conflict between groups - the haves and have-nots. Hence, sudden change is considered positive as it challenges inequalities that are entrenched by institutions designed to keep the oppressed from taking over. (2) The Industrial Revolution is an ideal historical example of a social and economic change that occurred that marked the widespread development of new technologies, transportation, communication systems and the growth of factories and mass production. It is here during this time where urbanisation, labour rights and women's rights took centre stage. In general, social changes can occur through hard work of activists or simple generational change. Examples of important social changes include the fight for gender equality, religion, free expression, or demographic and cultural changes (helpfulprofessor.com.)

Social Change Terminology in a Greater Context: Social Movements, Social Reform, Societal Evolution, Cultural Change and Social Progress

There are many additional areas of focus used in conjunction with social change that make up the parts to the whole of society. A Social Movement for example is a *"loosely organized group campaigning or supporting a social goal, typically for the implementation or the prevention of a change in society's structure or values."* A Social Reform on the other hand describes movements organised by members of a society who aim to create social change. Both are necessary to create lasting change.

Societies also have been proven to change over time which is described as Societal Evolution which is *"the change of cultures and societies over time, explained by evolutionary theories."* To dive deeper we can begin to examine cultural change that occurs in society, a term that is used by sociologists to describe *"the way society changes. Society takes on new cultural traits, behaviour patterns, customs and social norms and develops new social structures because of changing cultural norms."* Lastly, social progress is defined as *"a society's capacity to meet the basic needs of its citizens. Social progress is the foundation of a society that allows its citizens to enhance and sustain a decent quality of life and reach their full potential."* This is an important aspect of social change that we will touch upon more further in this chapter as we all have either a known conscious or subconscious unique purpose here on earth and an untapped potential inside of us that is waiting to be unleashed to the world for the greater good to assist in helping social humanity evolve to its highest potential one person, one family, one community at a time.

Social Dysfunction Dismantled

For us as a society to even begin to think about moving in the direction towards making positive lasting change in our world, we must look at what is working well, *"the current state"* and how it can be improved as well as what is dysfunctional and no longer working well to support the citizens of our communities at a local and then greater global level. Social dysfunction refers to a situation when something does not contribute positively to the maintenance of society and causes disharmony. Something is dysfunctional if it inhibits or disrupts the working of the system as a whole or another part of the system. For example, when a family becomes abusive (instead of providing love and care), then it is said to be dysfunctional. Social dysfunctions can have various causes, but they primarily arise because society is unable to fulfill the needs of all its members.

Crime is an example of societal dysfunction, meaning that it affects the entire society. Victims of crime may face physical harm, trauma, or financial losses, which can have long lasting detrimental effects on their life. Lastly, crime makes people feel unsafe and isolated in their communities and this fear can undermine social cohesion.

As per Merton, each system in a society has a specific unique function and is associated with other systems - all of these rely upon each other. When these systems work together properly, it leads to social stability. Everything on our planet within societies is connected and if one part or component of the system becomes hindered or even abolished all together, the other systems or areas must adjust to compensate for this loss or dysfunction overtime leading to social instability. (3)

We must work to strive towards balance and in creating a functioning sustainable society one step, one person at a time by beginning to focus on supporting the three main pillars of a sustainable society in some way which includes the genuine authentic allocation of human resources and bringing greater awareness and education in the form of extreme poverty reduction, global gender equality and wealth redistribution just to name a few concrete examples. Each one of these pillars are gargantuan global issues that one could most easily write an entire book publication on each topic alone. According to the 2024 Sustainability Trends Report (4), the social pillar, or 'people,' emphasizes fair business practices for employees and the community and fosters fairness, human rights and embraces diversity including boosting positive reputations and trust. The environmental pillar, or 'planet,' or the ecological pillar encourages the responsible use of resources to protect the environment, our planet as a whole and its diverse ecosystems. The economic pillar, or 'profit,' involves creating economic value that also considers environmental and overall social costs involved and fosters cultivating prosperity and progress responsibly through sustainable inclusive growth which involves the applied concept of risk management. All these pillars are interconnected, each influencing and depending on the others. Like a tripod, the structure topples when one is removed; we require efforts and a laser focus on all to stand strong as a functional society now and for generations to come hereafter.

To begin to tackle the larger problems and dysfunction that exists in our world, we need to begin to take a cold hard look at ourselves individually FIRST before we can even begin to expand this on an internationally collective scale. We must choose to show up fully as ourselves and to be real, vulnerable and authentic with all that we have been through in our past and are going through that makes us who we are today. Our beliefs and values have most times been corrupted by society that pulls us out of alignment from what matters in life and deemphasizes the importance of building human relationships and connections in our world which leads to building trust which is, in my humble opinion, part of the whole solid foundation block to every business and or relationship on the planet. Without trust, there is also dysfunction, isolation and brokenness. We must first learn to unconditionally love all parts of the person we see in the mirror every day and show up as we are with no strings attached to the rest of the world - with no masks, facades, or ulterior selfish motives. We must begin to dismantle and remove all that may be potentially contributing to this dysfunction and move towards being real in each moment with each and every interaction with all others to work collaboratively in harmony and unity together to empower and grow greater authentic communities consisting of connectedness and love for all people - a community that is free from dysfunction, layered illusions and corruptions of our world.

It All Starts with You!

The biggest catalyst towards positive change starts with consciously showing up just as you are. YOU, alone and what you choose to move towards and act on today matters more than you think as you are a role model and leader in your community and what you do people will take notice and begin to model as well. It starts with your thoughts as they will become your words, your words will become your actions and your actions will become your destiny. It is your destiny and purpose that leads to living a life on fire overflowing with fulfilment, joy, love and aligned purpose in each passing moment.

We are born innocent and free when we are entering into the world as newborn babies. As we grow up into toddlers, adolescents, young adults and finally into full grown adults, we have transitioned from innocence to most times unknowingly being corrupted by the imposed perceptions, limiting beliefs and expectations from others onto us by our parents, families, friends, media, music, teachers, sports, the movie industry and many others. Overtime, as we grow older and wiser through lived life experiences, we may or may not recognize the many perceptions projected onto us that we have somehow unconsciously taken on as our innate *"truth"* of who we really are which is just an illusion. This causes a massive need for concern and call for immediate overall deep reflection on the part of everyone to determine where your individual behaviours, speech and beliefs that are operating from that isn't in fact the "*real*" you at all.

Steps to Activating and Creating Positive Social Change

The first step to creating positive social change is to bring awareness to yourself and to get crystal clear on who you really are, not just what the world has conditionally told you need to be. Take a few minutes now to write down all your top morals and values and all that you consider to be the most important to you on a deep heart level not just what is coming to you from your mind and ego. This is what we will call your *"Attributes of Excellence (AOE.)"* Some examples may include honesty, authenticity, respect, integrity, or perhaps to always work hard and do your best, no matter what. For you to bring about positive change in the world for others, you first must do this for yourself as you can only help support others to the level you have first done the work on yourself. Once your AOE list above is complete, you can then proceed to move onto the second step of this process below.

The second step is to choose your top three morals/values from your Attributes of Excellence (AOE) list above that you would like to focus on becoming for a minimum of the next three months. Hand write them down with blue ink on a blank white sheet of paper and paste it on your mirror in your bathroom or somewhere you will see it numerous times throughout the day. This will be mandatory to move on to the last and final step of this change activation process.

The last step to create positive social change is to write three different key action items under each of the three items and include what that entails for each one. For example, if one of your top AOE's is kindness, you could write down one action to say or do something kind for someone every day, at least once. Then you need to make sure to commit to doing at least one action each day AND noticing and acknowledging it by writing it down. It is also important to notice when others do at least one of your items on the list of actions you just created and document this as well. I highly advise to use a chart to keep track of all the things you have done for a month and what others have shown you that is in alignment with your personal AOE list. This is key to reflect on this at the very beginning and end of each day, end of each week and then again at the end of the month. Take time to also make a point of celebrating both the big and small wins and your progress daily, both big and small wins. If you happen to miss a day just acknowledge it and commit to starting again the next day, do not feed attention to this and just keep optimistically forging ahead. The key here is consistency and moving forward with momentum to reach the three-month goal or longer, as you wish. Once you are past the first month or so you will have ingrained a newly formed conscious positive habit that will hopefully become your newfound reality. Just think of what the world would be like if we all collectively decided to do this exercise every day? What a radically different world we would live in and one that would be continuously moving towards positive change to mutually better ourselves and impact humanity. Commitment, consistency, compassion and action are key here as all components are required to make lasting positive changes in our world.

In addition, The Social Change Model of Leadership is based on seven dimensions, or values, called the *"Seven C's"*: consciousness of self, congruence, commitment, common purpose, controversy with civility, collaboration and citizenship. All seven of these values work together to accomplish lasting change. Social change can evolve from several different sources, including contact with other societies (diffusion), changes in the ecosystem (which can cause the loss of natural resources or widespread disease), technological change (epitomized by the Industrial Revolution, which created a new social group) and population growth and other demographic variables. Social change is also spurred by ideological, economic and political movements.

Our Past Lived Experiences Have Moulded Us into Who We Are Today

I'd like to share a brief story with you. Years ago, I was chosen as one of the speakers to present on a leadership panel which consisted of top politicians from across the globe. At the end of my presentation, I was asked if I were to change any one thing from my past what would it be and why? I thought about this for a moment and quickly concluded that my answer was in fact very simple indeed and that I would not change a SINGLE thing from my past. I am certain that my answer startled the moderator as they verbalized, they had not heard this answer before from anyone and I was politely asked to elaborate. I began by sharing that I had been through many incredible ups and horrific downs over the course of my life and had concluded that no matter what I went through, I learned something greater about myself and had become stronger in character and so many other ways because of each situation I had endured and overcome. It is through our lived experiences and pain endured and successes triumphed where we come to know who we really are from the *"inside out"* not the *"outside in"* free from the worldly projections, illusions and expectations from others.

It is from this place we begin to finally experience true joy and freedom as a uniquely made individual who is a part of something so much greater than just ourselves, someone who is also a part of creating positive social change for the betterment of all of humanity. Not just for today, or for tomorrow, but for many generations to come. This is the legacy we all desire and are hungry to create that, lives inside each one of you reading this. The sky is the limit and the potential you must do great things in this world to impact others is infinite and endless. Focus on compassion, unconditional love for self and all others and be authentic and real with all those you cross paths within each moment. As my great grandfather once said to me when I was only five years old that has stuck with me my entire life: *"Always leave every situation better off than how you found it."* This is a philosophy I have chosen to live my life by, and I hope you will choose the same or alternatively one that is also meaningful for you.

Ways to Create Social Change in Your Community

Some of the critical factors of positive social change include demographic, technological, cultural, political, economic and education areas of focus within society. Other ways to create and enact social change within your community include:

- Supporting a grassroots activism and advocacy are essential in creating any positive social change. Local people have the best knowledge of their own local context, challenges and systems. Make a point to connect with others and keep up with the local trends.

- Collaborate and work together with others to create a strong network of like-minded individuals. Mutually support and encourage one other every step of the way along the journey. Have and initiate conversations with others of varying demographics.

- Support sustainable measures within your local community and beyond for example, by reducing your environmental footprint.

- Share your unique story and network with others as together we are stronger than we are apart. Be genuine, care for and help others when we the opportunity presents itself and do not be afraid to step outside your comfort zone to stand up or speak up for a good cause or what you believe. Be a changemaker.

- Get creative and join culture initiatives in your community such as art exhibitions, music theatres and music festivals, just to name a few.

Reshaping the Future of Humanity and Next Steps Forward

Our minds our powerful and it all starts in our minds and thoughts we think followed by the choices you make and the actions you take. I will leave you with an old indigenous story tale to illustrate the importance of choosing our thoughts and path forward wisely.

The Story of Two Wolves

An old Cherokee is teaching his grandson about life. *"A fight is going on inside me,"* he said to the boy. *"It is a terrible fight and it is between two wolves. One is evil – he is anger, envy, sorrow, regret, greed, arrogance, self-pity, guilt, resentment, inferiority, lies, false pride, superiority and ego."* He continued, *"The other is good – he is joy, peace, love, hope, serenity, humility, kindness, benevolence, empathy, generosity, truth, compassion and faith. The same fight is going on inside you – and inside every other person, too."* The grandson thought about it for a minute and then asked his grandfather, *"Which wolf will win?"* The old Cherokee replied, *"The one you feed."*

Whether or not it's your first time of hearing this story, it serves as an imperative and important reminder of the sheer power we have over our experiences, choices in life to do good and in hanging positive thoughts and mindset in general. It's all too easy to default feeling like a helpless victim in challenging situations and difficult circumstances in our lives. As humans, we want to better understand our negative thoughts, feelings and experiences, so we inherently and sometimes automatically place blame on other people, objects, or events to take it away and deflect it temporary from ourselves. We look outward (instead of inward) to try to make better concrete sense of what's going on inside of us. We do this all the time most times subconsciously without even trying. Why? It's our instinctual way of coping and feeling more in control of uncontrollable situations that are most times difficult to handle in our world.

The major problem with this overall approach, however, is that it takes away our personal responsibility and freedom of choice and adds to the societal dysfunction as discussed above. In our overt attempt to feel more in control (by faulting and blaming others for our uncomfortable experience), we strip ourselves of our own power and truth of who we really are and why we are here as our unique purpose on this planet in the first place. That intrinsic power from deep within us is lost the moment we become dependent on other people or even on things to make us feel a certain way. Whether that feeling is positive or negative, we are no longer taking sole responsibility for our own emotions or experiences when we believe that they are a result of anything other than our own choice that comes externally from the world.

By beginning with your thoughts and by exercising your freedom of choice, you can make a life-changing decision of which wolf you want to feed. Take a moment to reflect now as we close out this chapter to ponder the following questions:

- Do you choose to feed the wolf who is hungry for anger, envy, sorrow, regret, greed, arrogance, self-pity, guilt, resentment, inferiority, lies, false pride, superiority and ego?

- Did you know that this evil wolf is also known your inner critic?

It is the one who tells you that you are a failure and will never succeed at anything you try, it the one who says that no one will ever really love you or understand you just as you are. This wolf is an overall representation of your depression, your shame, your guilt, anxiety and of your low self-esteem and self-worth. Begin by asking yourself: Do you WANT to continue to feed this wolf? Are you feeding it already? Take note and become aware of where you are at today, right here right now in this exact moment. It is only through greater awareness of self first that we will begin to move towards making greater positive change in our world.

In summary, by cutting off this wolfs food supply (aka our thoughts), you will be making a conscious empowered choice to use your energy and resources for the betterment of all of humanity including choosing thoughts, feelings and emotions that serve you in more healthy productive empowering ways. While you can recognize the negative emotions occurring within you, you don't have to attach to them or continue to give them attention. Shifting your focus immediately when you notice it coming in is a clear sign to that wolf that you are not interested in feeding it or giving it food any longer. You are taking back your power. Once you decide this you can begin teaching others how to do this as well. This will become like a ripple effect of goodness out into the world spreading from one person at a time to another and so on. Remember to be patient and gentle with yourself throughout this process as it may take some time for that wolf to fully lose its strength and power, but he will surrender and let loose once and for all - as will your unhelpful thoughts and emotions that once empowered and fed it. Once you finally stop fixating on them, they will organically drift away.

So, what about the other wolf? Well to keep it simple, it certainly isn't going to feed itself. Just as you would practice with not feeding the bad wolf, it is imperative that you exercise your freedom of social choice and decide to *"nourish"* the good positive wolf of joy, peace, love, hope, serenity, humility, kindness, benevolence, empathy, generosity, truth, compassion and faith. We all too often look to external objects for our fulfillment and happiness. We develop expectations that these things (a new job, a relationship, a lavish vacation, a brand-new pair of sunglasses, a new vehicle, etc.) will finally make us feel the way we want to feel which is not the truth. And while this thought process and practice may bring momentary gratification and satisfaction, it isn't realistic to maintain this for long-term.

Happiness isn't a conditional state. It's a state of being. True lasting happiness is known as *"joy"* comes from making an active consistent choice to be happy, rather than depending on external things to make you happy only temporarily. The more that we seek out happiness and look for it as if it is a treasure we will find, the less we are feeding the good wolf that is inside of us as this is who we are that represents our full potential we all have yet to uncover. You already have everything you need to be happy because you are whole and complete just as you are, right here, right now. The feeling and experience of true joy comes from feeding the good positive wolf from within. As it grows and becomes bigger and stronger it will be better equipped to handle all of life's challenges that are thrown at us. Choose to feed the good wolf inside of you and choose everyday to empower and encourage others to feed this good wolf as well as this is the light that lies inside of you and that the world needs you to shine brightly now more than ever. Your light will become a mirror for many others to model to allow them permission to also shine brightly leading to a myriad of positive social change behaviours that will catapult and cascade into a ripple effect of infinite light and goodness across all of humanity that will be globally witnessed in communities near and far from all corners of the earth.

When we focus on doing our part one step at a time starting at the local level within communities, we begin to create positive social change in all areas until we then gradually elevate from where we are at to collectively reshaping humanity towards victory and positive change for all. We are all so intricately connected, one positive change will continue to affect another and another in the hope that one day we will all live connected harmonious diverse societies relatively free from dysfunction centred around love and support for all of humanity.

Reference

(1) Harper, D. (2011) Structural functionalism. University of Leicester: School of Management. Management Journal, 25(6), 101-115.

(2) Savur, M. (1975) Sociology of conflict theory. Social scientist, p. 29-42.

(3) Merton, R. K., & Merton, R. C. (1957.) Social theory and social structure. New York: Simon and Schuster.

(4) 2024 Sustainability Trends Report

(5) Wilterdink, N. and Form, W. May 27, 2024. Encyclopedia Britannica: Social Change

Nadene Joy

Nadene Joy is a global advisor, leadership strategist, business coach, philanthropist and world-class Changemaker who is passionate about bringing greater wealth, wisdom, hope, love, purpose and joy into the world one person, one leader at a time. She sits as a Board Director and Advisor to many leading nonprofit organizations in her local community and across the world. Nadene has been globally recognized and was presented with the prestigious Global Bizz Business Excellence Award, Woman of Substance Award from The St. Mother Teresa University and the TISGS Award of Business Excellence in Social Impact under the Patronage of His Excellency H.E. Sheikh Eng. Salem Bin Sultan Al Qasimi in Dubai.

Not only is Nadene Joy a world class professional, but she is also involved on many societies, boards and organizations. She is Vice President of Community Relations for the Project Management Institute (PMI) Regina/South Saskatchewan Chapter, is a member of The International Society of Female Professionals (ISFP), a Professional Geologist registered with APEGS and is an International CEC Ambassador. Nadene Joy has mentored and professionally worked alongside some of the most influential leaders of our time including Joe Foster, Founder of REEBOK and has been featured on numerous top media appearances such as USA TODAY and iHeart radio in NYC, FOX40 and The Los Angeles Tribune just to name a few.

She is devoted to bringing greater mental health awareness, being the voice for vulnerable citizens in society, support for men, women and children as well as empowering communities through outreach, project management, greater access to education and positively uplifting the lives of all others she encounters. Nadene believes wholeheartedly that one person at a time can make a difference through the actions we choose to take today in this present moment which leads to great change for many and radically redefines what society defines as *"Hope for Tomorrow"* into a newfound reality and truth of *"Hope for Today."*

LinkedIn: //linkedin.com/in/nadenejoy
Web: www.NadeneJoy.com   Email: Nadene@NadeneJoy.com

Afterword

"We can easily forgive a child who is afraid of the dark. The real tragedy of life is when men are afraid of light."
Plato

This book can be a healing balm if you allow it to speak to you, challenge you and present a new perspective. It echoes to humanity the experience of connection, growth, lessons and hope. Most people feel that life happens by default and minimum proactive action. That is untrue. If you zoom into the life of Hannah from The Bible: She prayed in the spirit for a child **(FAITH)** and then she procreated with Elkanah **(WORKS.)** The result was the birth of Samuel **(FRUIT.)** You must strategically align your actions with your convictions to harvest a rewarding life.

Do not allow the circumstances of life to stop you from fulfilling God's plan and purpose for your life. You may feel as if you don't have it within you and that you don't have what it takes, either the strength or resources, to fulfill your purpose. The Apostle Paul in the Bible felt the same way, but he never allowed it to stop him. Paul never allowed his limits to constrain his vision. He understood the strength to do these things was not vested in him. He said, *"I can do all things through Christ who strengthens me."* Philippians 4:13. Recognise that you do not have to be at the top of our game to fulfill your commitment. Just have a willing heart to try, to do better than yesterday and make a material difference in some way.

As we close the chapters of *"Echoes of Humanity,"* I am filled with gratitude for the journey we have shared through the exploration of our collective human experience. This book sought to be more than just a compilation of words; it aimed to resonate with the very core of our existence, leaving behind echoes that reverberate within the chambers of our hearts and minds. Throughout these pages, we have embarked on a profound odyssey - traversing the highs and lows of human emotions, contemplating the intricate dance of individual stories within the grand tapestry of humanity. It is my hope that these echoes have not only reached your ears but have also found a home in your soul, stirring contemplation and kindling a deeper connection to the shared human narrative.

In the diverse narratives and perspectives presented, we have glimpsed the resilience of the human spirit, witnessed the beauty of empathy and confronted the shadows that linger in our collective history. These echoes serve as reminders that, despite our differences, we are bound together by the threads of a common humanity.

As you take a moment to reflect on the words within these pages, consider the echoes they may have awakened within you. Perhaps you have found solace in shared experiences, discovered new perspectives that challenge your preconceptions, or felt a renewed sense of purpose in contributing to the ongoing story of humanity.

The echoes persist beyond these written words - into the conversations sparked, the actions inspired and the connections forged. They invite us to be more mindful of our impact on the world and to recognize the power each individual holds in shaping the collective narrative. In the symphony of human existence, let these echoes be a melodic reminder that we are all participants in a grand composition. Our stories, like notes, blend to create a harmonious resonance that transcends the boundaries that often divide us. May the echoes of humanity continue to resonate within you, urging you to contribute your unique melody to the ever-evolving song of our shared existence.

As we navigate the complexities of our modern world, the significance of fostering a culture that uplifts emotional well-being becomes increasingly evident. The insights shared within these chapters inspire a collective responsibility to create a more compassionate and understanding world. By integrating these principles into our daily lives, we not only enhance our own existence but also contribute to a broader movement toward a more empathetic and interconnected global community.

In essence, this book serves as a catalyst for change, inviting readers to reflect on their individual capacities to influence positive transformations within themselves and the world at large. The overarching mission presented is not merely a lofty ideal but a tangible roadmap for those who seek to make a meaningful difference. May the principles discussed within these pages inspire a wave of intentional action, fostering a future where elevated emotional frequencies become the cornerstone of a more harmonious and compassionate world.

"12 Mighty Orphans" is a compelling film that takes inspiration from true events and unfolds a remarkable underdog story. Set against the backdrop of the Great Depression, the movie introduces us to the Fort Worth Masonic Home, a struggling orphanage with a football team known as the Mighty Mites. The story revolves around the determined and passionate coach, Rusty Russell, portrayed by Luke Wilson, who transforms a group of underprivileged orphans into a formidable football team. The Mighty Mites defy the odds and societal expectations, proving that strength and resilience can emerge from the most unexpected places. As the team overcomes challenges on and off the field, the film explores themes of teamwork, perseverance and the transformative power of sports. With a mix of heart-warming moments and intense football action, *"12 Mighty Orphans"* is a poignant tribute to the indomitable spirit of those who rise above adversity and find victory in the face of daunting circumstances.

The orphans were stigmatised and treated like second class citizens. They were often referred to as *"inmates"* and they were cocooned in with agony and lurking inspiration. Abandonment revealed lives that were awash in tragedy. Wrath is often the camouflage that hurt is forced to wear and parade with. Always remember you will reap rage when you sow pain. These lads had so much shoved down their throats. They were forced to beef up and bear all. They got the silver lining when the coach arrived. Rusty Russell was an orphan himself, so he understood the pain and the plight. Russell used his lived experience to carve a positive social change. These orphans got a glimpse of hope and shaped a bright and successful future for themselves. Russell did not allow his personal pain to dispense unwholesome slop. Even though he was soaked in adversity he was only drenched for a moment. We roar like trumpets broadcasting our successes, but we mumble our defeat through shrivelled lips. Russell used his misfortune to change the narrative. Wow what an inspiration. Just because you plant something never be naive to think weeds will not grow as well. The journey of life is the same, you must be able to grow despite adversity. Weeds are everywhere! Thrive despite it. The presence of success does not negate problems. Progress under pressure, especially when you cannot control the external processes in your life, but you still must live with joy despite the lack. With parched lips, a dry tongue and a bleeding heart, you must keep on moving. Don't bask in over analysing the situation and introspecting your emotions. Take a step towards something dynamic and healthy.

You dream for strawberries, sugar and cream but you are given a field to toil and a cow. Then you make no correlation that elbow grease is mandatory. Life may have left you lacklustre, but you do not have to live this way permanently. Only you can end the season or help someone to a better future. We all crave connection in an era of disconnection, bond with others and understand what makes them tick. Help to change the future and create history that will inspire others. Allow the courtesy of God to become flamboyant in the story. Offer humanity a glimmer of optimism with swashbuckler and bravado no matter how humble your beginnings. Abundant living begins when priorities are altered, shifted to make room for others. Sometimes we speak and the words choose themselves and then our lives tell a greater tale. People will thrive the moment they feel appreciated, how do you value people? Never barter human authenticity for stamps of approval, change keeps you inventing. What you are not changing, you are choosing. You maybe choosing to keep people trapped in a bleak future.

Just as a universal drug, probable regret has a few hazardous side effects. When you live life on a selfish platform that only focuses on yourself then the line up to assemble negative emotions are very strong. Unhappiness sitting next to hatred perched beside guilt and bathing daily in regret. The purpose of life is to produce a better outcome for both you and humanity. My overarching mission is to raise the emotional frequency of people on a global scale by cultivating and enhanced leaning culture within individual introspection, community liaisons and conscious enhancements to the welfare of humanity. *"Men can be divided into two groups: one that goes ahead and achieves something and one that comes after and criticizes."* - Seneca. Take your pick! I envision to live out the rest of my life standing in the light of vulnerability and authenticity, I will embrace and equip anyone who courageously meets me there.

Most of us lead modest lives. We are not banking on an honour parade or hall of fame. However, this should never diminish our influence, for there are tons of people waiting for someone to make a material difference in their life. A simple gesture of gratitude, empathy, unconditional love, loyalty and trust. You can change the narrative for someone just because you took the time to show that you care. Too often we underestimate the power of a hug, a smile, a kind word a listening ear, an honest compliment, or the smallest act of caring, all of which have a potential to turn a life around. Always consider the continuous opportunities there are to make your love felt. Your outreach can transform a desponded person, they may wake up faster and bolder than ever... new intuitive energy may surround them.

Condition yourself to make a positive impact. Resembling an open tap – flood the world with positive energy, fresh consciousness and magnificent vibes. Opportunities present every day, ponder what is unfolding daily. Life altering prospects lurks everywhere. Leaving a profound legacy will always be in fashion. Pride, selfishness and greed are ancient history. Invite creative deliberations, enhanced habits and summon profound significance to fill your heart and actions. Transformation begins with you and it will echo for eternity. Care not for perfection but rather to make a positive difference. The moon in all her glory is so fine-looking but under a microscope the craters are pronounced. Always focus on the beauty not the ugly. Never blame the distraction. Improve the focus.

The world is chocked by people telling their version but not the ultimate truth. What would life look like if you narrated the story from every angle not just your vantage point. Do you have the capacity to be truthful about the whole gamut? Be authentic in a harsh world. Stand for justice so others don't have to die from the lack of it. If you find yourself in the thickest of eucalypts, be definite to take a moment to hear the cockatoos sing. To observe that the songs never stop despite the circumstances. Prompt yourself of the goodness of nature and be resolute to dispense light and love despite the ruins and keep trying to enhance the echoes that will stand in humanity forever.

In the archives of history, there are few figures as captivating as Hedy Lamarr. Renowned for her unparalleled beauty, Lamarr's legacy transcends the silver screen, extending into the realms of science, technology and innovation. Born Hedwig Eva Maria Kiesler on November 9, 1914, in Vienna, Austria, she would later adopt the stage name Hedy Lamarr, enchanting audiences with her acting prowess and stunning allure.

From a young age, Lamarr exhibited a remarkable intellect and curiosity that set her apart. She was drawn to the world of science and technology, harbouring a deep fascination for understanding how things worked. This insatiable thirst for knowledge would propel her on a journey that intersected with some of the most pivotal moments of the 20th century.

As World War II engulfed Europe, Lamarr's life took a remarkable turn, as she found herself not only on the silver screen but also at the forefront of technological innovation. It was during this time that she collaborated with composer George Antheil to develop a groundbreaking invention that would forever change the course of modern warfare.

Their invention, known as frequency hopping spread spectrum technology, was a revolutionary method of secure communication. Inspired by the erratic movements of piano keys, Lamarr and Antheil devised a system whereby radio signals could be rapidly switched between different frequencies, making it nearly impossible for enemies to intercept and decipher messages.

The implications of their invention were profound, offering a means of secure communication that could potentially thwart enemy efforts to jam or intercept critical transmissions. Recognizing the significance of their creation, Lamarr and Antheil submitted their patent to the United States Patent Office in 1941.

Despite their innovative contribution, the full potential of Lamarr and Antheil's invention would not be realized until decades later. In the years following the war, frequency hopping spread spectrum technology would find applications far beyond the battlefield, laying the foundation for modern wireless communication technologies such as Bluetooth, Wi-Fi and GPS.

Lamarr's brilliance extended far beyond her contributions to science and technology. She embodied a rare combination of beauty and intellect, challenging stereotypes and inspiring generations of women to pursue their passions fearlessly. Her journey from silver screen siren to pioneering inventor serves as a testament to the power of intellect and innovation to transcend boundaries and shape the course of history.

Throughout her life, Lamarr remained fiercely independent and unapologetically herself, refusing to be confined by the limitations imposed by society. Her legacy endures as a beacon of inspiration for all who dare to dream and defy expectations. From Hollywood icon to technological trailblazer, Hedy Lamarr's remarkable legacy continues to inspire and captivate humanity, reminding us of all the limitless potential that resides within each of us. Beauty, brilliance and battlefield innovation changed the world and her invention does not just echo in humanities current landscape - it is roaring!

In a world beset by challenges, from social injustices to environmental crises, the need for champions of change has never been greater. Each of us has the power to make a difference, to be a catalyst for positive transformation in our communities and beyond. Becoming a champion for change is not just about acting; it's about embracing a mindset of empathy, courage and unwavering commitment to creating a better world for all.

Cultivate Empathy: At the heart of being a champion for change lies empathy – the ability to understand and share the feelings of others. Empathy compels us to see beyond our own experiences and perspectives, to recognize the struggles and challenges faced by those around us. By cultivating empathy, we can forge meaningful connections with others and gain a deeper understanding of the issues that affect our communities.

Educate Yourself: Knowledge is a powerful tool for change. Take the time to educate yourself about the pressing issues facing society, whether it's systemic racism, climate change, or economic inequality. Seek out diverse perspectives and voices, engage in critical dialogue and remain open to learning and growth. By arming yourself with knowledge, you can become a more effective advocate for change.

Speak Up: Silence is complicity. As a champion for change, it is essential to speak up and use your voice to amplify the voices of the marginalized and oppressed. Whether it's challenging discriminatory practices, advocating for policy reform, or raising awareness about important issues, your words have the power to spark meaningful dialogue and catalyse action.

Act: Change begins with action. Identify tangible ways you can contribute to positive change in your community, whether it's volunteering with local organizations, participating in grassroots movements, or supporting causes that align with your values. Remember that even small actions can have a ripple effect, inspiring others to join you in the fight for a better world.

Lead by Example: Be the change you wish to see in the world. Lead by example through your words, actions and values. Embrace integrity, authenticity and compassion in all that you do and strive to inspire others to do the same. By embodying the principles of change you wish to promote, you can become a beacon of hope and inspiration for those around you.

Foster Collaboration: Real change requires collective effort. Seek out opportunities to collaborate with others who share your passion for creating a more just and equitable world. By working together, pooling resources and leveraging collective expertise, we can achieve far more than we ever could alone.

Embrace Resilience: The journey toward change is not always easy and setbacks are inevitable. Embrace resilience in the face of adversity and remember that progress is often nonlinear. Learn from failures, adapt to challenges and remain steadfast in your commitment to the cause. Change may take time, but with perseverance and determination, anything is possible.

Becoming a champion for change is not a one-time event but a lifelong journey fuelled by passion, purpose and a deep-seated belief in the power of collective action to transform the world. By cultivating empathy, educating ourselves, speaking up, acting, leading by example, fostering collaboration and embracing resilience, each of us has the potential to be a force for positive change in our communities and beyond. Together, let us rise to the challenge and create a future that is brighter, fairer and more just for all. With every lesson, you decide whether to mark it as the end of your greatest days or the beginning of your finest hour. I endeavour to leave the reader with a renewed spirit for creating the architecture for unexpected dialogue and opening new doors. Let every obstacle serve to create an inferno within to spark with pronounced intensity.

Famed actor Arnold Schwarzenegger posted a photo of him sleeping on the street under his famous bronze statue and wrote *"how times have changed."*

The reason he wrote the phrase was not only because he was old, but because when he was governor of California, he inaugurated a hotel with his statue. Hotel staff told Arnold, *"At any moment you can come and we will have a room reserved for you."* When Arnold stepped down as governor and went to the hotel, the administration refused to give him a room arguing that he should pay for it, since they were in great demand. He brought a sleeping bag and slept underneath the statue and explained what he wanted to convey: *"When I was in an important position, they always complimented me and when I lost this position, they forgot about me and did not keep their promise. Do not trust your position or the amount of money you have, nor your power, nor your intelligence, it will not last."* Trying to teach everyone that when you're *"Important"* in people's eyes, everyone is your *"Friend"*. Once you don't benefit their interests, you won't matter anymore. According to Arnold, *"Nothing lasts forever"*.

Yes, indeed seasons change but your lived experience can still speak volumes to the world long after the event. The power is in passing the lesson just like Arnold did. Thank you for joining us on this journey. May the echoes endure, connecting us across time and space and inspiring a future where our collective humanity shines brighter than ever before. *"When will our conscious grow so tender that we will action to prevent human misery rather than avenge it?"* - Eleanor Roosevelt.

Acknowledgments

It is with great pleasure and excitement that we present this literary masterpiece to you. The journey of curating this collection has been a labour of love, driven by our commitment to bringing you works of unparalleled quality and significance. Each piece within these pages has been carefully selected for its unique voice, compelling narrative and profound impact on the literary landscape. We owe a debt of gratitude to the talented authors whose dedication to their craft has enriched this anthology. Soman Rifkin for inclusion of her poem.

Moreover, we extend our appreciation to the diligent editorial and publishing Markey Writing Academy team whose discerning eyes and unwavering commitment to excellence have shaped this compilation.

Appreciation to Dr Christina DiArcangelo, for penning a heartfelt foreword. Helen Glen, Lyssa-Ann Clarke and Lynn Claudia Naidoo we are thankful for your efforts to write genuine book acclaims.

To all the readers: as we embark on this literary voyage together, we invite you to immerse yourselves in the richness of these narratives that span genres and traverse the depths of human experience. Your support as readers fuels our passion for championing outstanding literature and we trust that this collection will find a cherished place on your bookshelves, heart and it will become your tangible action plan. Breaking boundaries and taboos to let in light is something we all can do - THANK YOU for putting this book into action.

Kelly Markey

CEO: Markey Writing Academy
CEO: Beacon of Hope Mission
Publisher
Writer's Consultant
Global Bestselling Author
Top Executive Award: IAOTP
Women Changing the World Finalist
Brand Ambassador:
Global Movement of Hope
Winner: Book of the Year
kellymarkey.com